FREE *and* CLEAR

Understanding & Communicating God's Offer of Eternal Life

R. LARRY MOYER

kregel
PUBLICATIONS

Grand Rapids, MI 49501

Published by Kregel Publications, a division of Kregel, Inc., P.O. Box 2607, Grand Rapids, MI 49501. Kregel Publications provides trusted, biblical publications for Christian growth and service. Your comments and suggestions are valued.

For more information about Kregel Publications, visit our web site at http://www.kregel.com.

Cover design: PAZ Design Group
Book design: Nicholas G. Richardson

Library of Congress Cataloging-in-Publication Data
Moyer, R. Larry.
    Free and clear: understanding and communicating God's offer of eternal life / R. Larry Moyer.
        p.   cm.
    Includes bibliographical references.
    1. Salvation. 2. Future life—Christianity.
3. Evangelistic work. 4. Witness bearing (Christianity).
I. Title.
BT752.M68   1997   234—dc20   96-34200
                                                          CIP

ISBN 0-8254-3177-8

Printed in the United States of America

1 2 3 / 03 02 01 00 99 98 97

To my dear wife, Tammy,
without whom my ministry as a traveling
evangelistic speaker would not be possible.
Wherever I've been, she has always been there in spirit.
Only eternity will reveal how greatly God has used
her unwavering support to populate heaven.

Next to eternal life in Christ,
she is the most priceless gift
God could have ever given me.

Table of Contents

Acknowledgments

If I were to thank every person who assisted in some way in the writing of this book, the acknowledgments would be a book in themselves.

I am sincerely grateful to the many pastors and congregations who, as they gave me the opportunity to preach the Gospel as an expository evangelist, allowed me to verbalize from the pulpit what I discovered in my study. I'm also grateful to the new converts and those who have attended our training seminars. As they have been discipled, they have in turn led others to Christ. Their encouragement to put into print what was shared with them has meant everything.

I express appreciation as well to Dorian Cox, who gave invaluable assistance through her editing expertise. As we worked together, I came to appreciate her as one of the most gifted and knowledgeable women in the family of God.

I am indebted to Rebecca Hopper, John Cocoris, Joy Kupp, and Adria Ger for the part each of them played in pulling together this final manuscript. Without their assistance, it would have never gotten to the publisher.

Cam Abell, who has such a heart for the Gospel and for evangelism, was of much help in reading and rereading the manuscript. Knowing the biblical texts and knowing me, he was able to make sure the words on the pages said what I thought I had said.

Last but certainly not least, I want to thank those who read the final manuscript and gave me their honest and helpful feedback. Their eagerness to help lifted me greatly, and their critiques made this a better book.

Thanks for being such special brothers and sisters in the eternal family of God. Being with you on earth makes the thought of life together in heaven most exciting!

Introduction

I have two things in common with most Christians. First, evangelism sometimes frightens me. I don't know of anything more exciting than God using me to change another person's eternal destiny. But often when I consider the possibility of talking to someone about the Savior, I become frightened—that sweaty hands, nervous knees experience. It's usually fear of the unknown: I simply don't know how the person is going to respond. I don't know whether I'm going to gain a friend or lose one. And I'm an evangelist!

Second, it is easiest for me to understand something new when it is simple, clear, and to the point. "Stop making it so difficult," I often want to plead. Put it in language I can understand, and give it to me one point at a time. Don't throw "the whole ball of wax" at me at once. Give me one point, let me understand it, and then move on to the next point.

Therefore, I've had an intense desire to write a textbook on personal evangelism—one that anyone, anywhere can follow, yet one that can also be used on a college or seminary level. But I wanted to write it particularly for the people who are serious about evangelism—so serious that they want their lives to be used consistently by God to introduce others to Christ. My burden is for the person who says, "I'm scared. I don't evangelize, but I want to change that. Please help me learn how to do it so that month by month I can see God using me in some way to affect the lost."

This book is one way to further minister to the many people who have attended our training seminars throughout the world. It is also a way to thank the many people who have said to me, "Your thoughts on and your study of Scripture and your ability to express things simply have helped me. Would you ever consider writing a book and putting these things into print?" Those comments humbled me but encouraged me as well.

I wanted to look at the message we have for the lost for the simple reason that I became "freed up" when I clearly understood what the message was and how to communicate it accurately to someone else. I

9

no longer felt guilty that maybe I didn't tell them everything I should have. In helping thousands of people in evangelism, I discovered that they too experienced this same freedom when they clearly understood the message Christians have to share with the lost.

As I wrote this book, I handled Scripture very carefully. Evangelists are often not respected by Bible scholars. They feel that evangelists are too sloppy in the way they handle the Scripture. So I wanted this book to reflect the study and commitment I have to the clear exposition of Scripture. I didn't want to avoid the hard-hitting questions that those who evangelize will face: Do we have a right to tell people their good works will not save them? What about the verses that appear to teach that baptism saves? On what basis does a person know they're saved? What part does an open and public profession of Christ play in salvation? Can a person really be a Christian and be living in sin? If so, how do you deal with that kind of person—as one who is not saved or as a "backslidden Christian"? How can you talk about hell and expect people not to be scared away? How do you conquer fear? How do you demonstrate wisdom in your relationships and conversations with non-Christians? What do you do with a person the moment he or she comes to Christ?

Each chapter ends with a section called So What? I wanted to first examine each subject from a biblical context as simply and clearly as I could. Then I wanted to answer the question, "What difference does this make in the way I approach my neighbor, friend, coworker, relative, or person I sit next to on a plane?" I hope you enjoy the many real-life experiences in the So What? section that will bring the concepts of the chapter to life.

Interaction with other believers plays a big part in remembering, digesting, and applying what you've learned. I've also included group discussion questions at the end of each chapter so you can pull ideas and experiences together and profit from mutual interaction.

During the "Tell—Scotland" evangelistic campaign of the mid-1950s, a minister active in promoting the campaign wrote to the headquarters in Glasgow: "We have our committees organized, our literature prepared, our schedules set, our promotion underway. We are ready now to take part in 'Tell—Scotland.' But, pray tell me, what are we to tell Scotland?"[1] My prayer is that through this book, you will be free of excuses, be able to overcome the fear of evangelism, and know how to clearly communicate the Good News of Christ. I hope too that you will have a greater understanding of the things related to

---

1. Leighton Ford, *The Christian Persuader* (New York: Harper and Row, 1966), 93.

evangelism, such as prayer, wisdom, boldness, follow-up, and so forth. If these things happen, every moment spent in writing this manuscript will be worth it. And even more, I'll look forward to meeting the people that you've introduced to our tremendous Savior.

My sincere desire is that you will find this book tremendously helpful in your personal evangelism and that as a result you will commit your life in a fresh way to doing the most exciting thing on earth—clearly introducing others to Jesus Christ.

R. LARRY MOYER

Chapter One

When Is Good News the Good News?

As I neared the chapel, I perceived that someone was in the pulpit preaching, and who should the preacher be but my dear and venerable grandfather! He saw me as I came in at the front door, and made my way up the aisle, and at once he said, "Here comes my grandson. He may preach the gospel better than I can, but he cannot preach a better gospel; can you, Charles?"

—Charles H. Spurgeon
C. H. Spurgeon Autobiography
Volume 1: The Early Years 1834–1859

Some years ago, a commuter train stalled on the tracks moments before a freight train was due to arrive. A conductor ran to flag down the approaching train, and the passengers were assured that there was no need for worry. As they began to relax, the freight train suddenly came bearing down upon them.

The engineer of the freight train narrowly escaped death by jumping just before the impact. He later testified in court why he had not stopped: "I saw a man waving a warning flag, but it was yellow. I thought he just wanted me to slow down." Examining the flag in question explained the confusion. The flag had once been red, but long exposure to the sun and weather had turned it a dirty yellow color. The cause of the crash can be stated in one sentence: The message was not clear.

When I first read that story, I agonized because that same lack of clarity can occur in spiritual realms. When talking to non-Christians, we often use words and phrases such as, "The gospel is the good news that Christ wants to come into your life and give you happiness and meaning. Nobody knows how to run your life better than He does because He is the one who made you." "The gospel is forgiveness. God wants to wipe out the past and allow you to start all over. If you surrender your life to Him, He'll start right now." "The gospel concerns your eternal destiny. We are all headed to an eternal hell. But God has made it possible for us to go to heaven. All we have to do is invite His Son into our lives." Although we mean well in saying these things, we have not communicated the simple message that God wants us to share as accurately and clearly as we should have.

Why not? Why is there such confusion? Why is it so easy for us to make the message of the Gospel unclear?

C. H. Spurgeon put his finger on one cause of the confusion when he said, "When a man does not make me understand what he means, it is because he does not himself know what he means."[1] We are often unclear when we share the good news because we aren't sure how to define the good news.

First, we should understand the meaning of the word *gospel*.

THE WORD *GOSPEL* USED OUTSIDE THE BIBLE

Our word *gospel* is a translation of the Greek word *euangelion,* which simply means "good news." As we often greet someone today with the expression, "How are you?" it was not uncommon in biblical times for one person to address another with the question, "Have you any good news for me today?" It was even used to communicate news of victory in battle. When a messenger arrived from a battlefield with his face radiant, his spear decorated with laurel, his head crowned, and his right hand raised in greeting, it was known that he brought good news.[2] The phrase took on a religious connotation when the Cult of the Emperor was the state religion of the Roman Empire. The ruling Caesar was believed to be divine by nature; many Roman citizens believed his appearance brought good fortune to the whole kingdom. Therefore, the announcement of his birth, his enthronement, his speeches, and his decrees were all considered *euangelion*—"good news."[3]

THE WORD *GOSPEL* USED IN THE BIBLE

The word *gospel* used within Scripture sometimes has a nonreligious meaning, as in 1 Thessalonians 3:6: "But now that Timothy has come to us from you, and brought us good news *[euangelion]* of your faith and love, and that you always have good remembrance of us, greatly desiring to see us, as we also to see you." Paul only refers to the good news about the Thessalonian believers, not the good news of Christ.

The main use of *gospel* in the Bible, however, is in connection with a religious proclamation. The New Testament often refers to the "gospel of the kingdom." Matthew 4:23, for example, says, "Jesus went about all Galilee, teaching in their synagogues, preaching the gospel of the kingdom." This refers to the good news of the kingdom Christ would establish if the Jews received Him as their long-promised

Messiah (Luke 1:32–33). It was announced, "The Messiah is here and ready to establish His eternal kingdom if you are ready to receive it."[4]

The Jewish people as a whole, however, rejected Christ as their King, but at the end of the coming tribulation period, Christ will again present Himself to Israel as both the Messiah and King. Although Christ has been rejected by both Jews and Gentiles throughout the world, He has not rejected humankind. That is why the Bible also refers to "the gospel of the grace of God in Christ." Paul, facing persecution, told his worried friends, "None of these things move me; nor do I count my life dear to myself, so that I may finish my race with joy, and the ministry which I received from the Lord Jesus, to testify to the gospel of the grace of God" (Acts 20:24).[5] Since grace means unmerited favor, this message is good news concerning the unmerited favor of God toward us.[6]

Therefore, we find that there are two predominant themes surrounding the use of the word *gospel* in the New Testament. The Gospel of the kingdom is the good news that Christ has come to establish His kingdom. The Gospel of the grace of God is the good news that God, through Christ, has graciously made it possible for sinners to enter His kingdom. The two themes are distinguishable but inseparable because the Gospel of the kingdom includes the Gospel of the grace of God.

How do we explain this unmerited favor of God toward us? One of the most accurate and meaningful descriptions is given by Paul the apostle in 1 Corinthians 15.

WHAT IS THE GOOD NEWS OF THE GOSPEL?

When Paul preached in Athens, the Greek philosophers were offended at the very idea of a literal and physical resurrection (Acts 17:32). Paul wasn't very patient with such thinking. If there is no resurrection, he said, there is no Good News to preach.

To begin his discussion of the resurrection, Paul stressed the importance of the Gospel: "Moreover, brethren, I declare to you the gospel which I preached to you, which also you received and in which you stand, by which also you are saved" (1 Cor. 15:1–2). Paul was not dealing with a minor detail. The Gospel he was about to define is the one by which the Christians in Corinth were saved. This is not second-class material.

Having caught the readers' attention, Paul then continued, "If you hold fast that word which I preached to you—unless you believed in vain" (v. 2). You might ask if Paul was implying that if people backslide, they have lost their salvation or they were not saved in the first place. Not at all! When Paul said, "If you hold fast that word which I preached to you," he was thinking of the moment they came to faith in Christ, the moment they took a firm grip on his message. When he added, "Unless you believed in vain," he was not doubting the genuineness of their faith. Instead, his idea is "unless true believing led you nowhere." That does not happen, since faith in a Christ who is risen always produces salvation. God performs what He promises.

Paul now defines the Gospel: "For I delivered to you first of all that which I also received: that Christ died for our sins according to the Scriptures, and that He was buried, and that He rose again the third day according to the Scriptures, and that He was seen by Cephas, then by the twelve" (vv. 3–5). The facts concerning Christ are conveyed by four prominent verbs.

Christ Died

Paul said, "Christ *died* for our sins according to the Scriptures" (1 Cor. 15:3). Christ died as our substitute. Had He not taken our punishment, we would all bear it ourselves.

The idea presented here is illustrated in the story of a father who, with his twelve-year-old daughter and eleven-year-old son, hiked up Mount Ranier on Memorial Day weekend in 1968.[7] I've used it often in speaking because it so beautifully illustrates what Jesus did for you and me. An hour after they began the ascent, a blizzard struck high on the flanks of the great mountain, trapping the father and his two young children. The temperature dropped to twenty-two degrees with wind and snow blowing at sixty miles an hour. They could neither see nor move. A few steps in the wrong direction could be suicide. The three of them trampled out a six-foot circle and then anchored a tarp over the depression they made in the snow. The father helped his son and daughter into their sleeping bags and placed himself near the opening of their tiny cave to protect them from the wind. Three days later, a search party found the trio. The children were alive, but the father had died. The young girl told the search party, "Dad gave his life for us."

Christ died as my substitute and yours. Had He not died, we would have to suffer our own punishment. He died "according to the Scriptures," Paul said. Isaiah, for example, seven hundred years before Christ, prophesied His death when he said, "He was wounded for our transgressions, He was bruised for our iniquities" (Isa. 53:5).

Christ Was Buried

The second verb Paul used concerning Christ is that "He was *buried*" (1 Cor. 15:4). Since Paul did not repeat the phrase "according to the Scriptures," it is likely that he mentioned Christ's burial simply as proof that He died. The proof of death is burial.

Christ Rose

The third verb Paul used is that "He *rose* again the third day according to the Scriptures" (1 Cor. 15:4). This is the second time Paul used the phrase "according to the Scriptures." He wanted his readers to know that, just as Christ's crucifixion was not a surprise, neither was His resurrection. David predicted the resurrection of Christ when he said, "For you will not leave my soul in Sheol, Nor will You allow Your Holy One to see corruption" (Ps. 16:10).

Christ Was Seen

The fourth verb Paul used is "seen": "He was *seen* by Cephas, then by the twelve" (1 Cor. 15:5). Notice again that Paul did not repeat the phrase "according to the Scriptures." It is likely that just as Paul mentioned Christ's burial as proof that He died, he mentioned that Christ was seen as proof that He arose. In verses 5 through 8, Paul gave an account of the many individuals who saw the risen Christ. Stop and think about it! These were not people who had not known Him and, therefore, might have mistaken Him for someone else. These were people familiar with Him.

The Gospel—the Good News of Christ—is that *Christ died for our sins; Christ arose*. His burial is proof that He died. The fact that He was seen is proof He arose. So the Gospel in its simplicity is that Christ died for our sins and arose. These are the exciting facts we are privileged to announce. Christ wants to come into your life and give it meaning and happiness, and the Gospel does concern forgiveness. But we dare not overlook the fact that these have significance only as they are properly related to the facts of the Gospel. The clearest way to present the Gospel is to give the historical facts as they are given in the New Testament. The Good News we are privileged to announce is that "Christ died for our sins; Christ arose."

CONCLUSION

A noted Bible teacher once said, "Remember—you have not preached the Gospel until you have given people something to believe." What people are asked to believe is defined and expressed in 1 Corinthians 15: *The Good News is Christ died for our sins; Christ arose.*

The great emperor Napoleon had three commands he gave his messengers as they conveyed his messages to various sections of his army. Those three commands were, "Be clear! Be clear! Be clear!" Those who are entrusted with proclaiming the Good News of Christ must also be clear.

So What?

Now that we know what the good news is, so what? How should this effect how we share the Gospel with the lost? We know what the Gospel is, but we should also know that it has four unique qualities. It is objective, finished, proven, and never-changing.

First, the Good News is *objective*. It focuses on what Christ has done and not on what we want Christ to do in our lives. What happens when we become subjective and focus on our own desires? We attempt to persuade the lost to come to Christ based on what they have seen in Christians. What happens when they realize that Christians sin too? Have you ever heard someone say, "Christians are hypocrites"? Christians ought to make Christianity attractive, but they never make it credible. Even if Christians or individual churches were near-perfect, people would still go to hell when they died. The Good News, however, is that Christ died and arose. That is what makes Christianity credible. Through personal trust in Him, we can now go to heaven when we die. The Gospel has nothing to do with Christians, it has everything to do with Christ.

Second, the Good News is *finished*. Christ died for our sins, was buried, and arose from the dead. It's finished. Christ has already sacrificed Himself in our place. There was nothing we could do to reconcile our sin before God. Only a holy sacrifice could be acceptable to a holy God. We could never achieve that holiness on our own. Christ interceded on our behalf. Only He was the perfect and holy sacrifice.

Third, the Good News is *proven* historical fact. Christ's death and resurrection are a part of history. Jesus was born, grew up, had friends, became a teacher, performed miracles, died on a cross, was buried, rose from the dead, and was seen. No other religion can claim a God who has risen from the dead. This is unique to Christianity. And it is proven.

Fourth, the Good News is *never-changing*. Regardless of time or culture, the message remains the same. Make sure you're telling the right message, though. For example, if you tell people in New Delhi, India, that if they trust Christ, their lives will really be better, they will most likely think that you mean they will never know poverty or starvation again. Is that true? No. What is true? The clear Gospel—that Jesus took the punishment for their sins on the cross and rose again so that we may enjoy eternal life—will make them understand the Good News. They will come to understand that regardless of how difficult life on earth can be, they can be with Christ forever in eternity.

What happens when we lose the meaning of this objective, finished, proven, never-changing focus of the Gospel? The answer again is that the thrust of our message changes. Why did Christ die on the cross? So that individuals might have their marriages mended? No! So that individuals might be fulfilled? No! These things have occurred when individuals have trusted Christ, but unhappy marriages and unfulfilled lives are simply symptoms of an even larger problem—separation from God. Christ died on the cross for one reason—to bring everyone who trusts Him into a right standing with God. If we lose sight of that, we may neglect to tell people what they need most and in so doing, may not lead them to Christ at all. The first and foremost issue is not a broken marriage or an unfulfilled life, but separation from God. We must establish the issue of the cross and resurrection of Christ and the need to trust Him for eternal life. Christ's death and resurrection *are* the good news we are privileged to announce.

During an evangelistic outreach in Pennsylvania, a man responded to the invitation to trust Christ as his only way to heaven. In the counseling room, he unfolded his previous week's experience. Having messed up his life, he had responded to an invitation at another church to "come to Christ and He'll straighten up your life." He confided, "Things are better but something is still missing. I don't even know that I'm going to heaven." I went through the Gospel with him, explaining how Christ took his place on a cross and rose again. Because Christ's death completely paid for our sins, God was now offering him heaven for free. I stressed to him that before he ever concerned himself with what God wanted to do in the future for him, he first must concern himself with what God had already done for him. I explained that he must answer the question God was asking, "Will you accept what My Son did on the cross and trust Him for a right and eternal standing with Me?" He instantly exclaimed, "Nobody has ever shown me this. I didn't even know He died for me." He trusted Christ and rejoiced in what he knew to be a fact—heaven was his because of Christ's death and resurrection.

The Gospel as found and preached in the Bible concerns the objective, finished, proven, never-changing fact: Christ died and arose! Often, what we share with the lost is the entire Bible—everything from Genesis to Revelation. Yet we leave out the message God most wants the non-Christian to hear. The Bible *contains* the Gospel, but the Bible is not the Gospel. The Bible includes everything from God's creation of the earth in Genesis to His creation of a new earth in Revelation. The Gospel, however, is the message of the death of Jesus Christ for our sins and His resurrection. God could not have given us a simpler message. A simple message with such profound purpose—to save the lost.

Group Discussion Questions

- As you reflect upon opportunities you have had to present Christ to the lost, how have you allowed the conversation to drift away from the Good News of Christ's death and resurrection?

- Understanding the simplicity of the Gospel, how much biblical knowledge must believers accumulate, or how well must they be able to defend their beliefs before they can evangelize?

- In what ways should the simple gospel message effect your personal walk as a Christian? Be specific.

Chapter Two

What Is Sin?

It is related that William E. Gladstone (an esteemed British statesman), was once asked what was the great lack of modern life. He replied slowly and reflectively, "Ah, a sense of sin; that is the great lack of modern life."

—Herbert Lockyer
All the Parables of the Bible

Years ago, newspapers were filled with stories about Donald Harvey, a former nurse's aide in Cincinnati, Ohio. He pleaded guilty to killing twenty-four people by poisoning them with cyanide, arsenic, rat poison, and cleaning substances. However, in a televised interview, he dismissed suggestions that what he did was wrong. He described the murders as mercy killings in light of the victims' circumstances: "I visualized myself being in that same position, and laying there and suffering for years and no one cared to come and see me. And I thought I'd put them out of their misery, like I hope someone would put me out of my misery."[1]

Extreme as this example is, it shows that what seems wrong to one person may not seem wrong to another. The often-quoted statement "If it feels good, do it" is not merely a bumper sticker, it is the principle that governs many lives in every culture. Though we may not carry it to the point that Donald Harvey did, we all have inadequate conceptions of sin. We need an absolute standard by which to measure our thoughts, words, and actions. That standard is God's standard. What was true in the past is true in the present. We lack a true sense of sin.

Such a standard is certainly crucial for recognizing our need for the Savior. Spurgeon observed, "Before you can get a sinner saved, you must get him lost." Christ's own words verify this when He said to Zacchaeus, the sinful tax collector, "The Son of Man has come to seek and to save that which was lost" (Luke 19:10). To the Pharisees who regarded themselves as righteous, Christ said, "Those who are well have no need of a physician, but those who are sick" (Matt. 9:12). Unless, however, we can define sin biblically, we have no answer for the lost person who justifies his sinful condition by asking, "What right have you to judge?"

What is sin? How does God feel about sin? How should we feel about sin? What are the consequences of sin? How are guilt and sin related? These are all pertinent questions demanding biblical answers.

WHAT IS SIN?

The Bible looks at sin from different angles. Two prominent ideas surrounding the biblical teaching on sin are of *missing the mark* and *rebellion*.

Missing the Mark

One way God characterizes sin is "missing the mark" or "missing the divine standard." This is seen in the two predominant words for sin used in the Old and New Testaments.

The principal Hebrew word in the Old Testament for sin is *hatta't*, whose verb form is used in Judges 20:16 to speak of the 700 Benjamites who could sling stones without missing a target, however small: "Among all this people there were seven hundred select men who were left-handed; every one could sling a stone at a hair's breadth and not miss." The Hebrew word used here is *hatta't*. This idea of missing the mark characterizes not only this particular Hebrew word for sin, but the whole concept of sin in the Old Testament.[2]

Two examples from the Old Testament that depict sin as missing the mark are found in Psalm 51, which contains David's confession of his sin with Bathsheba. When Nathan confronted David with his adultery, David confessed to God, "Against You, You only, have I sinned, and done this evil in Your sight" (v. 4). David recognized that although his sin involved others, it was primarily against God. He confessed that God's standard is so exact and perfect that he had broken it from the time he was born. He said, "Behold, I was brought forth in iniquity, And in sin my mother conceived me" (v. 5). David recognized that from the moment of conception, man possesses a sinful nature causing him to act in ways that miss the mark of God's standard.

To convey the idea of missing the divine standard in the New Testament, the predominant Greek word *hamartia* is used and is simply translated "sin." One example of this word in the New Testament is Romans 3:23: "For all have sinned and fall short of the glory of God." Another reference communicating this same idea is Romans 3:9–12. There Paul said, "What then? Are we better than they? Not at all. For we have previously charged both Jews and Greeks that they are all under sin. As it is written: 'There is none righteous, no, not one; there is none who understands; there is none who seeks after God. They have all gone out of the way; they have together become unprofitable; there is none who does good, no, not one.'" Measured by God's standard, we have all missed the mark. We are all sinners.

Rebellion

Sin is also characterized in Scripture as rebellion. Two other frequently used words for sin in the Old and New Testaments bring out this idea of rebellion. In the Old Testament the Hebrew word *pesha'* (verb *pasha'*) is used to denote the willful breach of a relationship of peace or alliance. In 1 Kings 12:19 concerning Israel's renouncement of the dynasty of David, we are told, "So Israel has been in rebellion [*pasha'*] against the house of David to this day." Isaiah spoke of Israel's rebellion against God, depicting Israel as children rebelling against parental authority. "Hear, O heavens, and give ear, O earth! For the LORD has spoken: 'I have nourished and brought up children, And they have rebelled [*pasha'*] against Me" (Isa. 1:2).

In the New Testament this same idea of rebellion is conveyed by the Greek word *adikia*. Often translated "unrighteousness," *adikia* covers a wide range of injustices such as indecency, immorality, or the violation of a society's standards, laws, and regulations. Romans 1:18 indicates the variety of offenses this word covers. "For the wrath of God is revealed from heaven against all ungodliness and unrighteousness [*adikia*] of men, who suppress the truth in unrighteousness [*adikia*]."

One of the clearest passages that describes sin as rebellion against God is Romans 1:28–32:

> And even as they did not like to retain God in their knowledge, God gave them over to a debased mind, to do those things which are not fitting; being filled with all unrighteousness, sexual immorality, wickedness, covetousness, maliciousness; full of envy, murder, strife, deceit, evil-mindedness; they are whisperers, backbiters, haters of God, violent, proud, boasters, inventors of evil things, disobedient to parents, undiscerning, untrustworthy, unloving, unforgiving, unmerciful; who, knowing the righteous judgment of God, that those who practice such things are worthy of death, not only do the same but also approve of those who practice them.

Although we wrong our neighbor and society when we sin, it is ultimately a rebellion against God. His holiness has been violated when we sin, and though we may consider ourselves passively involved in what we have done wrong, He considers us the originators of the wrongdoing. In Leviticus 4:13, for example, God spoke of an unintentional sin among the congregation of Israel. He proposed a situation in which "the whole congregation of Israel sins unintentionally, and the thing is hidden from the eyes of the assembly." Whether it was intentional or unintentional, God called it sin: "When the sin which they have sinned becomes known, then the assembly shall offer a young bull for the sin, and bring it before the tabernacle of meeting" (v. 14).

Whenever, wherever, and however we sin, we have missed God's standard; we have rebelled against Him.

HOW DOES GOD FEEL ABOUT SIN?

The question is not, Does God know about our sin? Certainly He does. The psalmist confessed, "O God, You know my foolishness; and my sins are not hidden from You" (Ps. 69:5). How does God feel about our sin? The answer is that sin is absolutely and undeniably repulsive to God.

Nothing could make God's feelings plainer than the repeated statements in Scripture that sin is an abomination to God. In Deuteronomy 25, Moses exhorted the Israelites to be totally honest in their business dealings. Thinking of those who would be less than honest, he told them, "All who do such things, and all who behave unrighteously, are an abomination to the LORD your God" (v. 16). The Hebrew word for "abomination" literally means "a thing of horror." It is used in Psalm 88, a prayer for help written by a man close to death. His physical appearance was so repulsive that his friends avoided him. He said to God, "You have made me an abomination to them" (v. 8). That is, as he lay on his deathbed in such a condition, his friends considered him a thing of horror.

Sin is a thing of horror to God. It is so horrible that after God created man, and man became wicked, God regretted for a moment that He had ever made man. "The LORD was sorry that He had made man on the earth, and He was grieved in His heart" (Gen. 6:6). God went so far as to list sins that are particular objects of His wrath. Among them are homosexuality and other sexual perversions (Lev. 18:22–30), idolatry (Deut. 7:25), human sacrifice (Deut. 12:31), occult activities (Deut. 18:9–14), pride, lying, murder, and a deceitful and wicked heart (Prov. 6:16–19).

Why is sin such a horror to God? Simply because it is the opposite of everything that God is. Habakkuk 1:13 illustrates this contrast when the prophet confesses to God, "You are of purer eyes than to behold evil, and cannot look on wickedness." Sin is detestable to God's holiness. God being what He is—holy—makes sin what it is—horrible.

Understanding the truth of sin makes Christ's work at the cross that much more significant. A perfect God must demand a perfect and complete payment for sin, a payment no sinner could make. It took His all-righteous Son to atone for an all-sinful humanity. Nothing else would have sufficed, and no one else could have satisfied His holy demands.

HOW SHOULD WE FEEL ABOUT SIN?

God's feelings about sin are clear. But how should we feel about sin? What is repulsive to God ought to be repulsive to us. We should so revere and respect God that we find disobedience repulsive. Scripture refers to the "fear of God," a phrase that depicts reverential respect. It does not mean that one should cower in fear of God. When Moses called upon Israel to commit themselves totally to the Lord, he said, "And now, Israel, what does the LORD your God require of you, but to fear the LORD your God?" (Deut. 10:12). Moses told them that to fear the Lord would cause them "to walk in all His ways and to love Him, to serve the LORD your God with all your heart and with all your soul, and to keep the commandments of the LORD and His statutes which I command you today for your good" (vv. 12–13). Proverbs, which speaks fifteen times of the fear of the Lord, says, "The fear of the LORD is to hate evil; pride and arrogance and the evil way and the perverse mouth I hate" (8:13).

Why do people outside of Christ not have this view? On October 9, 1981, *The Dallas Times Herald* told of a gunman who fired on a police officer during a chase in Brooklyn, New York. Authorities claimed that while the officer lay bleeding on the ground, the crowd tried to rob him. Romans 3:18 describes such people as having "no fear of God before their eyes." Individuals outside of Christ are spiritually dead and blinded to their own sin. Their "deadness" is spoken of in Ephesians 2:1: "And you He made alive, who were dead in trespasses and sins." The deadness there is not physical but spiritual. Those who are dead physically cannot respond to physical things; those who are dead spiritually cannot respond to spiritual things. They are separated from God.

Paul wrote of their blindness: "But even if our gospel is veiled, it is veiled to those who are perishing, whose minds the god of this age has blinded, who do not believe, lest the light of the gospel of the glory of Christ, who is the image of God, should shine on them" (2 Cor. 4:3–4). In this usage, *blinded* means that Satan, the god of this age, has deprived them of insight. Unless the Spirit of God works in their lives, people outside of Christ do not see their need. As Paul said earlier, "The natural man does not receive the things of the Spirit of God, for they are foolishness to him; nor can he know them, because they are spiritually discerned" (1 Cor. 2:14).

Sin often appears pleasurable and inviting, even to the believer. Scripture warns of "the deceitfulness of sin" (Heb. 3:13). To contemporary society, a vice can appear to be a virtue. Covetousness can appear as cleverness. What may be pleasurable for a sinful moment will have a painful end. How many people have been lured by the deceitfulness of riches (Matt. 13:22) only to discover that those who live in the largest homes and drive the most luxurious cars have nothing of spiritual value? A Christian businessman once told me, "A man with two million dollars in the bank looked across the table at me and said, 'I'd give it all away if I could find happiness in my life.'"

How does a non-Christian come to understand the reality of sin? Such insight requires the ministry of the Holy Spirit. Christ said, "No one can come to Me unless the Father who sent Me draws him" (John 6:44). The Holy Spirit draws people to Christ and enables them to see their need.

John 16:7–11 speaks of the ministry of the Holy Spirit among unbelievers. Jesus prophesied,

> Nevertheless I tell you the truth. It is to your advantage that I go away; for if I do not go away, the Helper will not come to you; but if I depart, I will send Him to you. And when He has come, He will convict the world of *sin,* and of *righteousness,* and of *judgment:* of sin, because they do not believe in Me; of righteousness, because I go to My Father and you see Me no more; of judgment, because the ruler of this world is judged [emphasis added].

The Greek verb translated "convict" in John 16:8 appears seventeen times in the New Testament with various shades of meaning. It conveys ideas such as to expose, convince, reprove, and discipline.[3]

John listed three key truths that the Holy Spirit convicts the non-Christian of: sin, righteousness, and judgment.

First, the Spirit tells them that they are sinners. They have missed the mark of God's standard and rebelled against Him.

Second, the Holy Spirit reveals to unbelievers the standard of Jesus' righteousness. God measures everyone by the standard of perfection—perfection found only in the Son of God. By dying on the cross for our sins, rising from the dead on the third day, and ascending into heaven forty days later, Christ *proved* that He is the righteous Son of God. He could not have been received into God's presence if He wasn't righteous. To be accepted by God, one must measure up to Christ.

Third, the Holy Spirit convicts the non-Christian of judgment "because the ruler of this world is judged." When Christ died on the cross, God met victory and Satan met defeat. The good news is that sinners can be pardoned. The Holy Spirit makes this provision of being delivered from the penalty of sin known to non-Christians.

When people are convicted by the Holy Spirit and recognize the truth of their own sin, the righteousness of Christ, and the condemnation of Satan, they can then say with the tax collector of Luke 18, "God be merciful to me a sinner" (v. 13). As the Holy Spirit works in their hearts, they can be characterized by the curiosity of Nicodemus (John 3) or the attitude of seeking of Cornelius (Acts 10). A new convert, speaking of how the Holy Spirit convicted him, once said, "I heard it, I heard it, I heard it; then one day *I heard it!*" Because sin is so deceitful, non-Christians who are left on their own, being blinded and dead in their sin, never see their need. For that reason, God has to seek them out before they can be moved to seek Him.

WHAT ARE THE CONSEQUENCES OF SIN?

God is noted more for miracles than surprises. God promises that there will be consequences for our actions. His instructions to Adam in the Garden of Eden left no room for misunderstanding: "The LORD God commanded the man, saying, 'Of every tree of the garden you may freely eat; but of the tree of knowledge of good and evil you shall not eat, for in the day that you eat of it you shall surely die'" (Gen. 2:16–17). The moment that command was broken, God kept His word and physical death entered the world.

Today we suffer the results of Adam's sin. The sentence of death was handed down to the human race. Romans 5:17–18 tells us, "By the one man's offense death reigned through the one. . . . Therefore, as through one man's offense judgment came to all men, resulting in condemnation."

"Now, wait a minute," non-Christians have said. "Why should I be punished for what Adam did?" Lest God be considered unfair or cruel in judging all people for one man's sin, Scripture tells us that the reason we deserve death is not simply because of Adam's sin and the resulting condemnation; it is because of our own sin. "Through one man sin entered the world, and death through sin, and thus death spread to all men, because all sinned" (Rom. 5:12). Sin entered the world through Adam and penetrated the whole human race. The reason it spread was not merely that Adam sinned; we all sin. God therefore gives us what we deserve. We are forewarned, "It is appointed for men to die once, but after this the judgment" (Heb. 9:27). Judgment for the non-Christian is seen as everlasting separation from God in eternal torment: "Anyone not found written in the Book of Life was cast into the lake of fire" (Rev. 20:15). The lake of fire is spoken of in verse 10 as a place where "they will be tormented day and night forever and ever."

HOW DO WE KNOW WHEN WE SIN?

The primary means by which God shows people that they are sinners is to use the law. Romans 3:20 says, "By the law is the knowledge of sin." *Law,* when used in contexts that show people their sin, refers to the revelation of God's moral law, commonly referred to as the Mosaic law, as given in the first five books of the Old Testament. This law includes the Ten Commandments and also all the commands that God has dictated. Therefore, people may say, "I'm not as bad as most people," and may feel quite good about themselves, but when looking at themselves in light of the law, they must conclude, "All have sinned and fall short of the glory of God" (Rom. 3:23).

In this connection, it is worth observing the five Greek words used in the New Testament for "sin" and see how they are all used in reference to the law.

1. "For all have sinned *[hamartia]* and fall short of the glory of God" (Rom. 3:23).
2. "Moreover the law entered that the offense *[paraptoma]* might abound. But where sin abounded, grace abounded much more" (Rom. 5:20). *Paraptoma* implies that we have blundered in our attempts to keep the law.
3. "Being filled with all unrighteousness *[adikia],* sexual immorality, wickedness, covetousness, maliciousness; full of envy, murder, strife, deceit, evil-mindedness; they are whisperers" (Rom. 1:29). *Adikia* refers to the ways that the law has been broken.
4. "Whoever commits sin also commits lawlessness *[anomia]*" (1 John 3:4). *Anomia* refers to living outside of the law.
5. "The law brings about wrath; for where there is no law there is no transgression *[parabasis]*" (Rom. 4:15). *Parabasis* implies that we have overstepped the boundaries of the law.

The law raises the standard of righteousness above that of humanity. God demands perfection. Therefore, He is not concerned with *degrees* of failure. James, when rebuking those who showed partiality and favoritism within the assembly, said, "Whoever shall keep the whole law, and yet stumble in one point, he is guilty of all" (2:10). What about those for whom the Mosaic law was not in effect or who were not aware of it?

There is another law behind the law of Moses—our conscience.

When we sin our consciences testify against us that we have missed God's standard. Romans 2:14–15 makes this clear:

> For when Gentiles, who do not have the law, by nature do the things contained in the law, these, although not having the law, are a law to themselves, who show the work of the law written in their hearts, their conscience also bearing witness, and between themselves their thoughts accusing or else excusing them.

No one knows better than Christ the sinful condition of humanity and the need for them to be confronted with the truth of their sin. For that reason, He was direct in showing people their sinful condition. In a confrontation with the Pharisees, Jesus asserted, "You are of your father the devil, and the desires of your father you want to do" (John 8:44). To Zacchaeus, the sinful tax collector, Christ explained His mission by saying, "The Son of Man has come to seek and to save that which was lost" (Luke 19:10). Along with these words are Jesus' repeated warnings about the reality of eternal punishment in hell (Matt. 5:29–30; 10:28; 13:37–43; 13:47–50; 25:41–46; Luke 16:19–31).

Christ's message was basically positive. Christ invited people to heaven with Good News during His ministry. He did not scare them out of hell with bad news. At the same time, He was quick to show people their sinful condition so they could see more clearly their need for a Savior.

CONCLUSION

As seen in Scripture, *sin is missing the mark of God's standard of perfection and rebelling against Him.* Because sin is the opposite of everything God is and represents, it is absolutely repulsive to Him. Although when Adam sinned the sentence of death was handed down to the human race, we suffer the consequences of eternal separation from God because we too have sinned. Only the grace of God extended to us through the death and resurrection of Christ can deliver us. In light of how repulsive sin is to God, it ought also to be repulsive to us. A proper fear of God, where we hold Him in reverential respect, will give us the right perspective on both the holiness of God and the vileness of sin. Unless the Holy Spirit works in our lives, we will never see the reality of our sin. God uses the law, particularly the first five books of the Old Testament, and our consciences to show us that we are sinners.

When we understand sin as it is presented in Scripture, we can only look at ourselves and exclaim with Paul, "O wretched [person] that I am!" When we understand the grace and love of Christ toward us, we can say, "What a beautiful Savior He is."

So What?

Believers are aware that for a non-Christian to come to Christ, they must first realize that they are a sinner. We often overlook the practical lessons that can be learned by a careful examination of the biblical teaching on sin.

USING THE LAW

Did you notice the wisdom of using the law, particularly the Ten Commandments, to show people that they are sinners? Using the law shows that no one can compare himself to a sincere preacher, loyal friend, or moral neighbor. Instead, everyone must measure up to God and His standard of perfection. I was once trying to explain to a young man his need of the Savior. He responded, "I haven't been a very bad person." Using the Bible, I showed him that one of God's commands was never to take His name in vain, meaning never to use it in an irreverent way. When I asked him if he had ever done that, he admitted that he had. He was beginning to see that regardless of how much good he had done, he was nevertheless a sinner. Shortly thereafter he trusted Christ to save him. As an evangelist, I have found that the best way to show a lost person that he or she is a sinner is to use the law of God as He intended—to show need.

DEFINING SIN

We learned how helpful it is to define sin by using the one idea of sin most prevalent in the Scriptures—the idea of missing the mark. I have often explained to non-Christians that when the Bible says we have all sinned, it recognizes that we lie, lust, and hate, to name just a few examples. The word *sin* in the Bible has the idea of missing the mark of God's standard. In other words, God is perfect and we aren't. Let me explain. Suppose you and I were each to pick up a rock. Then suppose I were to say to you, "We will throw our rocks and hit the North Pole." Well, you might throw the rock farther but neither of us would hit the North Pole. Both of us would fall short. When the Bible says, "All have sinned and fall short of the glory of God," it means that God has set a standard. That standard is God Himself. We must be as holy as He is holy, as perfect as He is perfect. It doesn't matter how religiously we live, how good we are, or how hard we work, we *cannot* meet that standard.

Some people resist the idea that they share responsibility for Adam's sin. A person I was witnessing to while flying to Amsterdam in the Netherlands said to me, "I don't see why I should be punished for

Adam's sin. That's not fair." The idea of missing the mark helps them to see that the issue is broader than Adam's sin. They also do not measure up to God's standard of perfection. When it comes to sin, the difference between Adam and us is that he beat us to it! We are all sinners. I explained this to the person on the Amsterdam flight by saying, "Had Adam not sinned, you would have." He quickly responded, "You can say that again. I really know how to sin!"

Even though we suffer the results from Adam's sin and God is punishing us for our own sin, we must remember that He has intervened on our behalf. Therefore no one has a justifiable reason for thinking ill of God. After explaining the sentence of death that has been declared upon the human race, Paul added, "Much more those who receive abundance of grace and of the gift of righteousness will reign in life through the One, Jesus Christ" (Rom. 5:17). Through His Son's atoning death on the cross for our sins, God, in His abundant grace, extends the free gift of His Son's righteousness to all who will trust in Him. That righteous standing with God, which secures eternal life for us, has removed the necessity of condemnation. It is only when we refuse to accept Christ's punishment on the cross for our sins that we must suffer our own punishment.

A biblical study of sin also makes clear to us that we are sinners not because we "feel" guilty. Our guilt before God is not based on feeling. We are sinners because the facts say we are guilty. *Time* magazine once told of a woman who confessed to murder. When asked how she felt about the crime she had committed, she answered, "What I was doing was right. It was coming from love . . . I have no guilt in me. How can someone be killed out of love? . . . whatever I do and know is right when I am doing it feels good."[4]

The same magazine told of looting that occurred during a blackout in New York City. One thief told a *Time* magazine writer, "Well, I got a stereo worth $400, a dining room set that said $600 in the window, and some bedroom furniture, but not a whole suite. I got some tennis shoes, and a few things from the jewelry store, but I got there too late for anything really good. I got it all done in half an hour, that's how quick I was working." Adding it up he continued, "I'd put the total somewhere between $3,200 and $3,500." When asked if he had any remorse about what he had done, he replied, "I've got three kids and I don't have no job. I had the opportunity to rob and I robbed. I'd do it again. I don't feel bad about it."[5]

In both cases, were these two guilty? Certainly they were guilty but not because they felt guilty. They were guilty because the facts said they were guilty. In a similar fashion, you and I are not guilty before God because we feel guilty; we are guilty because the facts say we are guilty.

The simple declaration of Romans 3:23 is, "For all have sinned and fall short of the glory of God."

There is a final conclusion from a study of sin that will help us evangelize. I have sometimes been asked, "Do we talk to lost people about *sin,* meaning their sinful condition before God, or their *sins,* meaning the particular wrongs they've done?" Our study has revealed that being a sinner before God is a matter of both who we are and what we have done. As individuals who fall far short of God's standard of holiness and perfection, our condition is reflected in our conduct. As we have observed, God is specific in naming the ways we have failed Him, and we can also speak specifically to the lost about what they have done. As we do so, they will see who they are and will say with the tax collector of Luke 18, "God be merciful to me a sinner!" (v. 13).

Group Discussion Questions

- How would a Christian's proper attitude toward sin be likely to influence a non-Christian's view of sin?

- Since your coming to Christ, what view of sin has the Holy Spirit given you which otherwise you would not have had? What people or circumstances did God use?

- If we did not have a biblical standard for sin, what standard(s) would we tend to use? How would that change the way we regard sin?

- Are you hesitant to explain to a non-Christian that he or she is a sinner? What are your concerns? How has the content of this chapter affected the way you will explain sin to a lost person?

- Because Jesus Christ did not withdraw from you, a sinner, what does that tell you about your attitude toward and relationships with the lost? Be specific.

Chapter Three

What Is Saving Faith?

Oh, the many times that I have wished the preacher would tell me something to do that I might be saved! Gladly would I have done it, if it had been possible. If he had said, "Take off your shoes and stockings, and run to John O'Groat's," I would not even have gone home first, but would have started off that very night, that I might win salvation. How often have I thought that, if he had said, "Bare your back to the scourge, and take fifty lashes," I would have said, "Here I am! Come along with your whip, and beat as hard as you please, so long as I can obtain peace and rest, and get rid of my sin." Yet that simplest of all matters—believing in Christ crucified, accepting His finished salvation, being nothing, and letting Him be everything, doing nothing but trusting to what He has done—I could not get a hold of it.

—Charles H. Spurgeon
C. H. Spurgeon Autobiography
Volume 1: The Early Years 1834–1859

A friend of mine relayed to me an incident I've never been able to forget. A man confused about what he must do to be saved went to a pastor for help. He told the pastor, "One person says I must invite Christ into my heart; another tells me I must make Him Lord; another says surrender your life to Him; still another says I must take up my cross and follow." Leaning over the pastor's desk, he pleaded, "Please tell me, what must I do?" More than once have I seen that kind of confusion written across the face of a non-Christian.

The Gospel is concerned not only with what God has done for man but also with what God asks man to do. What has been declared must now be acted upon. But confusion about the Gospel is matched or exceeded by confusion on the subject of saving faith.

Why is it so difficult to understand saving faith? One reason for confusion is that saving faith is often examined with the subject of faith in general. Failure to observe that the Scriptures use the term "faith" in different ways and with different objects leads to much confusion.

The centurion's faith when requesting the healing of his servant (Matt. 8:5–13) is often confused with the thief's faith in requesting paradise (Luke 23:39–43). Faith in the realm of physical illness (James 5:15) is sometimes confused with faith in the realm of salvation (Eph. 2:8–9). Faith needed in a day of great tribulation (Matt. 10:22) is often confused with the faith by which one obtains eternal life (John 11:25–26).

Another difficulty is that the biblical use of "believe" is often confused with different common uses of the English word "believe." In almost any household during the course of a week, you may hear these comments:

> "I believe it's going to rain."
> "I believe I'll be able to come."
> "I don't believe it makes any difference."
> "I believe I gave him the wrong address."

For that reason, to mention "believing" in connection with Christ may convey little more than "speculation." However, the biblical use of the word "believe" deals with certainty.

The saying of particular words, phrases, or prayers also contributes to difficulty in understanding saving faith. People often have the impression that one is saved by saying something. As will be seen later, one does not need to *say* anything in order to be saved. Although particular words or phrases may be used to express to God what one has done, saying a prayer has never saved anyone!

Lastly, the study of saving faith becomes difficult because we are dealing with a subject that on the one hand is simple but on the other hand is complex. One writer refers to this when he says:

> In like manner the penitent sinner, feeling an immediate and unspeakable need, lays hold upon Christ. So simple is the act of faith. Yet subsequent reflection upon the soul's experience of believing will invariably discover its amazingly rich complexity; for we are conscious that we have believed the things concerning Christ, that He has become ours, and that we have become His.[1]

In light of the above, two conditions must be imposed on the study of saving faith. One is that the book which must be given priority in our study of saving faith is the gospel of John, the one book written for the explicit purpose of explaining how to be saved. The apostle made his purpose unmistakably clear when he wrote, "These are written *that you may believe that Jesus is the Christ, the Son of God, and that believing you may have life in His name"* (John 20:31). No other biblical writer gives this purpose the way John does as his reason for writing. Just as we turn first to the book of Revelation when studying end times, because the book's purpose includes the revealing of future events (Rev. 1:1–3, 19), so we should turn first to John when studying saving faith.

A second condition to the study of saving faith is that we are not answering the question, What is the minimum a person needs to know to be saved? That is another discussion. Instead, we are discussing the common characteristics of faith as presented in the gospel of John. Whatever the minimum is that a person needs to know in order to be saved, we should not set before people the minimum. Rather, the basic concept of saving faith as it is set forth in the gospel of John should be presented. Several observations need to be made.

THE OFFER OF ETERNAL LIFE

A study of the word "life" in the gospel of John reveals that of the thirty-six times the Greek word *zoe*, meaning "life," is used, twenty-eight refer unmistakably to eternal life. The emphasis in John is not on a wonderful or abundant life on earth, but on eternal life with God. Regardless of whether Christ was speaking to a person who made God the center of his or her life or to a person known for his or her sin, Christ made it clear that He was offering something the person did not already have. To Nicodemus, a Pharisee of good standing among the Jews and knowledgeable in the Old Testament, Jesus said, "As Moses lifted up the serpent in the wilderness, even so must the Son of Man be lifted up, that whoever believes in Him should not perish but have eternal life" (John 3:14–15). To the Samaritan woman, a social leper living in adultery, He declared, "Whoever drinks of the water that I shall give him will never thirst. But the water that I shall give him will become in him a fountain of water springing up into everlasting life" (John 4:14).

The primary concern of our message about Christ is not what kind of life people have here on earth, although that is important. Christ offers something people do not and cannot have without Him—life that never ends. The offer concerns *eternal* life.

CHRIST EXTENDS THE OFFER

In the gospel of John the main object of the word "believe" is Christ and His proclamation. Christ desires people to understand that He, as the Son of God, is specifically the Person who is extending the offer of eternal life.

Note again Christ's discussion with a woman of Samaria. Having come to a well, Christ talked to her about the water He had for her.

He said, "If you knew the gift of God, and who it is who says to you, 'Give Me a drink,' you would have asked Him, and He would have given you living water" (John 4:10).

Christ's words to her are striking. Note that He did not say, "If you knew the gift of God, and who it is who says to you, 'Give Me a drink,' you would have asked *His Father* and He would have given you living water." Nor did he say, "If you knew the gift of God, and who it is who says to you, 'Give Me a drink,' you would have asked of Him, and *He would in turn have asked the Father*." Christ identified Himself as offering her that gift.

John 5 gives further evidence that Christ must be recognized as the one who extends the offer of eternal life. The passage describes one of Christ's many clashes with the Jewish leaders, this one stemming from His healing a man on the Sabbath. That action might have been pardonable had not Christ then claimed equality with the Father (v. 18). After all, not even Abraham or Moses, both highly revered by the Jews, had done that. Instead of apologizing, Christ continues to press His claims: "As the Father raised the dead and gives life to them, even so the Son gives life to whom He will" (v. 21). What bolder claim could there be than that He, as the Son, can give life to whomever He desires! He rebuked the stubbornness and pride of the Jews, telling them, "You are not willing to come to Me that you may have life" (v. 40). If they wished to receive eternal life, He directed them not to the Father, although He claimed equality with Him; He directed them to Himself.

The point is, the gospel of John presents Christ as the one who is extending the offer of eternal life. He is not one who tells about the offer but cannot extend it. Christ presents Himself as the One who gives eternal life to those who receive it. He and His proclamation must be the object of our faith. He proclaimed, "I am the way, the truth, and the life. No one comes to the Father except through Me" (John 14:6).

CHRIST'S DEITY IS THE BASIS OF HIS OFFER

On what basis can Christ offer eternal life? What gives Him the right to extend such an invitation?

The gospel of John reveals that the basis of Christ's offer is His deity. There are three ways this is given attention in John's gospel: John as narrator stressed it, Christ Himself affirmed it, and others attested to it. John emphasized Christ's deity both as he began his book and as he closed it. As John 1:14 says, "The Word became flesh and dwelt among us, and we beheld His glory, the glory as of the only begotten of the Father, full of grace and truth." In this verse, two things are mentioned about Christ, both of which address His deity.

First, John says, "The Word became flesh" (1:14). In the Aramaic paraphrases of the Old Testament, "Word" was used as a designation of God just as it is here and in verse 1. The term "Word" thus speaks of Christ's divinity, while "became flesh" speaks of His humanity (v. 14). John stressed that Christ was God, come in flesh. Because He was God, He never sinned. Though He was man, He did not lay His deity aside when He became man. He was the divine Sovereign in human flesh.

John added, "And we beheld His glory, the glory as of the only begotten of the Father, full of grace and truth." His deity as He walked among the people was proven. Everything from His messages to His miracles confirmed that He was, indeed, the Son of God.

The note on which John began the gospel is also the note on which he ended it. In John 20:30–31 we read, "Jesus did many other signs in the presence of His disciples, which are not written in this book; but these are written that you may believe that Jesus is the Christ, the Son of God, and that believing you may have life in His name."

John did not write simply to give historical information about the Lord. Nor did he select the miracles he recorded merely to present Christ as a miracle worker. Instead, they are intended to show Jewish and Gentile readers that this Jesus is "the Christ." He is the long-promised Messiah who has fulfilled Old Testament prophecy. He is the Son of God. The miracle of the Resurrection—as well as the other miracles John recorded—shows that Jesus is indeed deity.

Direct statements from John are not the only way he stressed Christ's deity. He also recorded the testimony of Christ Himself, by which He declared His relationship to the Father. Having healed a man tormented with a thirty-eight-year infirmity, Christ found Himself in trouble with the Jews. They objected to His healing on the Sabbath Day. Christ answered, "My Father has been working until now, and I have been working" (5:17). In saying this, He asserted in unmistakable terms that He was equal with the Father. As a result, "the Jews sought all the more to kill Him, because He not only broke the Sabbath, but also said that God was His Father, making Himself equal with God" (John 5:18).

Not only did John stress Christ's deity and Christ Himself affirm it, others also attested to it. For example, John the Baptist said, "I have seen and testified that this is the Son of God" (John 1:34). Nathaniel, who had earlier questioned whether anything good could come out of Nazareth, declared, "Rabbi, You are the Son of God! You are the King of Israel!" (1: 49). When many who had surrounded Christ turned away from Him, Christ asked the twelve, "Do you also want to go away?" (6:67). Peter replied, "Lord, to whom shall we go? You have the words of eternal life. Also we have come to believe and know that You are the Christ, the Son of the living God" (vv. 68–69). Thomas's comment in chapter 20 is another example. When facing the risen Lord and the nail prints in His hands and the wound in His side, Thomas exclaimed, "My Lord and my God!" (v. 28).

The evidence speaks for itself. The authority of the offer of eternal life was Christ's. Being God—as Christ's own testimony and the testimony of others revealed—He was completely qualified to extend a gift that only God could give.

HIS DEATH AND RESURRECTION VERIFY THE OFFER

As we study the gospel of John, we discover that Jesus' death and resurrection were divinely designed to bring forth faith in His person and His offer, as in John 2:13–22. When pilgrims came to Jerusalem for Passover, they brought a variety of currency with which to buy animals for sacrifice. The outer courts of the temple became a noisy market for changing money and selling animals. In an act that did not help His standing on the popularity scale, Jesus drove the merchants and their animals out of the temple, tossed out the moneychangers' money, and overthrew their tables.

The Jews, angered by His actions, wanted to know what right He had to do such a thing (v. 18). Christ told them, "Destroy this temple, and in three days I will raise it up" (v. 19). They wondered how He could raise up in three days a temple that had taken forty-six years to build. What they did not understand was that He was referring not to their temple of stone but to His temple of flesh—His own body. His resurrection from the dead demonstrated His right to exercise authority because it proved He was God, sovereign over His temple in Jerusalem (cf. Rom. 1:4).

In light of that, John 2:22 says, "Therefore, when He had risen from the dead, His disciples remembered that He had said this to them; and they believed the Scripture and the word which Jesus had said." At this early stage in his book, John showed that Christ mentioned His own resurrection as the basis on which He would elicit faith.

Probably one of the clearest statements Christ made concerning the purpose of His death and resurrection is found in John 12. There He said, "And I, if I am lifted up from the earth, will draw all peoples to Myself " (v. 32). Christ was affirming that through the purpose and the manner in which He would die, He would ultimately be glorified. As Jesus had just told the disciples, "The hour has come that the Son of Man should be glorified" (v. 23), involving death and new life as a result (v. 24). It was the time of His death and resurrection that He had been pointing to throughout His ministry. Through the Cross, ultimate victory over Satan would be achieved (v. 31) and God's saving grace would be offered to both Jew and Gentile. Through Christ's atoning work on the cross and resurrection, He has proved His ability to give life to those who will receive it.

The comment has been made, "If the Resurrection is true, every other miracle Christ performed is true. If the Resurrection is not true, no other miracle matters." What is meant by this statement is that if Christ supernaturally arose from the grave, He is indeed God and can be trusted in everything He says and does. If He did not arise from the grave, nothing He professed to be and do matters, because He is not God as He claimed to be. Christ Himself made it clear that His offer was verified by His own death and resurrection. Having risen from the grave, He has every right to ask us to put our faith in His ability to give us life.

A DECISION MUST BE MADE TO APPROPRIATE THE OFFER

The offer of eternal life is made. Christ is recognized as the One extending the offer. The basis of that offer is His deity, death, and resurrection. But that, in itself, does not grant anyone eternal life. The offer must be accepted—the gift must be received.

The clearest illustration of this is once again in Christ's conversation with the woman of Samaria in John 4. "If you knew the gift of God, and who it is who says to you, 'Give Me a drink,' you would have asked Him, and He would have given you living water" (v. 10). The gift to which He referred is eternal life. It is He who would like to do the giving. What must she do? In Christ's words, simply ask—"You would have asked Him." His point was that He had what she needed if she would only receive it. She had to appropriate His offer.

Consider next the case of Nicodemus, one prominent in religious circles. Stressing the need to be born again, Christ said to him, "As Moses lifted up the serpent in the wilderness, even so must the Son of Man be lifted up, that whoever believes in Him should not perish but have eternal life" (John 3:14–15). One wonders why Christ used Moses and the serpent for His illustration. Could it be that Nicodemus had just finished teaching the passage in the synagogue? Whatever the reason, it is to Numbers 21 that Christ turned Nicodemus's attention. The children of Israel were on the way to the Promised Land. They were murmuring against God and were dissatisfied with the manna He sent them. To discipline them God sent fiery serpents among the people, resulting in many deaths. Moses then asked God to remove the serpents. God told Moses, "Make a fiery serpent, and set it on a pole; and it shall be that everyone who is bitten, when he looks at it, shall live" (v. 8).

In a similar fashion, because of man's sin, Christ would be lifted up on a cross. In order to be born again and experience eternal life, Nicodemus needed simply to "look and live," just as in Numbers 21 one had to "look and live." Jesus explained their "look" as simply believing in Him. Whoever believes in Christ will not perish, but will instead have eternal life (John 3:15).

To Nicodemus, the admonition to look and live would have been both personal and effective. Having fasted, prayed, faithfully attended the synagogue, observed the feasts, and honored the Sabbaths, he was tempted to look at what he had done to give him a right standing with God. Instead, he now discovered he must look to Christ alone for eternal life. He must believe in Him.

This same emphasis on the need to appropriate His offer appears in John 6:35. Christ said, "I am the bread of life. He who comes to Me shall never hunger, and he who believes in Me shall never thirst." Using the analogy of bread, He presented the need for people to take what He offered. Apart from this "coming" and "believing," their hunger and thirst could not be satisfied.

These passages and more show that the offer of the gift does not grant the listener eternal life. Instead, a decision must be made; the gift must be appropriated. In some instances, many responded at once. We are told, "Now when He was in Jerusalem at the Passover, during the feast, many believed in His name when they saw the signs which He did" (John 2:23).

CONCLUSION

We can now answer the question, What is saving faith?

It has two elements. The first is knowledge. It is self-evident that to believe in a person, you must know about the person. The fact that saving faith includes knowledge is not only evident from common sense. It is also plainly taught in Scripture. As Jesus told the Samaritan woman, "If you *knew* the gift of God, and who it is who says to you, 'Give Me a drink,' you would have asked Him, and He would have given you living water" (John 4:10). Similarly, Jesus told a crowd in Jerusalem, "Most assuredly, I say to you, he who *hears* My word and believes in Him who sent Me has everlasting life" (John 5:24). Other writers of the New Testament also told of individuals' hearing before they believed (Acts 18:8; Eph. 1:13). Saving faith is not without content or substance. Before one can believe in Him, one must *know* about Him.

The second element of saving faith is appropriation. Passages such as the ones studied earlier show that personal response is demanded. That response in essence is, "Believing that You have the gift of eternal life and You alone are able to give it, I willingly take what You have to offer." To convey this idea in introducing others to Christ, many use the word "trust." Not only is this consistent with what is meant by the Greek word translated "believe," it also readily identifies in a lost person's mind what God is asking him to do. Having heard the Good News of Christ's substitutionary death and His resurrection, the sinner is asked by God to trust Christ as his only means of salvation. When people trust Christ for salvation, they are relying on Christ's sacrificial work as their only means of a right standing with God. It is then that the benefits of Christ's death are applied to sinners and they are saved by the grace of God. Some people "believe" in our English sense of the word. They mentally assent to the fact that Christ died and arose, while depending on their good works to save them. "Believe" in the biblical sense of the word means that if one mentally assents to the fact that Christ died for his or her sins and arose, they trust in Christ alone to save them.

An illustration might help. Picture a luxury liner cruising in the Pacific Ocean. It begins taking on water and lifeboats become a necessity. Three passengers find themselves in different situations. The first has no knowledge that lifeboats save and therefore never steps into one. The second understands that lifeboats save but for some reason refuses to step into one. The third passenger not only understands the ability of a lifeboat to save, but accepts as being true that the lifeboat has the ability to save. The passenger therefore steps into the lifeboat and in so doing relies upon it as the means of salvation.

Which of the three is saved? The answer is obvious. The last passenger had knowledge and used it. *A person is saved when he or she understands the ability Christ has to save and acts on that knowledge by trusting Christ.* That is saving faith. One is not saved by simply understanding that Christ died and arose or even mentally assenting to that being a fact of history while depending on one's good life for salvation. One is saved when as a sinner deserving of hell, one has trusted Christ alone for salvation.

So What?

Next to a study of the Gospel, the study of saving faith has done more than any other in helping me know how to approach non-Christians in light of what God is asking them to do.

A study of saving faith emphasizes the importance of being clear in talking to others about the Lord. God the Father ordained that His Son die on a cross to pay the penalty for our sins and raised Him to life again. He now asks each person to come to Him as a sinner and trust Christ as his or her only means to a right standing with God. Therefore in inviting men and women to come to Christ, we must invite them to do what the Scriptures ask them to do—trust Christ to get them to heaven. We must make that clear. And to be clear, we must avoid misleading and confusing phrases. Invitations such as "accept Christ,"[2] "give your life to Jesus," "pray to receive Christ," and "invite Jesus into your heart,"[3] are not only not used in Scripture but can result in a person's trusting in a prayer or depending on something he or she did instead of trusting Jesus Christ and what He did.

During an evangelistic outreach in Texas, when I invited those who wanted to trust Jesus Christ to talk with me, a teenager responded. I asked him, "Why did you respond?" He answered, "I've come to realize that I need to be saved." I said to him, "Tell me a little bit about yourself." "Well," he said, "when I was very small, I bowed my head and invited Christ into my heart." So I said to him, "Now let me ask you something extremely important. Have you been trusting Christ or have you been trusting a prayer to save you?" His reply was distressing. "I did not even know Christ died for me. I thought God liked that prayer so much that if you simply said that prayer, you'd go to heaven. I've never understood you have to trust *Christ* to save you." Giving people the kind of message that boy received can be damaging and misleading.

Similarly, in an outreach in Iowa, the man who ministered in song before my message trusted Christ afterward. He explained what happened. "Years ago I went forward in a church to 'accept Christ.' I thought what that meant was that you felt Christ was a great person and you would try to live as good a life as He did. If you did, you'd then go to heaven. I never knew that you had to trust in Christ alone to save you." Again, we must avoid dangerous and misleading phrases.

Although by using these phrases some have meant that we need to appropriate the gift of eternal life by depending on Christ for salvation, such phrases can be so misleading that they are better off forgotten. Unlike the various phrases used about salvation in the New Testament, these confusing terms can convey everything but dependence on Christ as one's only means of having eternal life. We must not use confusing terminology when we can speak clearly.

I once presented the Gospel to a man who said, "Oh, I believe that." Sensing what his problem was, I said, "Yes. I'm convinced you do. You believe Jesus Christ died for your sins and arose in the sense that it was an actual historical event. But you're depending on your good works to save you." He quickly agreed. I continued, "That's the problem. 'Believe' in the biblical sense of the word means that if you mentally assent to the fact that Christ died for your sins and arose, you trust in Him alone to save you." He responded, "Oh, I see what you mean. I've never understood that before." As we talked, I had the joy of seeing him transfer his trust from his good works to Christ alone to save him.

I was one of many privileged to be invited to Amsterdam '86, one of the most rewarding and spiritually profitable conferences I have ever attended. While there I asked an evangelist from a third world country, "How did you come to know the Lord?" He told me of a fearful experience in the jungle from which he had been delivered. Concerned if he genuinely knew what it meant to be saved, I questioned him further: "Well, have you come to a point in your life that you know were you to die, you'd go to heaven?" Immediately he responded, "Oh, I wouldn't say that." So I continued, "Well, if you were to stand before God and He were to ask you, 'What must you do to get to heaven?' what would you tell Him?" He answered, "I've lived a good life, gone to church, and tried to do what was right."

Because the meeting we were both attending was about to begin, a friend and I arranged another time to meet and talk with him. When that time came, however, the evangelist didn't appear; apparently he had forgotten. He, by his own confession, had, like many others, *missed the whole message* of his need to trust, not his own goodness or merit, but Christ, for salvation.

When people come to see their need to trust Christ, many who evangelize consistently have found it helpful to have them verbalize that to God. In simple prayer, they can tell God that they now understand that they are sinners for whom Christ died and arose and are now trusting Jesus Christ to save them. The previous study would remind us to explain to an individual that saying such a prayer has never saved anyone; trusting Christ saves. Prayer is simply the way to confess to God what one has done. For that reason, many who utter such a prayer are actually saved seconds or minutes before they pray, because they have already transferred their trust to the person of Christ as their only way to heaven. Verbalizing to God their trust in Christ, though, can be a great encouragement as they begin verbalizing it to their friends.

We also see the need to make sure our perspective is that of the gospel of John. God's offer concerns eternal life. God is not offering earth with heaven thrown in but heaven with earth thrown in. He does not give us what we need the least; He gives us what we need the most. Many non-Christians lead empty, purposeless lives. They would agree with the man who said, "I ended up at the top of the ladder and at the bottom of life." Others, though, are basically satisfied with life. If we talk with them about spiritual things they may remark, "I'm happy the way I am." But the primary concern of our message about Christ is not what kind of life people have here, whether it be with meaning or without. What Jesus Christ offers is something we do not have and cannot have without Him—life that never ends. Six months before he died of cancer, John Wayne said on national television, "It's kind of irritating to see I was a good-looking forty-year-old and suddenly I can look over and see this seventy-one-year-old. I'm not squawking. I just want to be around for a long time." What people need most is what Christ promises—eternal life. Therefore, so as not to take away from the supremacy of the gift and the depth of love in the offer, we must be sure we offer the lost what Christ offers them—eternal life.

The gospel of John reveals that there is no way a person can come to God for salvation apart from coming to Christ. The Bible gives no one the option of a conviction that says, "I believe in God. I just don't believe in Christ." Such a belief only causes one to remain in a lost condition. If a person wants to come to God, he or she must come to Christ. Christ could not have been any clearer than when He said, "I am the way, the truth, and the life. No one comes to the Father except through Me" (John 14:6).

Something else we learn is how to respond to the person who asks, "How do you know Christianity is right? The Mormons say they're right, and the proponents of Islam claim they're right. Jehovah's Witnesses claim they're right. How do you know whom to believe?" The answer is not so difficult as it is sometimes made to be. No religion is any better than the foundation on which it rests. Christianity stands or falls on an empty tomb. As the previous study proved, Christ used His own resurrection to solicit faith in Himself. Anyone asked to put faith in another should first ask, "Where's his empty tomb?" Anyone who struggles with who Christ is should study the evidence for the resurrection.

Frank Morison was one who did just that. As an English journalist and a man respected for his intellectual ability, he once stated that he could write a book disproving Christianity and set himself to the task. And as a man of integrity, he carefully collected and studied all the facts. When he was through, he became a believer in Jesus Christ, having been convinced by the resurrection. The first chapter of his book, *Who Moved the Stone?* is entitled, "The Book That Refused to Be Written."

Years ago, I was touring the visitors' center at the Mormon temple in Salt Lake City with a group of young people. Our guide was a commercial airline pilot. As he conducted the tour, I asked him, "What would you say is the basis on which Mormonism rests? On what foundation does it stand or fall?" He politely and accurately answered, "I would have to say, Joseph Smith." I then said to him, "Please do not misunderstand this, but I find that astounding." "Why do you say that?" he asked. I explained that I realized airline pilots were necessarily intelligent individuals. I then added, "It amazes me that you apparently have no reservations about placing everything you believe on someone whom you have no proof rose from the grave. If he did, you are all right. If he did not, you have never been worse off." I will never forget his reaction. Looking rather fearful and despondent, he replied, "I've never thought about that before."

Many people have walked the earth claiming to be the Messiah. Christ is the only one who proved it with an empty grave.

A study of saving faith also makes clear to us that if a person says, "I've always been a Christian," and sincerely means that, what he has basically said is, "I've never become one." No one is born a Christian; everyone is born a sinner (Ps. 51:5). Any person who hears about the offer of eternal life and recognizes his or her need must appropriate that offer personally. Nobody can receive it for someone else. Even birth into a Christian family will not give a person a right standing with God. Since all have sinned, all must suffer the consequences of their own wrongdoing or receive the benefits of Christ's punishment on a cross in their place. People do not have to do anything to suffer everlasting separation from God. Their sin has already condemned them. But a person must do something to live forever. He or she must appropriate the gift of eternal life by trusting in Christ.

At the same time, a study of saving faith makes clear that one dare not go to the other extreme and insist, "If you do not know the date you were saved, you are not saved." More will be said about this in our study of how a new believer can have assurance of salvation, but such an assertion has no biblical support. When Scripture discusses God's free and guaranteed offer of eternal life, it points to a fact, not a date. Whom are you trusting in right now? If you are trusting Christ alone to get you to heaven, you are saved regardless of when and where you crossed the line, though there was indeed a specific place and time. God knows when and where that was, but nowhere does Scripture say that you have to know. John 3:16 says, "For God so loved the world that He gave His only begotten Son, that whoever believes in Him should not perish but have everlasting life." It does not say, "Whoever believes in Him and *knows the date . . .*"

As in so many areas, a careful look at Scripture keeps us on target in what we are saying to lost people and helps us respond accurately and biblically to their questions and struggles.

As the New Testament does, let us be sure we make it clear to the lost that they must appropriate the offer of eternal life by believing. Coming to God as a sinner, a person must trust in Christ alone to save him or her. Now I'll be the first to admit that you and I would not have made it that simple. But then we don't love the way He does. Because He loves us so much, He has made it so simple that even children can understand.

Group Discussion Questions

- From your understanding of the content of this chapter, can a non-Christian be saved anywhere at any time? Why?

- As you consider terminology you have used in the past in explaining to non-Christians what they must do to be saved, how could that terminology have been confusing or misleading to them?

- Instead of seeing the issue of eternal salvation as being that of trusting Christ alone to save them, how do unbelievers tend to view what they must do to be saved? What do you think has caused this confusion?

Chapter Four

What Do We Tell the Lost?

The greatest favor we can do for any human being is to introduce [them] to Jesus Christ.

—Paul Little
What and Why Book

A lost person does not need to know how to *live* the Christian life as much as they need to know how to *enter* it. If we are not careful, we can confuse people by putting the "cart before the horse." We may attempt to tell a non-Christian in fifteen minutes everything it has taken us fifteen years to learn.

For that reason, after having studied the subjects of sin, the Gospel, and saving faith, we now have to bring all these together and ask ourselves, "What, then, do we tell the lost?" Or to put the question another way, "If someone had only five minutes to live and wanted to know how to get to heaven, what does the New Testament instruct us to tell him or her?" That's an interesting question to ask and a rewarding one to answer.

According to what we've learned in the Scriptures, people without Christ need to come to grips with three things.

THEY MUST RECOGNIZE THAT THEY ARE SINNERS

Sin, as noted earlier, is both rebellion against God and a failure to measure up to His standard of perfection. Before anyone can come to Christ, he or she must become aware of being lost. The person who is not thirsty sees no need for water. Similarly, until people see themselves as sinners, they see no need for a Savior.

The account of the feast at Levi's house (Luke 5:27–32) demonstrates that people must first recognize themselves as sinners. The Pharisees and scribes thought that Christ was mistaken in inviting Levi, a tax collector, to be one of His disciples. Tax collectors were despised by everyone because they collaborated with Rome and used their position to rob and cheat the people. But Levi accepted Christ's invitation and "gave Him a great feast in his own house. And there were a great number of tax collectors and others who sat down with them" (v. 29). Disdainfully, the Pharisees asked Jesus, "Why do You eat and drink with tax collectors and sinners?" (v. 30). To associate with one tax collector was deplorable, but for Jesus to mingle with a houseful of tax collectors and sinners was disgusting to the Pharisees. Christ's answer left no room for misunderstanding when He addressed their concerns, "Those who are well do not need a physician, but those who are sick. I have not come to call the righteous, but sinners, to repentance" (vv. 31–32).

Because the Pharisees were righteous in their own eyes by their obedience to Old Testament laws and their own regulations, they saw no need for a Savior. Christ described them as individuals who "outwardly appear righteous to men, but inside . . . are full of hypocrisy and lawlessness" (Matt. 23:28). The tax collectors and sinners, on the other hand, recognized how sick they were in sin. Having no hope themselves, they were able to look and listen to the One who was their only hope.

Another example of someone being aware of their own sinfulness is Christ's description of a Pharisee and a tax collector (Luke 18:9–14). As the two men went to the temple to pray, the Pharisee gave God a list of all the sins he had not done, as well as a list of the good deeds he had done. The tax collector, on the other hand, simply cried out, "God be merciful to me a sinner!" Referring to the tax collector, Christ declared, "I tell you, this man went down to his house justified rather than the other."

In coming to Christ, individuals must first see themselves as sinners in need of salvation.

THEY MUST REALIZE THAT CHRIST ALONE IS THE REMEDY

Problems without solutions produce hopelessness. It is essential that we recognize that we are sinners, but it is equally essential that we understand there is a remedy. Velma Barfield awaited trial in a North Carolina prison for poisoning four people, including her mother and fiance. One thought tormented her: "Nobody could ever love me. Not after what I've done." Overwhelmed by her guilt, she contemplated suicide. To know you are a sinner and yet not understand there is a solution for your sin is to feel trapped for eternity. Eventually, by God's grace, someone came along who loved her enough to share with her the Good News of Christ's saving power. When she walked to the electric chair to die for her crimes, she went as a sinner saved by the grace of God, looking forward to eternity in heaven.[1]

Sinners must understand God's one and only remedy for their sin. God declares that they be left with a message of hope. For that reason, the gospel of John is replete with emphasis on Christ as Savior. In the opening chapter, we are greeted with John the Baptist's witness concerning Christ: "Behold! The Lamb of God who takes away the sin of the world!" (1:29).

This Good News is viewed from three different angles in Scripture. First, the "manward" aspect, spoken of in Scripture by the term *reconciliation,* means that through His death and resurrection, Christ has made it possible for His enemies to become His friends. As 2 Corinthians 5:18–19 puts it, "Now all things are of God, who has reconciled us to Himself through Jesus Christ, and has given us the ministry of reconciliation, that is, that God was in Christ reconciling the world to Himself, not imputing their trespasses to them, and has committed to us the word of reconciliation."

Second, the "Godward" aspect, termed *propitiation* in Scripture. Propitiation means that a holy and all-righteous God was satisfied with His Son's death as sufficient payment for sin. Christ is "the propitiation for our sins, and not for ours only but also for the whole world" (1 John 2:2).

Third, the "sinward" aspect, called *redemption,* meaning that God delivered sinners from slavery to sin by the payment of Christ's own blood. Peter referred to this when he said, "Knowing that you were not redeemed with corruptible things, like silver or gold, from your aimless conduct received by tradition from your fathers, but with the precious blood of Christ, as of a lamb without blemish and without spot" (1 Pet. 1:18–19). These are three different ways of looking at what Christ did on the cross.

How then are these three aspects conveyed to a lost person? By simply doing what the people of the New Testament did: proclaim the Gospel— the death and resurrection of Christ. Paul testified, "Moreover, brethren, I declare to you the gospel which I preached to you, which also you received and in which you stand, . . . For I delivered to you first of all that which I also received: that Christ died for our sins according to the Scriptures, and that He was buried, and that He rose again the third day according to the Scriptures" (1 Cor. 15:1, 3–4).

Note the extremely significant account in Acts 17 of an incident that occurred during Paul's second missionary journey. After Paul went from Macedonia to Greece, he waited for Silas and Timothy to join him in Athens. In verse 16 we are told that Paul's "spirit was provoked within him when he saw that the city was given over to idols." Idols were so abundant that some have wondered if there weren't more idols than people. What, therefore, did he do? The next two verses explain.

> Therefore he reasoned in the synagogue with the Jews and with
> the Gentile worshipers, and in the marketplace daily with those

who happened to be there. Then certain Epicurean and Stoic philosophers encountered him. And some said, "What does this babbler want to say?" Others said, "He seems to be a proclaimer of foreign gods," because *he preached to them Jesus and the resurrection* (Acts 17:17–18, emphasis added).

When the message of Christ's death and resurrection is proclaimed as the remedy for sin, we communicate a message that is both simple and powerful. The newest believer can communicate that message to others, but even the most mature believer is unable to grasp completely the magnitude of what they are telling a lost person when they explain, "Christ died for our sins and arose."

THEY MUST TRUST CHRIST ALONE TO SAVE THEM

A remedy must be accepted by the one who needs it. A doctor capable of performing lifesaving surgery cannot do so until the patient submits to the doctor's careful hand. A person of wealth desiring to help out a friend financially cannot do so unless the friend is willing to receive assistance. Similarly, someone who understands that he or she is a sinner and also understands that Christ took his or her punishment on the cross and rose from the grave does not automatically have a right standing with God. The Scriptures show that a person must believe this truth and receive God's free offer of eternal life. As noted earlier, the issue is an eternal one—one who rejects Christ faces eternal condemnation. One who receives His offer receives eternal life.

It is for this reason that the Bible instructs the sinner to believe. Christ told the people, "He who believes in Me has everlasting life" (John 6:47). The word in English that embodies the meaning of the Greek word for *believe* when it relates to salvation is "trust." Sinners, facing eternal separation from God and recognizing that Christ bore the punishment for their sins on the cross and arose the third day, must trust Christ alone as the only means of salvation. By trusting in Christ and His finished work on the cross, sinners are telling God, "Your Son is my only hope of salvation. Without Him, I am lost." The moment an individual comes in simple faith, he or she stands before the almighty God reconciled, redeemed, and no longer subject to His wrath. The simple promise of John 3:36 is true: "He who believes in the Son has everlasting life."

CONCLUSION

Throughout the New Testament, the one who speaks on behalf of God speaks as a dying man to dying men. As he does so, his message comprises three subjects: the sinfulness of men, the substitutionary death and resurrection of Christ, and the need for personally trusting Him as Savior.

So What?

Every time I think about the simplicity of the gospel message, I get a renewed "fire" to tell it to somebody else. Nothing has affected my motivation more than the simplicity of the message.

The thrust of our message to lost people should be God's offer of eternal life. A non-Christian might say, "What relevance does the offer of eternal life have to the life we live here and now? I have so many problems right now. Don't bother me with the hereafter." The answer is that it has everything to do with our life on earth. The apostle Paul acknowledged, "If in this life only we have hope in Christ, we are of all men the most pitiable" (1 Cor. 15:19). What sense is there in suffering ridicule because we identify ourselves with Christ? What sense is there in using anything from our mind to our money for Christian causes? Why not be like everyone else and go after money, fame, and leisure? The assurance we have of life everlasting gives purpose, meaning, direction, and a future outlook to our lives here.

Its relevance is also seen in the fact that we are never prepared to live until we are prepared to die. How can we experience life at the fullest knowing tomorrow the doctor may diagnose a lump under our skin as malignant? A lost person once said to me, "I don't care about life hereafter. I just want happiness right now." I asked him, "Do you really think it is possible to have happiness now if you don't know where you are going when you die? Stop and think about it. Everything in life can be going great, then one day you get up and discover a lump on your body you have never seen before. You go to the doctor and he gives you three months to live." The lost person looked at me and said, "I see what you mean." How can we be excited about the future with the realization that we may be wiped out in an automobile accident? How can an invalid experience a fulfilling life knowing his physical condition keeps him from enjoying the activities others enjoy? Having eternal life changes our perspective. An invalid's condition becomes temporary. Death separates two Christians for only a limited time. Understanding Christ's promise of eternal life enables one to live as a person prepared to die and die as a person prepared to live.

The story is told of D. L. Moody being in a boat on Lake Michigan when a storm arose. The other passengers became quite upset while Moody remained calm. When asked why he was not fearful, he replied, "I have a sister in Chicago and one in heaven. I don't care which one I see first."

The discussion of the relevance of life eternal to life today need not stop there. Eternal life consists of the Person of God Himself taking up residence within us. Imagine that—God Himself living in us! That is why we live forever. We have not given Him our life; He has given us His. As Paul wrote to the believers in Galatia, "I have been crucified with Christ; it is no longer I who live, but Christ lives in me; and the life which I now live in the flesh I live by faith in the Son of God, who loved me and gave Himself for me" (Gal. 2:20). Some problems are bigger than we are, but no problem is bigger than God. So even though things go wrong, we can live with calmness. Paul could therefore say, "I know how to be abased, and I know how to abound. Everywhere and in all things I have learned both to be full and to be hungry, both to abound and to suffer need. I can do all things through Christ who strengthens me" (Phil. 4:12–13). A Christian looks forward to being with the Lord in heaven but enjoys His presence and its benefits now. Eternal life has every relevance to life lived today—so much so that without it, there is not real life now.

We also observe that if we are genuinely concerned about the evils of our day—homosexuality, adultery, abortion, drugs and alcoholism, just to name several—we have a responsibility before God and an obligation to the lost to announce the Good News of Christ's death and resurrection. To claim that we are bothered by the hideous sins of our day and not be willing to walk across the street and tell a neighbor about Christ is inconsistent at best and hypocritical at worst. We must do as Paul did when he saw a city given over to idols—tell them of Jesus' death and resurrection.

Many, as they consider the need to explain sin, substitution, and saving faith to a lost person, ask, "Is there a method of presenting the Gospel that puts all this together in a way easy to explain it to a non-Christian?" The following is the simple "Bad News/Good News" approach that I have developed and found very helpful. Nothing else I have used or taught has helped people more than this. Perhaps you will want to adopt this method and use it in presenting the Gospel to the lost.

HOW TO PRESENT THE GOSPEL[2]

I normally spend several moments getting to know the person as we discuss family, job, and background. Discussing these areas is very helpful in relating to the lost and will provide a turning point to talk about spiritual things. In order to present the Gospel, I ask a question.

Opening Question: Has anyone ever taken a Bible and shown you how you can know that you're going to heaven? May I?

Transition Point: The Bible contains both bad news and good news.

The bad news is something about you. The good news is something about God. Let's discuss the bad news first.

I. Bad News
    A. You are a sinner.
        1. *The verse:* Romans 3:23 says, "All have sinned and fall short of the glory of God."
        2. *The illustration:* When the Bible says that you and I have sinned, it means that we lie, we lust, we hate, we murder, etc. The word *sin* in the Bible means "to miss the mark." In other words, God is perfect and we are not. Let me explain. Suppose each of us were to pick up a rock, and I were to say to you, "We'll throw our rocks and hit the North Pole." Well, you might throw farther than I, or I might throw farther than you, but neither of us would hit the North Pole. Both of us would fall short. When the Bible says, "All have sinned and fall short of the glory of God," it means that God has set a standard. That standard is God Himself. We have to be holy as He is holy, perfect as He is perfect. But it doesn't matter how religiously we live, how good we are, or how hard we work, we cannot meet that standard. All of us have sinned and fall short of the glory of God.
    B. The penalty for sin is death.
        1. *The verse:* Romans 6:23 says, "The wages of sin is death."
        2. *The illustration:* Suppose you were to work for me one day and I were to pay you fifty dollars. Fifty dollars would be your wages. That's what you have earned. The Bible is saying that because you and I have sinned, we have earned death. We are going to die and be eternally separated from God.

Transition Point: Since there was no way you could come to God, God decided to come to you.

II. Good News
    A. Christ died for you.
        1. *The verse*: Romans 5:8 says, "But God demonstrates His own love toward us, in that while we were still sinners, Christ died for us."
        2. *The illustration*: Let's say that you were in the hospital dying of cancer. I could come to you and say, "I want to do something for you. We'll take all the cancer cells from your body and put them into my body." What would happen to me? (Pause) Right! I would die. What would happen to

you? (Pause) Right! You would live. Why? (Pause) Yes! Because I took the thing that was causing your death and placed it upon myself, and I died as your substitute. The Bible is saying that Christ came into the world, and He took the sin that was causing your death and placed it upon Himself, and He actually died in your place. He was your substitute. The third day He arose as proof that sin and death had been conquered.

B. You can be saved through faith.
  1. *The verse*: Ephesians 2:8–9 says, "By grace you have been saved through faith, and that not of yourselves; it is the gift of God, not of works, lest anyone should boast."
  2. *The illustration*: The word *grace* means undeserved favor. *Saved* means to be delivered from the penalty of sin. Now you may be wondering, "What is faith?" The word *faith* means "trust." For example, you weren't here when that chair was made and you didn't examine how it was built before you sat down. You are simply trusting the chair to hold you. Putting your faith in Christ means trusting Him to save you—not trusting your church membership, your good life, or your baptism to get you to heaven, but trusting Christ and Him alone. Your trust has to be in the One who died for you and arose. It is then that God gives you heaven as a free gift.

III. Conclusion
  A. Question: "Is there anything keeping you from trusting Christ right now?"
  Note: If the person seems hesitant, take a 3x5 card and number from one to five on the left-hand side. Ask the individual to list a few things that keep him or her from trusting Christ right now. Then answer each objection. For example, if a man writes, "I don't know what my wife will say," you might say to him, "I can understand that, but let me ask you something. Do you love her? (Pause) Then, obviously if you knew you were going to heaven, you would want her to know she was going to heaven, too. But just as you can't come back from some place you have never been, you can't introduce her to somebody you don't know. So what you ought to do is trust Christ and then tell her about Him." The point is that you need not push. If the Holy Spirit does not bring nonbelievers to Christ, you cannot. But you can pursue; you can help them think through what is keeping them from trusting Christ.

B. Decision to trust Christ: "Would you like to pray right now and tell God you are trusting His Son as your Savior?"

Note: I ask new believers to tell me how I can go to heaven to make certain they understand it. If they do, I then do one of two things. I either lead them in prayer or have them pray. But before doing either, make certain that they understand that saying a prayer has never saved anyone. Prayer is only *the means* by which a person tells God that he or she is trusting Jesus Christ as his or her Savior.

Prayer: "Dear God, I come to you now. I know that I am a sinner. I believe Christ died for me and rose from the grave. Right now, I trust Jesus Christ alone as my Savior. Thank you for the forgiveness and everlasting life I now have. In Jesus' name, amen."

C. Assurance:
  1. Turn to John 5:24, "Most assuredly, I say to you, he who hears My word and believes in Him who sent Me has everlasting life, and shall not come into judgment, but has passed from death into life."
  2. Have the new believer examine all the verbs of that verse by asking the following questions:
     a. "he who *hears* My word"—Did you do that?
     b. "and *believes* in Him who sent Me"—Did you believe what God said and trust Christ as your Savior?
     c. "*has* everlasting life"—Does that mean later or right now?
     d. "and *shall not* come into judgment"—Does that say "shall not" or "might not"?
     e. "but has *passed* from death into life—Does that say "has passed" or "shall pass"?
        "In other words, you *now have* everlasting life on the basis of fact, not *feeling.*"
  3. Encourage them to commit this verse to memory.

Group Discussion Questions

- How would leaving out the need of seeing ourselves as sinners, the remedy found in Christ's atoning sacrifice, or the necessity of trusting Christ to save us present an inadequate message to the lost? How specifically would the communication of the gospel message to them be hindered if any of these three were ignored?

- As well as you can remember, how many times did you hear the gospel message before you came to Christ? How did each time you heard it build upon what you already knew?

- In what ways would your presentation of the Gospel to a lost person be changed if you knew that he or she had only a few minutes to live? How should the reality of life and death affect our witness?

- Think of particular unbelievers you know. In which of the three areas—sin, substitution, and faith—do you see them the most confused? How are you now better prepared to help them?

Chapter Five

What Is the Biblical Basis for Assurance of Salvation?

The children of God are not perfect, but we are perfectly His children.
—D. L. Moody

New believers are overwhelmed! When they realize the simple truth of the Gospel, they often want to tell someone else about it. Their excitement becomes contagious. I personally do not know of a more exciting person to be around.

But most of them will testify that being excited does not mean they don't struggle. Life can be difficult as new believers seek to expel from their lives what should not be there and add what should be present. Their warm words about Christ will often fall on the cold and deaf ears of those who are convinced that their relative or friend has become a "religious fanatic." Those unimpressed with the testimony of new converts would have them think that they have had merely an "experience" with no validity. Worst of all, there will be times when Satan himself causes new believers to doubt that they are indeed members of the family of God forever. In fact, those first few weeks after new converts come to Christ can be some of the most exciting—and difficult—they've ever had. They must make adjustments to a new life, say no to temptations, and face many challenges.

How new believers respond to such challenges can determine to a large extent whether their Christian growth is stimulated or stymied. If there is one question that must be settled in their minds in order to "grow in the grace and knowledge of our Lord and Savior Jesus Christ" (2 Pet. 3:18), it is the question of their assurance of salvation. It is virtually impossible for new believers to make strides spiritually if they don't have the matter of their eternal destiny settled.

How does the New Testament provide us with assurance of salvation? On what basis can we *know* we are saved?

CAUTION: WHAT IS *NOT* THE BASIS OF ASSURANCE

Christians often explain assurance of salvation to new believers something like this: "Now that you are a Christian, you will be able to love others like you never have before. Jesus said in John 13, 'By this all will know that you are My disciples, if you have love for one another.' In fact, now since you've come to Christ, you won't have difficulty forgiving other people, the way you used to. Day by day you will see things changing in your life and know that you are a child of God."

Wait a minute! Is that the basis on which we are to give people assurance of their salvation? If so, why does 1 Corinthians speak of Christians being so unloving that they were even taking one another to court (1 Cor. 6:1–8)? Why does Acts 15:36–40 speak of Paul and Barnabas having such a severe disagreement that they resolved it by parting ways? Were Paul and Barnabas not Christians?

Such examples should prompt us to reevaluate our understanding of the basis of assurance. Granted, God wants each believer to be a fruitful and producing Christian. As Galatians 5:25 says, "If we live in the Spirit, let us also walk in the Spirit." The fruit of such a walk is earlier defined as love, joy, peace, longsuffering, kindness, goodness, faithfulness, gentleness, self-control (vv. 22–23). Nowhere in Scripture, however, are these things the basis for determining if one is saved.

WHAT IS THE BIBLICAL BASIS OF ASSURANCE

How then does Scripture give assurance to new believers? On what basis can they be assured that they are indeed children of God?

The answer is as simple as the very message that saved them. Consider the repeated emphasis of being confident in our salvation.

> But as many as received Him, to them He gave the right to become the children of God, even to those who believe in His name (John 1:12).

> For God so loved the world that He gave His only begotten Son, that whoever believes in Him should not perish but have everlasting life (John 3:16).

> He who believes in Him is not condemned; but he who does not believe is condemned already, because he has not believed in the name of the only begotten Son of God (John 3:18).

> Most assuredly, I say to you, he who hears My word and believes in Him who sent Me has everlasting life, and shall not come into judgment, but has passed from death into life (John 5:24).

And this is the will of Him who sent Me, that everyone who sees the Son and believes in Him may have everlasting life; and I will raise him up at the last day (John 6:40).

Most assuredly, I say to you, he who believes in Me has everlasting life (John 6:47).

Jesus said to her, "I am the resurrection and the life. He who believes in Me, though he may die, he shall live. And whoever lives and believes in Me shall never die. Do you believe this?" (John 11:25–26).

But these are written that you may believe that Jesus is the Christ, the Son of God, and that believing you may have life in His name (John 20:31).

To Him all the prophets witness that, through His name, whoever believes in Him will receive remission of sins (Acts 10:43).

To demonstrate at the present time His righteousness, that He might be just and the justifier of the one who has faith in Jesus (Rom. 3:26).

Therefore we conclude that a man is justified by faith apart from the deeds of the law (Rom. 3:28).

But to him who does not work but believes on Him who justifies the ungodly, his faith is accounted for righteousness (Rom. 4:5).

Therefore, having been justified by faith, we have peace with God through our Lord Jesus Christ (Rom. 5:1).

Knowing that a man is not justified by the works of the law but by faith in Jesus Christ, even we have believed in Christ Jesus, that we might be justified by faith in Christ and not by works of the law; for by the works of the law no flesh shall be justified (Gal. 2:16).

For you are all sons of God through faith in Christ Jesus (Gal. 3:26).

> In Him you also trusted, after you heard the word of truth, the gospel of your salvation; in whom also, having believed, you were sealed with the Holy Spirit of promise (Eph. 1:13).

> For by grace you have been saved through faith, and that not of yourselves; it is the gift of God, not of works, lest anyone should boast (Eph. 2:8–9).

> And be found in Him, not having my own righteousness, which is from the law, but that which is through faith in Christ, the righteousness which is from God by faith (Phil. 3:9).

> However, for this reason I obtained mercy, that in me first Jesus Christ might show all longsuffering, as a pattern to those who are going to believe on Him for everlasting life (1 Tim. 1:16).

One can see from the Scriptures that faith and assurance go hand in hand. Once an individual trusts Christ, he or she is saved. The one question individuals must answer to determine if they are forever a child of God is, Have I trusted Christ alone as my only way to heaven? If they have, they are as certain of heaven as if they had already been there for a thousand years. As John put it:

> This is the testimony: that God has given us eternal life, and this life is in His Son. He who has the Son has life; he who does not have the Son of God does not have life. These things I have written to you who believe in the name of the Son of God, that you may know that you have eternal life (1 John 5:11–13).[1]

ASSURANCE BASED ON FAITH ALONE IS CONSISTENT WITH THE NATURE OF SALVATION

It should not surprise us that eternal life is guaranteed the moment we trust Christ. Assurance on the basis of faith supports three of the most prominent characteristics of our salvation as presented in Scripture.

The first is that God's saving love is not based on our performance, but on His Son's atonement. When an individual comes to Christ, God looks back to the cross and accepts sinners based on that sacrifice. The work of the cross does not say, "I love you *if* . . ." It says, "I love you—*period!*"

Consider 2 Corinthians 5:21: "For He made Him who knew no sin to be sin for us, that we might become the righteousness of God in

Him." When God's judgment against sin fell, it fell on Christ. God treated the One who had never sinned as though He were the guiltiest sinner of all. Christ took our punishment and died in our place. Since our attempts at righteousness will not satisfy God, Christ clothes us with His righteousness in such a way that when God looks upon us, He does not see our sin; He sees only the righteousness of His Son Christ. This same truth is taught in Romans 4:5: "But to him who does not work but believes on Him who justifies the ungodly, his faith is accounted for righteousness." *Accounted* means that something is "reckoned to our account." Because of Christ's atoning work on the cross, the moment we trust in Him as our only means of salvation, God puts to our account the righteousness of His Son. At the moment of salvation God looks back and receives a person on the basis of the atoning work of Christ.

It is not reasonable that our good or bad performance should alter the assurance of salvation. Regardless of how a Christian may behave, Christ is perfect. Therefore, upon accepting His atoning work on the cross, even the worst sinner is secure in Him. If one were not secure in Christ at the moment of faith, the unconditional character of God's love would be anything but unconditional. Equally, the completeness of Christ's work on the cross would be anything but complete.

A second characteristic of salvation that gives us assurance is that the free offer of life eternal is just that—a free offer. As has been noted to the woman of Samaria in John 4, Christ so simply said, "If you knew the gift of God, and who it is who says to you, 'Give Me a drink,' you would have asked Him, and he would have given you living water" (v. 10). That same theme is repeated in Revelation 22:17 where John, as he closed his unfolding of end-time events, said, "And the Spirit and the bride say, 'Come!' And let him who hears say, 'Come!' And let him who thirsts come. And whoever desires, let him take the water of life freely." The apostle Paul sounded that same note of freeness when he referred to "being justified freely by His grace through the redemption that is in Christ Jesus" (Rom. 3:24).

A third characteristic of our salvation is that God's gift is backed by a promise. If we trust His Son, the promise is, "I give them eternal life, and they shall never perish; neither shall anyone snatch them out of My hand" (John 10:28). We are secure because God, through His promises, holds us. We do not hold Him. When we have come to Him in faith, eternal life is ours. No one is greater than God, and no one is able to remove us from His hands. He said, "My Father, who has given them to Me, is greater than all; and no one is able to snatch them out of My Father's hand" (John 10:29).

WHAT ABOUT SCRIPTURE THAT
APPEARS TO TEACH OTHERWISE?

When faced with verses throughout the New Testament that are clear that salvation is both given and guaranteed upon faith alone, individuals often struggle with verses that appear to teach otherwise. Ten main passages should be considered. As one studies these, one comes to see that assurance of salvation is indeed based on faith. I want to spend some time on these passages because there should be no doubt in our minds that we have assurance of our salvation.

Luke 8:4–15

The parable of the sower and the seed, found in Matthew 13:18–23, Mark 4:1–9, and Luke 8:4–15, is one of the most familiar parables. Of the three accounts of this parable, the gospel of Luke tells us the most about the condition of the four soils.

> And when a great multitude had gathered, and others had come to Him from every city, He spoke by a parable: "A sower went out to sow his seed. And as he sowed, some fell by the wayside; and it was trampled down, and the birds of the air devoured it. Some fell on rock; and as soon as it sprang up, it withered away because it lacked moisture. And some fell among thorns, and the thorns sprang up with it and choked it. But others fell on good ground, sprang up, and yielded a crop of hundredfold." When He had said these things He cried, "He who has ears to hear, let him hear!" Then His disciples asked Him, saying, "What does this parable mean?" (Luke 8:4–9).

The seed is a symbol of the Word of God, and the soil is a symbol of the person who receives the Word. Christ explains that there are usually four different types of responses when the seed is sown.

Concerning the first soil, we are told that when some by the wayside hear, "the devil comes and takes away the word out of their hearts, lest they should believe and be saved" (Luke 8:12). These, by Christ's own admission were indeed non-Christians; they had not believed.

Concerning the second soil, we learn that, "the ones on the rock are those who, when they hear, received the word with joy; and these have no root, who believe for a while and in time of temptation fall away" (Luke 8:13). Bearing in mind that verse 12 told us that those symbolized by the first soil were prevented from believing and were, therefore, unbelievers, we may conclude that those of the second soil were in fact saved by believing. The problem was that when temptation or "tribulation or persecution" (Matt. 13:21) comes along, they "fall away"

(Luke 8:13) or withdraw (as the verb can be translated) from affliction. They are believers who readily testify for Christ in a church service, but then when faced with hardship or the ridicule of relatives, lose that excitement or stumble (as Matthew 13:21 puts it) in their growth. How many believers do you know who would fall into that category?

The third soil presented a different problem. Christ explained further, "The ones that fell among thorns are those who, when they have heard, go out and are choked with cares, riches, and pleasures of life, and bring no fruit to maturity" (Luke 8:14). Following the progression Luke uses, these people went beyond the point of salvation to bearing fruit. The issue in verse 14 is the degree of fruitfulness, not salvation. Their fruitfulness became choked by the cares, riches, and pleasures of life. Although they are believers, they did not progress to a point of spiritual maturity. We all know people like this. Some of us may have fit into this category at one time or another.

The fourth soil presents an account of a growing believer. We read, "But the ones that fell on the good ground are those who, having heard the word with a noble and good heart, keep it and bear fruit with patience" (Luke 8:15). It is rather interesting how the degrees of fruitfulness vary. Some produce "a hundredfold, some sixty, some thirty" (Matt. 13:23). This soil pictures believers saved by the grace of God and progressing to various degrees of fruitfulness.

What is the point of this parable? The difference is in the *soil,* not the *seed.* The difference is in each heart that hears the Word. Far from taking away assurance on the basis of faith, it affirms that one is saved simply by believing, as in the case of the last three soils, or lost by not believing, as in the case of the first. Having trusted Christ, we need to endeavor to be like the last soil, which gives the seed of the Word all the liberty it needs to produce growth.

John 8:31

When Christ said, "If you abide in My word, you are My disciples indeed," was He saying that if one does not abide in His Word one is not saved? Jesus was speaking to believers. As He preached His message concerning who He was and people's need to come to Him, "many believed in Him" (John 8:30). Jesus then told those who believed in Him, "If you abide in My word, you are My disciples indeed" (v. 31). The word *disciple* simply means "learner." Belief results in salvation; abiding in the Word results in true discipleship. Only as we abide in Christ can we also experience the freedom from being slaves to sin (vv. 34–36).

Abiding in Christ's Word is not a condition of salvation. Jesus stresses abiding in His Word as a condition of discipleship.

John 15:6

What exactly did Christ mean when He stated in John 15:6, "If anyone does not abide in Me, he is cast out as a branch and is withered; and they gather them and throw them into the fire, and they are burned"? If we do not abide, we will be thrown into the fire. Does that mean those who are unfruitful are no longer saved or were not saved to begin with?

We must examine the end of the paragraph, which says, "By this My Father is glorified, that you bear much fruit; so you will be My disciples" (John 15:8). Christ was speaking about discipleship, not salvation. This is understandable, since He was addressing the eleven apostles (cf. John 13:1–31). He was not addressing non-Christians or even a mixed audience, but believers who considered themselves His disciples. It is also worth noting that seven times within the first eight verses of John 15, the word *abide* appears—the same word used twenty-six times in 1 John. This, along with Christ's own explanation in 15:8, assures us that He was speaking about fellowship with Christ, not salvation.

The passage is filled with imagery—the vine, the branches, the fruit. The entire paragraph portrays the process of pruning. Dead wood is cut away. The branches that are bearing fruit are cut back so that the clusters of grapes may be rich and full. In order to be fruitful, branches must draw sap from the vine.

Similarly, disciples need to abide in Christ if they are to be fruitful. As they do, they experience answered prayer (v. 7). Undoubtedly, the things they ask of Him are what He desires for them because they are living in close fellowship with Him. His desires and their requests are in harmony with each other. Disciples who do not abide in Him suffer the opposite—even the danger of divine discipline referred to in verse 2 as "every branch in Me that does not bear fruit He takes away." Verse 6 seems to picture a progression of the most unfortunate kind. There is a loss of that abiding relationship, that closeness or fellowship ("he is cast out as a branch"), the loss of spiritual freshness and vitality ("and is withered"), and divine discipline ("they gather them and throw them into the fire, and they are burned"). Since the entire passage involves an image set in the context of discipleship, fire must be taken as a portrayal of divine discipline instead of portraying the literal fires of hell. Other passages in which fire portrays the disciplinary action of God include Deuteronomy 4:23–24 and Hebrews 12:28–29.

The branch that is fruitful experiences the hand of God in a delightful way: "Every branch that bears fruit He prunes, that it may bear more fruit" (John 15:2). The Greek word for *prune* means to "make clean." Men who labored in Palestinian vineyards often had to wash from the branch deposits of insects, moss, and other parasites that could hinder the plant's growth and fruitfulness. As Ryrie states, "In pruning, the wise and loving vinedresser removes all useless things that would sap the strength of the branch and keep it from bearing more fruit."[2] Similarly, it is the Word Christ uses to cleanse the lives of believers and encourage their growth. He said to them, "You are already clean because of the word which I have spoken to you" (v. 3). As disciples experience the cleansing effect of the Word, their fruitfulness is enhanced.

Far from taking away a believer's assurance of salvation on the basis of faith, John 15:6 powerfully reminds believers of the need for an abiding relationship with Christ in order to be fruitful. As Christ stated, "Without Me you can do nothing" (v. 5).

Colossians 1:21–23

Colossians 1:21–23 appears to say that people can be certain they are going to heaven only if they "continue in the faith." We read:

> You, who once were alienated and enemies in your mind by wicked works, yet now He has reconciled in the body of His flesh through death, to present you holy, and blameless, and irreproachable in His sight—if indeed you *continue in the faith,* grounded and steadfast, and are not moved away from the hope of the gospel which you heard [emphasis added].

Paul says that Christ has reconciled Christians through His death (v. 21) that He might present them "holy, and blameless, and irreproachable in His sight" (v. 22). Paul desired that having come to Christ, the Christians at Colosse would now come to maturity and lead holy lives. As he went on to say, "Him we preach, warning every man and teaching every man in all wisdom, that we may present every man perfect in Christ Jesus" (v. 28). The Greek word for *perfect* means "mature," as seen in 1 Corinthians 2:6 and 14:20. Only if believers go past conversion to maturity will they be prepared to give account of themselves before God and be holy, blameless, and irreproachable in His sight. They should seek to be blameless in the same sense that church leaders were exhorted to be blameless in 1 Timothy 3:2.

How though could they reach such maturity? They must close their ears to false teachers, such as those referred to in Colossians 2:16, 18, 21–23, and refuse to be "moved away from the hope of the gospel which [they had] heard" (1:23). Paul therefore pleaded for steadfastness on their part, urging them to cling to the Gospel they had heard and received from the beginning.

These verses assure us that once having come to Christ, we are reconciled and are assured of our salvation. Being His, we are then to grow to a point of maturity, so that we may stand holy, blameless, and irreproachable in His sight and are well pleasing to Him (2 Cor. 5:9).

2 Corinthians 13:5

Paul said to the Corinthians, "Examine yourselves as to whether you are in the faith. Prove yourselves. Do you not know yourselves, that Jesus Christ is in you?—unless indeed you are disqualified." Since the apostle admonished his readers to prove themselves, was he not telling them that only by looking at their lives and finding evidence of salvation could they determine if they were truly saved? This is unlikely, since when Paul wrote to the Corinthian church, he was writing to people he deemed to be Christians. In his first letter to them, he addressed the Corinthians as "those who are sanctified in Christ Jesus," "enriched in everything by Him in all utterance and all knowledge," "eagerly waiting for the revelation of our Lord Jesus Christ," "called into the fellowship of His Son, Jesus Christ our Lord" (1 Cor. 1:2, 5, 7, 9).

In 2 Corinthians 13:5, the Corinthians were challenging the apostle's authority: "You seek a proof of Christ speaking in me" (v. 3). One chapter earlier Paul had to remind them of the proving signs of his apostleship (12:12) and present the agonizing truth that the more he loved them the less they loved him (12:15).

The passage, therefore, is a highly emotional one. Paul instructed the Corinthians to examine themselves instead of him. He said, "Do you not know yourselves, that Jesus Christ is in you?—unless indeed you are disqualified."

The word *disqualified* means "being disapproved." Paul used it of himself in the area of being rewarded for faithful service when he said in 1 Corinthians 9:27, "But I discipline my body and bring it into subjection, lest, when I have preached to others, I myself should become disqualified."

In 2 Corinthians 13:5 he presented the possibility of the Corinthians failing to live obediently for the Savior. Notice how earlier he spoke of not finding them "as I wish" and pointed to their "contentions, jealousies, outbursts of wrath, selfish ambitions, backbitings, whisperings, conceits, tumults; . . . uncleanness, fornication, and licentiousness" (12:20–21). No wonder he closed this epistle to them by pleading, "Become complete. . . . be of one mind, live in peace" (13:11).

Paul was concerned that they should see abundant manifestations of Christ's work in themselves. To be "in the faith" means to be conducting themselves within the convictions and spheres that they knew should be part of their Christian experience. The phrase *Jesus Christ in you* here is not raising the issue of their salvation, but instead the need to live obedient, God-honoring lives that would manifest Christ working in them and merit eternal reward.

Hebrews 3:12–14

Certain passages in the book of Hebrews have caused readers alarm. For example, Hebrews 3:12–14 says,

> Beware, brethren, lest there be in any of you an evil heart of unbelief in departing from the living God; but exhort one another daily, while it is called *"Today,"* lest any of you be hardened through the deceitfulness of sin. For we have become partakers of Christ if we hold the beginning of our confidence steadfast to the end.

These verses are set in the context of a discussion of Israel's failure that led to the forty years of wandering in the wilderness (Num. 13–14). The writer of Hebrews wanted his readers to guard themselves against the hard-heartedness that characterized the Israelites in the wilderness. With that in mind he exhorted them to encourage "one another daily . . . lest any of you be hardened through the deceitfulness of sin" (v. 13).

What then is the meaning of verse 14? "Partakers of Christ" could be translated "partners with Christ," since it means to share as in a companionship. The article "the" is before the word "Christ" in Greek. The context of Hebrews (especially Hebrews 5–8) appears to give this use of "Christ" the sense of "the Messiah." What the writer means by our being "partners" with the messianic King is clarified by looking at earlier verses in the same chapter and, interestingly enough, meeting some of the same terminology (vv. 5–6) as that found in verse 14. Earlier we read:

> Moses indeed was faithful in all His house as a servant, for a testimony of those things which would be spoken afterward, but Christ as a Son over His own house, whose house we are if we hold fast the confidence and the rejoicing of the hope firm to the end.

Moses faithfully exercised his responsibilities within the tabernacle, which was but a shadow of the house over which Christ presides, which has the universe as its sphere. Believers share in His dominion over the created order, which Christ will forever rule. Whatever that function on our part involves, we must hold on to our confidence and hope as both verses 6 and 14 exhort.

In no way was the writer doubting his readers' salvation or implying they could forfeit their salvation. He was simply stating that the privilege of serving with Christ and in some way ruling with Him is based on remaining faithful to Him. The thought is not unlike that of Revelation 2:26–27, where we are told, "He who overcomes, and keeps My works until the end, to him I will give power over the nations— 'He shall rule them with a rod of iron.'"

It is understandable that the writer of Hebrews should follow verse 14 with a quote from Psalm 95:7–8—a call to worship and obedience. Faithfulness means privileges, privileges having to do with our partnership with Christ in His eternal rule.

Hebrews 6:4–6

If there is one thing Hebrews 6:4–6 tells us, it is that we are secure in Christ the moment we place our faith in Him to save us. Yet many have thought that the paragraph says the opposite. It reads:

> For it is impossible for those who were once enlightened, and have tasted the heavenly gift, and have become partakers of the Holy Spirit, and have tasted the good word of God and the powers of the age to come, if they fall away, to renew them again to repentance, since they crucify again for themselves the Son of God, and put Him to an open shame.

To say this paragraph describes people who "tasted" salvation, meaning that they heard the Gospel and were close to trusting Christ, but never did, represents an inconsistency in interpretation. The Greek word for *tasted* is also used in Hebrews 2:9 concerning Christ: "But we see Jesus, who was made a little lower than the angels, for the suffering of death crowned with glory and honor, that He, by the grace of God, might *taste* death for everyone" (emphasis added). Can we say that Christ merely tasted death in the sense that He came close to dying, but never actually died? Hardly! The word *tasted* was an established idiom for the experience of knowing the Lord. Peter says, "As newborn babes, desire the pure milk of the word, that you may grow thereby, if indeed you have tasted that the Lord is gracious" (1 Pet. 2:2–3).

If we attempt to understand the word *enlightened* in a similar way, describing individuals who were "almost Christians," how do we explain the author's use of the same word in Hebrews 10:32? *Enlightened* is translated "illuminated" as the author describes the readers' genuine conversion experience. We read, "But recall the former days in which, after you were illuminated, you endured a great struggle with sufferings." Along the same lines the word for partakers is also used in Hebrews 3:1 to describe the readers' relationship to their heavenly calling, even characterizing them as "holy brethren." He stated, "Therefore, holy brethren, partakers of the heavenly calling, consider the Apostle and High Priest of our confession, Christ Jesus." The use of these words elsewhere makes it extremely difficult to see anyone other than believers in view in 6:4–6.

Who then is a person who has "fallen away" whom it is impossible to renew to repentance? The author pictures a Christian who has in one way or another strayed from the Lord. Granted, a person who appears to have strayed from the Lord may have never trusted Christ, but that is not the individual in view here. This individual has indeed trusted Christ but has strayed from Him. That this was a real possibility is brought out in such places as Hebrews 3:12–13, which says, "Beware, brethren, lest there be in any of you an evil heart of unbelief in departing from the living God; but exhort one another daily, while it is called, 'Today,' lest any of you be hardened through the deceitfulness of sin." Addressing them as brethren, the writer makes it clear that in his mind the problem is not that they do not know God; it is that knowing Him they could depart from Him. In chapter 6 the writer again warned of the danger of becoming sluggish when he said, "We desire that each one of you show the same diligence to the full assurance of hope until the end, that you do not become sluggish, but imitate those who through faith and patience inherit the promises" (vv. 11–12).

Depending on how far a Christian strays from the Lord, it may be impossible to renew such a person to repentance—to bring him to a change of mind. First John 5:16 speaks to that possibility when it warns, "If anyone sees his brother sinning a sin which does not lead to death, he will ask, and He will give him life for those who commit sin not leading to death. There is sin leading to death. I do not say that he should pray about that" (cf. 1 Cor. 11:30). That an individual would trust Christ and then turn his back on Him is a New Testament possibility—and a most dangerous condition for a believer to be in. One can stray so far from God that it is impossible to bring him back and God has no choice but to discipline him with physical death.

Why? Christians who do so are said to "crucify again for themselves the Son of God, and put Him to an open shame" (Heb. 6:6). They approach the cross like those who crucified Him did—they expose Christ to public shame. But since they are actually believers, they are inviting upon themselves the judgment of God. The analogy that follows becomes most fitting. In verses 7 and 8 the passage continues, "For the earth which drinks in the rain that often comes upon it, and bears herbs useful for those by whom it is cultivated, receives blessing from God; but if it bears thorns and briers, it is rejected and near to being cursed, whose end is to be burned." The readers were familiar with burning a field to destroy unfruitful growth so that fruitfulness could begin. The ultimate end is good, not bad, just as when God disciplines His children; His desire is to make them fruitful. Although the judgment of God upon a believer is not pleasant, it yields positive and fruitful results. The situation described here is not unlike that of John 15:6.

Interestingly enough, the writer continues, "But, beloved, we are confident of better things concerning you, yes, things that accompany salvation, though we speak in this manner" (Heb. 6:9). Instead of threatening them with the possibility that they may not be Christians, this passage is designed to warn Christians of the danger of apostasy. Instead of taking away the security of one who has put his trust in Christ and then falls out of fellowship with Him, it instills security. If we should fall away, we are in danger of discipline, not damnation. At the same time, it warns believers very strongly of the danger of being a recipient of the disciplinary action of God. The writer does not specify what form this discipline may take. Sickness, physical death, and hardships of all kinds could be imagined.

Instead of doubting the security of the believer, Hebrews 6:4–6 drives home the severity of departing from the Savior. As Hebrews 10:29 warns, "Of how much worse punishment [than the Israelites received], do you suppose, will he be thought worthy who has trampled the Son of God underfoot, counted the blood of the covenant by which he was sanctified [or set apart] a common thing, and insulted the Spirit of grace?" Such a warning ought to cause us to do what the writer urged when he began the discussion leading to Hebrews 6:4–6—"go on to perfection" (v. 1)—that is, go on to maturity in Christ.

Hebrews 12:14

If eternal life is both free and guaranteed (John 4:10; 10:28), why would the writer of Hebrews exhort, "Pursue peace with all men, and holiness, without which no one will see the Lord"?

The context again becomes most crucial. The writer recognized how spiritually weak his readers could be at times and warned them of the chastening hand of God. It is abundantly clear that the writer was talking to believers from his advice not to disregard God's discipline, which applies to His children: "If you endure chastening, God deals with you as with sons; for what Son is there whom a father does not chasten?" (v. 7). He assured them that God's chastising has positive results: "Now no chastening seems to be joyful for the present, but grievous; nevertheless, afterward it yields the peaceable fruit of righteousness to those who have been trained by it" (v. 11).

With that in mind, the writer of Hebrews encouraged them to help strengthen weaker Christians (vv. 12–13). This would renew spiritual vitality. Christians also renew spiritual vitality by pursuing "peace with all men, and holiness, without which no one will see the Lord." There are two ways of understanding the last part of that verse, both of which are in keeping with the context. First, when believers are in God's presence, they will be holy as He is holy (1 John 3:2). That realization ought to make us want to be as holy as possible now. If that is what we are going to be like forever, why not seek holiness now? Second, those who seek to live pure and holy lives are the ones who have the best perception and understanding of God's will, His ways, and His works. Christ admonished, "Blessed are the pure in heart, for they shall see God" (Matt. 5:8). The pure in heart are those who recognize their justified condition before God and seek to be pure in their walk before Him—actions, attitudes, and motives all involved. Such a walk enhances spiritual perception. One scholar comments, "The pure in heart are the single-minded, who are free from the tyranny of a divided self, and who do not try to serve God and the world at the same time. From such it is impossible that God should hide Himself."[3]

For that reason the writer of Hebrews continued by vowing that one who is unfaithful to God, such as one who responds bitterly to His chastening hand, can adversely affect others. He said, "Looking diligently lest anyone fall short of the grace of God; lest any root of bitterness springing up cause trouble, and by this many become defiled" (12:15).

In light of the writer's admonition to pursue peace and holiness, the remainder of chapter 12 is most stimulating. It recalls the frightening physical manifestations seen when God revealed Himself on Mount Sinai. In contrast the writer says, "You have come to Mount Zion and to the city of the living God, the heavenly Jerusalem, to an innumerable company of angels" (v. 22). Since we enjoy the ever new spiritual and heavenly blessings due to our position in Christ, we dare not "refuse Him who speaks" (v. 25). Our response must be to "serve God acceptably with reverence and godly fear" (v. 28).

The writer of Hebrews, in urging Christians to pursue holiness, was laying a path whereby spiritual vitality could be renewed and the chance of falling short of what the grace of God desired for them would be reduced.

James 2:14–26

Perhaps no other passage in Scripture has been used more than James 2:14–26 to assert that if a person's life is not characterized by good works, then he or she is not saved. After all, what else could James mean when he says, "But do you want to know, O foolish man, that faith without works is dead?" (v. 20).

It might be helpful to put the passage before us as we prepare to consider it:

> What does it profit, my brethren, if someone says he has faith but does not have works? Can faith save him? If a brother or sister is naked and destitute of daily food, and one of you says to them, "Depart in peace, be warmed and filled," but you do not give them the things which are needed for the body, what does it profit? Thus also faith by itself, if it does not have works, is dead. But someone will say, "You have faith, and I have works." Show me your faith without your works, and I will show you my faith by my works. You believe that there is one God. You do well. Even the demons believe—and tremble! But do you want to know, O foolish man, that faith without works is dead? Was not Abraham our father justified by works when he offered Isaac his son on the altar? Do you see that faith was working together with his works, and by works faith was made perfect? And the Scripture was fulfilled which says, "Abraham believed God, and it was accounted to him for righteousness." And he was called the friend of God. You see then that a man is justified by works, and not by faith only. Likewise, was not Rahab the harlot also justified by works when she received the messengers and sent them out another way? For as the body without the spirit is dead, so faith without works is dead also.

If we take these verses to say that we are not saved unless our lives are characterized by good works, we meet once again with insurmountable problems. One is that in context, James never questioned his readers' possession of eternal life. That he understood them to be believers is plain one paragraph earlier, where he warned Christians about the danger of being snobbish. He said, "My brethren, do not hold the faith of our Lord Jesus Christ, the Lord of glory, with partiality" (2:1). Even in the paragraph we are discussing, James began by addressing his readers as "brethren" (2:14).

In James 4:11, two chapters later, James exhorted Christians, "Do not speak evil of one another, brethren. He who speaks evil of a brother and judges his brother, speaks evil of the law and judges the law. But if you judge the law, you are not a doer of the law but a judge." If James 2 is indeed teaching that unless a person's life is characterized by good works, he is not saved, why did James not simply declare his readers lost, since speaking evil of a brother is certainly not "good works" and they were apparently guilty of this and other sins?

Another problem is that we may have too quickly assumed that wherever "save" is used in James it refers to salvation from damnation. Do we assume this with James 5:15, where we are told, "The prayer of faith will save the sick"? If so, we also have to assume that anointing with oil in 5:14 becomes an essential part of the salvation process and that an individual is sick because he is a non-Christian. Suddenly we become uneasy with our interpretation, and rightly so.

We must determine what James 2:14–26 is saying by looking first at the flow of the letter as a whole. After introducing the subject of trials and hardships and the purposes for which they are and are not intended, James sets forth what might be called the outline of his epistle in 1:19–20: "Therefore, my beloved brethren, let every man be swift to hear, slow to speak, slow to wrath; for the wrath of man does not produce the righteousness of God." The three qualities most needed in our lives when undergoing trials are being swift to hear, slow to speak, and slow to anger. So James 1:21–2:26 discusses the need to be swift to hear, James 3:1–18, the need to be slow to speak, and 4:1–17, the need to be slow to wrath. James 5:1–20 constitutes a fitting conclusion to the exhortations concerning trials and the need to look at them from God's perspective.

James 2:14–26 fits into the section of the epistle in which James discussed the need to be swift to hear. Only as Christians do what James called "receive with meekness the implanted word" (1:21) will it be possible to "save your souls." The Greek idiom "save your souls" (*sosai tas psuchas humon*) is a phrase that in English can also be rendered "save your lives." Mark 3:4 uses it in this sense: Jesus said, "Is it lawful on the Sabbath to do good or to do evil, to save life *[psuchen sosai]* or to kill?" The Septuagint, a Greek translation of the Old Testament, also gives it this meaning in Genesis 19:17; 32:30; Job 33:28, and Psalms 31:7; 72:13; and 109:31.

The idea behind the phrase *save your souls* is that of being saved from damage to one's life. That meaning becomes apparent when we notice that James 5:20 uses the same phrase and even adds the clarification "from death." Speaking concerning a Christian who has known the truth, wandered from it, and then turned back, James said, "Let him know that he who turns a sinner from the error of his way will save a soul from death and cover a multitude of sins." The point is that when believers maintain a proper receptivity to the Word, they are able to save their lives from the damaging consequences of sin.

For James, the only way to receive the Word is to *do* the Word. So he began his section on being swift to hear by saying, "But be doers of the word, and not hearers only, deceiving yourselves" (James 1:22). Hearing the Word will not save us from the consequences of sin in our lives—only doing it will accomplish that. He goes on to list specific ways that one can do what the Word says. Among the things he mentions are controlling the tongue (1:26), taking care of orphans and widows (1:27), and not showing partiality toward others (2:1–13).

James 2:14 continues his emphasis on doing what the Word says. James wanted to stress that faith cannot be a substitute for obedience. Individuals can be genuinely saved (as they are in this passage), but those who do not put their faith to work will suffer the consequences of sin in daily living. They will not be justified before other people because no one will be able to see what they believe.

For that reason, James asked two pertinent questions. "What does it profit, my brethren, if someone says he has faith but does not have works? Can faith save him?" (2:14). The answer anticipated is "No!" and an illustration drives the point home: "If a brother or sister is naked and destitute of daily food, and one of you says to them, 'Depart in peace, be warmed and filled,' but you do not give them the things which are needed for the body, what does it profit? Thus also faith by itself, if it does not have works, is dead" (vv. 15–17). Since empty words have never clothed a naked body or fed an empty stomach, James asked, "What does it profit?" or in other words, "What good does it do?" Likewise, "faith by itself, if it does not have works, is dead" (v. 17). We have often been too analytical in trying to determine what James meant by *dead* and in doing so have missed the obvious. Faith in Christ that is not put to work in the marketplace of life through obedience will still take one to heaven. John made that clear (John 6:47). But it will not save one from the consequences of a sinful life. It is dead in that it is not active, productive, fruitful.

The next verses, James 2:18 and 19, have often been misunderstood and even used out of context because the first four words have been overlooked: "But someone will say." James responded to one who might object to his argument. The objector attempts to say that there is no significant connection between faith and works. The wording indicates that verses 18 and 19 are the objector speaking. Notice how James began verse 18 by saying, "But someone will say" and began verse 20 by saying, "But do you want to know, O foolish man."

It helps in understanding the objection to read "by" in verse 18 (as a large majority of Greek manuscripts of James do) instead of the word "without." Verse 18 would thus read, "'You have faith, and I have works.' Show me your faith by your works, and I will show you my faith by my works." The one objecting is making the point that an individual can no more display his set of doctrinal beliefs by his actions than another person can, out of his works, give you his creed. Who can look at a person's works and know anything about his doctrinal convictions? The objector simply argues that faith and works have no relationship. What clinches the argument, as far as the objector is concerned, is to look at people and demons. Both believe there is one God; that is, they are both monotheists. But believing there is one God has no connection with what they do, since a person might "do well," but demons do great iniquity despite their trembling fear of punishment from God.

How does James answer such an objector? James was wise enough to know how foolish it is to argue with foolishness. He simply asked the objector, "But do you want to know, O foolish man, that faith without works is dead?" (v. 20).

Once again, James gives illustrations to drive his point home, using Abraham, one of the most respected names in Jewish history, and Rahab, noted for the part she played in the conquest of Jericho. As James cited these two examples, it is clear he was talking about justification by works. But justification in what sense? In this context, James was speaking of the need for obedience in order to avoid the consequences of sin. Therefore he is discussing another kind of justification, one seen right here on earth before people in which faith is alive in works. For that reason, he said in verse 24, "You see then that a man is justified by works, and not by faith only." Justification by faith gives a person a right standing with God, but justification by works saves him or her from the consequences of sin in this life and before others shows faith to be active.

Abraham is a most fitting example. James argues, "Was not Abraham our father justified by works when he offered Isaac his son on the altar? Do you see that faith was working together with his works, and by works faith was made perfect? And the Scripture was fulfilled which says, 'Abraham believed God, and it was accounted to him for righteousness.' And he was called the friend of God" (vv. 21–23). Interestingly enough, the word "perfect" in verse 22 translates a word meaning "mature." Abraham had a right standing with God long before offering Isaac, as we know from Genesis 15:6, which James quoted. But by Abraham's works his faith became mature. One such work was his simple obedience to God when told to offer his son Isaac upon the altar (Gen. 22). Any father can identify with how Abraham must have felt. Convinced, though, that God knew what He was doing and could resurrect his dead son (Heb. 11:19), Abraham acted in obedience and his faith matured. As a result, the Scripture (Gen. 15:6) was fulfilled.

"Fulfilled" conveys the idea "filled to the full." Abraham's works showed as nothing else could the part his faith played in his obedience. Now God and also people, like those described in 2 Chronicles 20:7 and Isaiah 41:8, could call him the friend of God. Abraham would still have had a right standing with God had he refused to offer up Isaac. But by an obedience that "saves the life," he earned the title "friend of God," by which he has been known for centuries. In this way he was justified (before people) by works.

We should not see as unusual a differentiation between knowing God and being the friend of God, since Christ said, "You are My friends if you do whatever I command you" (John 15:14). Through faith we obtain an eternal relationship with God. Only through works can we obtain a closeness or an intimacy that is noticeable even to others. If we desire intimacy with God, we must act in obedience to Scripture. Justified by faith in Genesis 15:6, Abraham was justified by works in Genesis 22. The first justification saved him from damnation in hell; the second saved him from the consequences of sin that a disobedience would have produced.

Rahab made another fitting illustration. Her faith is spoken of in Hebrews 11:31: "By faith the harlot Rahab did not perish with those who did not believe, when she had received the spies with peace." When Rahab received the spies Joshua had sent to Jericho (Josh. 2:1), she could have fled herself after hiding them under the flax on her roof; she could have betrayed their presence or conceivably murdered them. But she had heard what the Lord had done for the Israelites and had come to believe that the Lord was giving them the land of Canaan and that the Lord their God "is God in heaven above and on earth beneath" (v. 11, cf. vv. 9–11). How was her faith, which she had prior to meeting the spies, seen to be alive? It was, as James tells it, "when she received the messengers and sent them out another way" (2:25). In so doing, did she save herself from hell? In no way. What she saved was her own life and the life of her family from the physical consequences of sin that disobedience would have produced. Had she failed to obey the spies, although nothing would have changed in terms of her eternal relationship with God, she would have been dead physically. Instead, when all of Jericho came under divine judgment, she and her family lived. She lived because she had a living faith, not a dead faith.

Now James drew his conclusion to the argument just presented: "For as the body without the spirit is dead, so faith without works is dead also" (James 2:26). The human spirit keeps the human body alive. Without that life-giving spirit, all you have is a corpse. Works also keep faith alive and healthy. The fact that James is not discussing whether a person is a believer is proven by this verse. In order for a corpse to be dead it must have once been alive. Likewise, in order for faith to be dead, it, too, must once have been alive.

James argues biblically for what practical experience and observation prove. A person can be a Christian and yet have a dead faith, which is an extremely serious matter. A dead faith does not save one from the current consequences of sin, even the consequence of physical death, nor does it justify us before others. On the other hand, a living faith, seen in works of obedience, saves a life from the consequences of disobedience. James was not arguing that a person without works has no assurance of belonging to Christ. And he was certainly not suggesting that we become children of God on the basis of faith plus works. He would have agreed with Paul. "But to him who does not work but believes on Him who justifies the ungodly, his faith is accounted for righteousness" (Rom. 4:5). Salvation from hell is not the issue in the context of this paragraph. James is instead warning against something that confronts every Christian—the danger of not keeping our faith lively through works of obedience.

We need only faith to obtain eternal life, but we need faith and works to be saved from the consequences of sin and to be declared right in the sight of others. If we do not perform good works, that does not mean we have not trusted Christ; however, it does mean that we are disobedient. Good works reflect a healthy, living faith that others can observe. Once we have trusted Christ, God commands us to do good works. As we do, we are justified before people, who now have every right to call us "friends of God."

1 John 3:6

John wrote, "Whoever abides in Him does not sin. Whoever sins has neither seen Him nor known Him." Would this verse tell a believer living in sin that he or she is not a true member of God's family?

If we jump to that interpretation, we face a tremendous problem. Three verses later, continuing along the same line, John says, "Whoever has been born of God does not sin, for His seed remains in him; and he cannot sin, because he has been born of God" (1 John 3:9). What believers would dare to say that since they have trusted Christ, they have never sinned again? John in fact addresses the possibility of sin in his fellow believers and children in the faith by saying, "My little children, these things I write to you, that you may not sin. And if anyone sins, we have an Advocate with the Father, Jesus Christ the righteous" (2:1).[4]

Some attempts have been made to explain 1 John 3:6 on the basis of understanding the present tense to read, "Whoever *sins* and *continues* to sin has neither seen Him nor known Him." The explanation is then offered that only if people continue in sin are they not Christians. But where in Scripture is "continued" defined? Are we talking about a month, a year, two years, ten years? Such a view calls for subjective conclusions that we are not given the liberty to make. It would then make it impossible to know that we have eternal life as 1 John 5:13 instructs. What then was John saying? The understanding of 1 John 3:6 is found in looking at the theme of 1 John, which is quite different from the theme of the gospel of John. John wrote his first epistle to tell people how they can live in close fellowship with the One who saved them. As he said in the opening verses of his epistle, "That which we have seen and heard we declare to you, that you also may have fellowship with us; and truly our fellowship is with the Father and with His Son Jesus Christ. And these things we write to you that your joy may be full" (1 John 1:3–4). With that purpose of fellowship with the Father in mind, the word *abide* is used a total of twenty-six times—most interesting in a book containing only five chapters!

John's point in 1 John 3:6 is that sin is never the product of seeing or knowing God. Sin is committed when, as believers, we walk in darkness and act out of rebellion or ignorance. Sin never results from an abiding experience. It results from an experience, however long it may be, when we were not abiding in the sinless person of the Savior. It occurs when we are acting out of our original capacity for sinning rather than our new capacity for righteousness.

When the context of 1 John is understood, not only does 1 John 3:6 make sense, but many other verses in 1 John do also. First John 3:15 says, "Whoever hates his brother is a murderer, and you know that no murderer has eternal life abiding in him." A Christian can hate a brother in Christ, but the hate is not the result of abiding in Christ. Verse 17 tells us, "But whoever has this world's goods, and sees his brother in need, and shuts up his heart from him, how does the love of God abide in Him?" One can be a Christian and be coldhearted toward a brother and his need (how often have we ourselves been that way?), but no Christian can *abide* in Christ and be such. First John 2:4 says, "He who says, 'I know Him.' and does not keep His commandments, is a liar, and the truth is not in him." "The truth is not in him" because he is not abiding in Christ. Only as a believer abides in Christ is the truth operative in them. Two verses later John says, "He who says he abides in Him ought himself also to walk just as He walked" (v. 6). Disobeying His commandments is not the result of an abiding experience. First John 4:20–21 admonishes us:

> If someone says, "I love God," and hates his brother, he is a liar; for he who does not love his brother whom he has seen,

how can he love God whom he has not seen? And this commandment we have from Him: that he who loves God must love his brother also.

John is in no way doubting his readers' salvation, as shown in the fact that he addresses them as brethren. He simply makes the point that one cannot love God and not love his brother. Instead, if we are abiding in Him, loving the Father means we have to love His family.

First John 3:6 and other verses in 1 John do not negate the assurance of salvation on faith alone. Instead, they stress the need to abide in Christ. Only when we abide in Him can we live the way God wants us to live.

CONCLUSION

God is not making a bargain; He is offering a free gift. When people receive that free gift by trusting in Christ alone for salvation, they are forever His. A well-known preacher of years past, C. H. Spurgeon, is quoted as saying that he was so sure of his salvation that he could grab onto a cornstalk, swing out over the fires of hell, look into the face of the devil, and sing, "Blessed assurance, Jesus is mine."

A person who wants to know if he or she is a Christian has only to answer one question: Am I trusting Christ alone for my eternal salvation?

So What?

Clearly understanding the biblical basis of assurance is vital not only to understanding salvation, but also to subsequent growth in the Christian life. It is when people understand the security found in their relationship with Christ that they are prepared to experience the dynamic of spiritual growth.

Some Christians often struggle with what is commonly referred to as eternal security. They sometimes hear others adamantly insist that "once saved, always saved" cannot be biblical. Too often this conclusion was arrived at from a study of Christians instead of a study of Scripture. Seeing Christians whose lives do not maintain a certain standard, some cannot fathom that such persons would remain saved—and part-owners of heaven. They overlook three things. First, God's offer of eternal life is not based on our performance; it is based on His. Second, to take away the eternality from the gift is to take away the gift. God's offer is not an offer of life, but an offer of *eternal* life. Third, since that offer is backed by the power of God, one can clearly see why it is eternal. The One who saves us apart from what we do is big enough to keep us apart from what we do.

Deity is so closely tied to the gift of eternal life that to deny the eternality of the gift is in essence to deny the deity of Christ. When speaking to individuals who do not believe in eternal security, we must determine whether they understand the Gospel. There are those who, having previously trusted their good works to get them to heaven, progress to a point of trusting Christ *and* their good works to get them to heaven. No one is ever saved until one comes to a point of trusting Christ alone for salvation. When the substitutionary death of Christ and His resurrection are understood, the security of the believer, besides being biblically proclaimed, makes sense. If nothing we do obtains eternal life other than receiving it as a gift, it stands to reason nothing we do keeps it. Otherwise the gift is not a gift. God extends to us nothing less than the free and *guaranteed* gift of eternal life upon faith in Christ.

I spoke with a young woman at the end of an evangelistic service. As we talked, she explained that she felt Christ is the way to heaven but did not believe that once saved you could never lose salvation. Taking the Bible and showing her several verses in the gospel of John, I explained that salvation is not granted on the basis of Christ making a bargain by saying, "If I do this for you, what will you do for Me?" Instead He is offering a gift and saying, "May I give you heaven?" Since we do nothing other than to receive it, we do nothing to keep it. We are eternally secure because God does not save us based on our performance, but based on His Son's performance. It was as though a light came on for her! We prayed together, and she told God she was trusting Christ alone to take her to heaven and embarked on a path of steady spiritual growth. A year later I asked her, "When you reflect upon that night, do you feel you simply gained assurance of your salvation or did you actually trust Christ that night?" Her answer was most revealing: "There's no doubt in my mind I was saved that night. I realize that previously I had been trusting Christ and my works to get me to heaven instead of Christ alone."

I once asked a relative who struggled with eternal security, "What would I have to do for God *not* to save me?" I suggested things such as stealing one thousand dollars to stealing ten million dollars, murdering one person to what has become all too familiar, gunning down a crowd of people. He confessed that God can save a person regardless of what he has done if he simply comes to Him as a sinner. There is no sinner that God cannot save. I then remarked, "But what you're saying by your disbelief in eternal security is that He'll save you regardless of what you've done in the past but toss you back based on how you perform now." I vividly remember his facial expression as he said, "I guess I've never thought about that before."

When I'm speaking with either someone who is struggling with eternal security because he or she has not come to completely understand the Gospel or with someone I sense may be trusting Christ and works to get to heaven, I've found this illustration helpful. I draw three circles. One stands for works, the second stands for Christ and works, and the third stands for Christ alone. The diagram looks like this:

I then explain, "There are some people who trust in their works to get them to heaven." Pointing to the second circle, I say, "There are some who trust in Christ and their works to get them to heaven." Pointing to the third, I say, "There are some who trust Christ alone to get them to heaven. Where are you?"

Those who do not understand the Gospel usually point to the middle circle. If they do, I explain as I point to the first circle, "When people are trusting their works to get them to heaven, they are saying, 'Christ's death was totally unnecessary.' After all, if any amount of anything we did could get us to heaven, God was foolish and cruel to allow His Son to suffer such an agonizing death on the cross." Pointing to the second circle, I comment, "If we are relying on Christ and works to get us to heaven, we are telling God, 'Your Son's death on the cross was a big disappointment. I have to finish what He started—paying for my sins. He paid for some of my sins; I have to pay for the rest.'" As I point to the third circle, I explain, "If we are trusting Christ alone to get us to heaven, we are agreeing with God that His Son's death was sufficient to pay for everything wrong we've done." I then explain that we are never saved until we are relying on Christ and Christ alone as our only means of salvation. Christ did not make the down payment for our sins; He made the *full* payment as He said in John 19:30, "It is finished." It is exciting when people begin to see the beauty of God's grace in providing a means of salvation.

Others insist that their struggle does not concern eternal security. Instead their difficulty concerns what is sometimes referred to as the perseverance of the believer. Perseverance means continuing as a Christian (pray, go to church, study the Bible, etc.). Many believe that if people do not persevere in Christian living, they were never Christians in the first place. As the previous study revealed, Scripture does not approach assurance on the basis of good conduct. If one examines salvation on the basis of actions, conduct, and feelings, one will never be sure.

The simple question, "Have I trusted Christ as my only basis for a right standing with God?" must be asked first. Only when one has trusted Christ alone can someone then rightly ask, "Why am I not growing?" As he or she thinks that through or receives the counsel of others, the person may find several things that are hindering the spiritual walk. Dealing with those hindrances appropriately, one can once again grow in the Lord.

One other item that results from a careful study of assurance deserves mention. Some stress that individuals are Christians only if they know the date they were saved. As noted in our study of saving faith, when Scripture gives assurance of salvation, it goes back to a *fact,* not a *date.* If a person is trusting Christ alone to get to heaven, regardless of when and where he or she "crossed the line," he or she is eternally His. Many know the date; others don't. Undoubtedly still others are wrong about the date.

I often use a story to illustrate this point. Having grown up in Pennsylvania, I moved to Dallas, Texas, to attend graduate school. I met my wife and settled there. Let's suppose she and I were returning to Pennsylvania to visit my family. When we cross the state line, it is nighttime. I am driving and my wife is sleeping. When she awakens, she sees a sign that says "Harrisburg Cafe." Harrisburg is the capitol of

Pennsylvania. Does the fact that only I know the moment and place we crossed the line change the fact that we are both in Pennsylvania? Not in the least! Similarly, just because one person knows the date and place he or she was saved and another does not, it does not change the fact that they are both saved. When Scripture discusses God's free and guaranteed offer of eternal life, it goes back to a fact, not to a date.

Nowhere does this become more important than when dealing with children. Consider children who come to know Christ when they are five or six years old. Sooner or later as their understanding increases, they comprehend better the meaning of what Christ did for them on a cross. At those times they may wonder whether or not they understood salvation earlier and were actually saved. The way parents respond to them at those times is often dangerous. Remembering a date or time when the young person said a prayer or walked an aisle, they respond, "But don't you remember what you did on such-and-such?" The fact is, they often do not. Besides, that can be very faulty ground for assurance. No one can relive history. Suppose what a parent thought happened—that the child trusted Christ—did not actually happen. A child needs to be reminded that if he or she is trusting Christ to get to heaven, he or she is saved, even though the initial moment of trust may not have been as early as the child or the parents thought.

Some use the analogy of a birth certificate. Should you ask an individual, "Whose child are you?" he or she will most likely give a parent's name. If you then ask, "How do you know that?" he or she may reply, "My mother had me," "They told me so," "I grew up in their family," or something similar. None of those reasons is an absolute guarantee that he or she belongs to the parents, since human beings can lie. If one keeps pressing and says, "You have one proof that you are their child that would stand up in a court of law; what is it?" he or she will answer, "A birth certificate." That's right. A single piece of paper is assurance of being a certain person's son or daughter. God too has given us a sheet of paper, far better than a birth certificate because it is without any error. He wants us to take His Word in the Scripture that having trusted Christ, we can rely on Him to keep the promise of John 5:24. Having trusted Christ, we need to trust the Word.

After such a study as this, one might ask, "But when people see evidence of the Holy Spirit at work in their lives, should they not be encouraged that they are indeed Christians?"[5] Most definitely. But nowhere is that the basis upon which to determine whether we are saved, and understandably so. Should believers stray from God, their lives may not bear the fruit it otherwise would. Such people need to be alarmed, but if they are believers, their lack of growth is the problem, not their salvation. Also, the life of people may give evidence of what many would call "the Holy Spirit at work," while all their good works may be deeds done in the flesh—deeds they are depending on to get them to heaven.

We often hear that nothing in life is guaranteed. The Scriptures prove that to be untrue. God guarantees that if we will trust Christ, nothing on earth or in heaven will change our eternal destiny. We are His forever. As Paul so emphatically declared: "I am persuaded that neither death nor life, nor angels nor principalities nor powers, nor things present nor things to come, nor height nor depth, nor any other created thing, shall be able to separate us from the love of God which is in Christ Jesus our Lord" (Rom. 8:38–39).

Group Discussion Questions

- Think of times you have been disappointed with yourself in your Christian walk and your lack of gratitude to God for the gift of forgiveness. Why can you also be grateful that your assurance of eternal life was not conditioned on how you behaved during those times?

- How does a proper understanding of assurance contribute to victory in a person's Christian life?

- If God had left it up to us to devise the plan of salvation, what would we have likely demanded?

- Why do lost people often miss the simplicity of the salvation message? How does the way other people demonstrate love often give them an inadequate view of how God responds to them? Give specific examples.

Chapter Six

What Is Repentance?

When David Brainerd, the outstanding missionary to the American Indians, was summarizing his ministry among them and message to them, he said, "I never got away from Jesus and Him crucified in my preaching. I found that once these people were gripped by the great evangelical meaning of Christ's sacrifice on our behalf, I did not have to give them any instructions about changing their behavior."
—Our Daily Bread, April 1977

Those wanting to clearly present the Gospel of grace to the lost realize that unbelievers have to admit they are sinners, recognize that Christ died in their place and rose again, and trust in Christ alone for salvation. Where does repentance fit in? What does repentance mean? Do you simply have to change your mind and admit you are a sinner or do you have to be sorry for your sin and even turn from your sin?

There are varying opinions on repentance. Students of the Scriptures differ not only over what the word means, but also over whether repentance is essential to salvation.

UNDERSTANDING PART OF THE PROBLEM

In order to understand repentance as it relates to salvation we must deal principally with two Greek words used in the New Testament. One is the noun *metanoia,* and the other is the verb *metanoeo.* What contributes to the difficulty is that no English word communicates all that the Greek writers meant by these two words. The word *repent,* which to most of us conveys the idea of remorse or sorrow, is far more in line with the meaning of a third word, *metamelomai.*[1]

A. T. Robertson acknowledged this when he wrote:

The tragedy of it is that we have no one English word that reproduces exactly the meaning and atmosphere of the Greek word. The Greek has a word meaning to be sorry *(metamelomai)* which is exactly our English word repent and it is used of Judas (Matt. 27:3).[2]

William Howard summarized the frustration of Bible translators even more descriptively when he said,

> It is evident that repentance is a mistranslation of *metanoia*. This fact was never more apparent than during the English and American revisions of the King James version of our Bible. Frequent debate centered around this word and it was the opinion of many that a suitable English equivalent should be sought for the Greek expression. It was agreed, however, that no one English word was sufficient to convey all that lay in the Greek. And, although it was admitted that the translation was poor, it was felt that the common term should be retained in the hope that it would come to convey all that its Greek derivative expressed. Several English words were suggested to the revisers, among them resipiscence (derived from a word meaning "to come into one's senses"), but manifestly none of them was appropriate. It seems to be the present task of the expositor, then, to pause at the reading of this word and reiterate all that it is really intended to mean.[3]

It is essential that we understand the importance of repentance to evangelism. Paul the apostle declared, "Truly, these times of ignorance God overlooked, but now commands all men everywhere to repent" (Acts 17:30).

Let's look first at repentance in the New Testament (because of its relationship to salvation) and then the Old Testament. In so doing we seek to understand what the term means.[4]

REPENTANCE IN THE NEW TESTAMENT

As noted earlier, principally two Greek words are translated "repent" in the New Testament. One is *metanoia* and the other is *metanoeo*. Let's look first at these two and then at the third word, *metamelomai*.

Metanoia *and* Metanoeo

Metanoia and *metanoeo* are used fifty-eight times.[5] Concentrating on uses in an evangelistic context, we find there are several objects with which the two words are used. Sometimes the objects are implied; at other times they are stated. The following list gives examples of uses with stated objects.

The Object of Repentance	Example
God	Paul was diligent in "testifying to Jews, and also to Greeks, repentance toward

	God and faith toward our Lord Jesus Christ" (Acts 20:21).
Idols	"But the rest of mankind, who were not killed by these plagues, did not repent of the works of their hands, that they should not worship demons, and idols of gold, silver, brass, stone, and wood, which can neither see nor hear nor walk" (Rev. 9:20).
Particular Sins	"They did not repent of their murders or their sorceries or their sexual immorality or their thefts" (Rev. 9:21).
Deeds	"And they blasphemed the God of heaven because of their pains and their sores, and did not repent of their deeds" (Rev. 16:11).
Dead Works	"Therefore, leaving the discussion of the elementary principles of Christ, let us go on to perfection, not laying again the foundation of repentance from dead works and of faith toward God" (Heb. 6:1).

What about instances when the object is implied? Often the implied object is the Person of Christ. For example, in Acts 2:38 we find, "Then Peter said to them, 'Repent, and let every one of you be baptized in the name of Jesus Christ for the remission of sins; and you shall receive the gift of the Holy Spirit.'"[6] A study of the context here clearly reveals that the object of their repentance is the Person of Christ. William Evans comments:

> Thus, when Peter, on the day of Pentecost, called upon the Jews to repent (Acts 2:14–40), he virtually called upon them to change their minds and their views regarding Christ. They had considered Christ to be a mere man, a blasphemer, an imposter. The events of the few preceding days had proven to them that He was none other than the righteous Son of God, their Savior and the Savior of the world. The result of their repentance or change of mind would be that they would receive Jesus Christ as their long promised Messiah.[7]

A study of *metanoeo* and *metanoia* shows that the idea of a change of mind is clearly there. The references and objects cited earlier reveal, if nothing else, that God is asking for a change of mind regarding Himself, idolatry, particular sins, deeds, and dead (useless) works.[8]

For that reason it would be difficult for a Bible teacher to preach one sermon on the word *repentance* because its object is not always the same. Whereas one person may be asked to repent of making and worshiping an idol, another might have to repent of his dead works—works not based on faith but on hopes of earning God's favor. R. A. Torrey has appropriately said, "What the repentance or change of mind is about must always be determined by the context."[9]

Just as interesting as its varying objects are the accompanying actions with which repentance is used. Observe the following list:

Accompanying Action	Example
Believe	"The time is fulfilled, and the kingdom of God is at hand. Repent, and believe in the gospel" (Mark 1:15).
Baptism	"Then Peter said to them, 'Repent, and let every one of you be baptized in the name of Jesus Christ for the remission of sins; and you shall receive the gift of the Holy Spirit'" (Acts 2:38).
Conversion	"Repent therefore and be converted, that your sins may be blotted out, so that times of refreshing may come from the presence of the Lord" (Acts 3:19).
Faith	"Testifying to Jews, and also to Greeks, repentance toward God and faith toward our Lord Jesus Christ" (Acts 20:21).
Turning to God	"But declared first to those in Damascus and in Jerusalem, and throughout all the region of Judea, and then to the Gentiles, that they should repent, turn to God, and do works befitting repentance" (Acts 26:20).
Remission of Sins	"That repentance and remission of sins should be preached in His name to all nations, beginning at Jerusalem" (Luke 24:47).

Sometimes, however, the word is used alone. In Acts 17:30 we are told, "Truly, these times of ignorance God overlooked, but now commands all men everywhere to repent." One would almost expect

Paul in this passage to say, "Repent and be saved" or "Repent and believe." Instead he simply states that God commands people to repent. Of greatest concern is how the word *repentance* is used in reference to belief. The gospel of John, written explicitly to tell how to obtain eternal life, says, "Most assuredly, I say to you, he who believes in Me has everlasting life" (John 6:47). So where does repentance fit in?

There are times when repentance includes believing and other times when it is *distinct* from believing. When it includes believing, the speaker apparently assumes that the listener understands that to repent is also to believe on Christ. Notice how the words of Christ, Paul, and Peter verify this.

Christ spoke of repentance in Luke 15:7 as he told a parable about a lost sheep. He concluded, "I say to you that likewise there will be more joy in heaven over one sinner who repents than over ninety-nine just persons who need no repentance." Since faith in Christ is the means of salvation, if the angels are rejoicing over repentance, faith must be included in that.

As Paul stood on Mars Hill and spoke to the people of Athens, he explained that God would judge the whole world by the resurrected Christ. As he rebuked the thought that the Godhead is something similar to gold, silver, or stone—all of which are carved by humankind—he warned them:

> Truly, these times of ignorance God overlooked, but now commands all men everywhere to repent, because He has appointed a day on which He will judge the world in righteousness by the Man whom He has ordained. He has given assurance of this to all by raising Him from the dead (Acts 17:30–31).

What is it that he asked them to do regarding sin? Believe? No, he simply mentions repenting from sin. We know that Paul knew that believing in Christ is the means to eternal life (Acts 13:39), so it is logical to assume that repentance includes believing. To repent in Acts 17 is to believe in Christ.

Peter spoke of repentance in a similar way in 2 Peter 5:9. People had become a bit disgruntled and had raised questions about the promise of Christ's coming. In explaining one reason Christ had not returned, Peter told them, "The Lord is not slack concerning His promise, as some count slackness, but is longsuffering toward us, not willing that any should perish but that all should come to repentance." Since we know from Peter's statement to Cornelius in Acts 10:43 that he understood that belief in Christ is the sole requirement for salvation, he too was using repentance as part of believing.

It may be concluded that when used in salvation contexts, *metanoia* and *metanoeo* either imply faith or are associated with faith. These ideas are sometimes difficult to separate but they can be distinguished. For example, Nicodemus was told that in order to have eternal life, one must believe (John 3:15). However, this required that Nicodemus repent concerning his view of himself and his understanding of how one entered the kingdom of heaven. He had to see himself as a sinner under condemnation for having rejected Christ (v. 18). Even Christ's reference to Moses and the lifting up of the serpent in Numbers 21 served to show Nicodemus his hopeless condition and the need for salvation outside of his own merits. He then had to recognize Christ as the One lifted up on the cross in his place as his only way to heaven. Otherwise, he could not exercise faith and enter the kingdom of God.[10]

It now becomes clearer why the word *repent* is never mentioned in the gospel of John and *repentance* is mentioned only once in Romans. Lewis Sperry Chafer noted this:

> The Gospel by John, which is written to present Christ as the object of faith unto eternal life, does not once employ the word repentance. Similarly, the Epistle to the Romans, which is the complete analysis of all that enters into the whole plan of salvation by grace, does not use the word repentance in connection with the saving of a soul, except in 2:4 when repentance is equivalent to salvation itself.[11]

If repentance is involved in salvation, to genuinely repent is to believe in Christ as the only way to heaven.

Metamelomai

Metamelomai is used six times in five verses.[12] Only once is it used in a salvation-related context. In Matthew 21:32 Christ says, "John came to you in the way of righteousness, and you did not believe him; but tax collectors and harlots believed him; and when you saw it, you did not afterward *relent* and believe him" (cf. Acts 19:4, emphasis added).

A study of the six uses of *metamelomai* reveals that, first, it most definitely involved a change of mind. When Christ told of two sons who were commanded by their father to go work in the vineyard, He said that the second son "answered and said, 'I will not,' but afterward he *regretted* it and went" (Matt. 21:29, emphasis added).

A second feature of *metamelomai* is that the idea of sorrow is sometimes involved. Concerning the actions of the one who betrayed Christ, we are told:

Then Judas, His betrayer, seeing that He had been condemned, was *remorseful* and brought back the thirty pieces of silver to the chief priests and elders, saying, "I have sinned by betraying innocent blood." And they said, "What is that to us? You see to it!" Then he threw down the pieces of silver in the temple and departed, and went and hanged himself (Matt. 27:3–5, emphasis added).[13]

One must be careful how far the issue of sorrow is carried since in only two of the verses where the word *metamelomai* is used is sorrow actually stressed. The dominant idea appears to be the need for a change of mind regardless of the extent to which remorse is felt.

REPENTANCE IN THE OLD TESTAMENT

Although Hebrew does not have a word equivalent to the Greek word for *repent,* ideas surrounding the concept of repentance are certainly in the Old Testament. They take two basic forms.

There is a ritualistic form of repentance that shows a lack of seriousness in one's relationship to God. In other words, ceremonial fasts were sometimes observed as if the people were repenting but with little regard for the need of obedience to God (Zech. 7:1–7).

There is also the form of repentance that has the idea of conversion and bears a relationship to the New Testament use of the word *repentance.*[14] The term used for this was not one the prophets originated. Instead they used a secular term *(shub)* to express what they had in mind. *Shub* usually carried the idea of turning back, returning. For example, after Abraham's conversation with the Lord concerning the wickedness of Sodom and Gomorrah, "Abraham returned *[shub]* to his place" (Gen. 18:33).

It began to be used figuratively to express a person's spiritual relationship to God whether of turning away from God or turning toward God. After the children of Israel rebelled on the edge of the Promised Land, they were told not to enter it, "for the Amalekites and the Canaanites are there before you, and you shall fall by the sword; because you have turned away *[shub]* from the LORD, the LORD will not be with you" (Num. 14:43). In contrast, the Spirit of God said through Azariah, "For a long time Israel has been without the true God, without a teaching priest, and without law; but when in their trouble they turned *[shub]* to the LORD God of Israel, and sought Him, He was found by them" (2 Chron. 15:3–4).

It is also instructive to observe that in the Old Testament, as in the New, when eternal salvation was stressed, faith was the focus. The predominant passage most often quoted in explaining the Old

Testament concept of salvation is Genesis 15:6. Concerning Abraham's conversion we are told, "And he believed in the LORD, and He accounted it to him for righteousness." This is the Old Testament passage Paul cited in Romans 4:1–8 in explaining that eternal salvation is by grace and not by works. Abraham knew he had done many good works. Yet he also knew that none of those good works would merit him a right standing with God. By simple faith, the same way one is saved in the New Testament, he trusted God, relying on Him to forgive his sins. How much Abraham understood the means by which his sins would be atoned (Christ's death and resurrection) is difficult to say. He knew, however, that one could be justified only by faith and not by works.[15]

When discussing salvation, the emphasis of the Old Testament, as in the New, is on faith.

A DEFINITION OF REPENTANCE

From the above study of the concept of repentance in the Old and New Testaments, three conclusions may be drawn: (1) Repentance clearly means to change the mind. (2) The object of repentance is not the same in every context, but is nonetheless in one way or another "Godward." (3) In salvation contexts, repentance either implies faith or is associated with faith. Therefore, when used in a soteriological context, repentance means to change one's mind about whatever is keeping one from trusting Christ and trust Him as the only means of salvation. Some may have to change their minds about their very concept of God. That is, they have to realize that He is indeed God and Christ is indeed His Son. Others may have to realize that their works cannot save them. Still others may have to change their minds about the seriousness of particular sins, admitting to God that they are indeed sins. But once an individual has changed his or her mind about whatever is keeping them from trusting Christ and trusts Him for salvation, both faith and repentance have taken place.

With that in mind, a passage such as Acts 20:21 becomes most understandable. As Paul gathered with the elders of Ephesus, he reminded them of the content of his gospel message. He said, "testifying to Jews, and also to Greeks, repentance toward God and faith toward our Lord Jesus Christ." One must remember that Paul ministered to the generation of people who had crucified the Lord (Acts 2:36). Therefore he preached to them about the need to change their minds about God, to recognize that Christ is indeed His Son, and to trust in Christ alone for their salvation. Instead of presenting what some have taken to be two different aspects of salvation—repentance and faith— he is simply presenting two inseparable concepts. Should they repent about God, recognizing Christ is the One God declared Him to be (Rom. 1:4), they must trust in Christ alone for their salvation. At this point two questions must be answered.

Is Sorrow a Condition of Repentance?

When coming to Christ, one should be sorrowful over one's sin and how it dishonors God. But there can be sorrow without repentance. Teary eyes alone are not evidence that someone has changed his or her mind about sin or the Savior. The question that is therefore debated is, Is genuine sorrow a requirement for genuine repentance?

The answer depends on how one defines *sorrow*. If by sorrow one means acknowledging that one is a sinner deserving of punishment, the answer is yes. For example, in Mark 2 Christ attracted the tax collectors and sinners to Himself and, in so doing, disturbed the proud scribes and Pharisees. When asked how He could eat and drink with such a deplorable group of people, He replied, "Those who are well have no need of a physician, but those who are sick. I did not come to call the righteous, but sinners, to repentance" (v. 17). The problem of the scribes and Pharisees was that they were unwilling to admit they were sinners—unlike the thief on the cross who said of himself and the other thief, "We receive the due reward of our deeds" (Luke 23:41).

If by sorrow one means that there must be visible signs of sadness, such as tears, the answer is no. It is conceivable that a person might come to God as a sinner after changing his mind about Christ or whatever is keeping him from Christ, and yet not have visible signs of sorrow. It is interesting that even in the notable conversion of the thief on the cross, nothing is said of tears. Yet the thief recognized both the error of his way and the deity of Christ. Tears are commonly associated with our English word *repentance* but are not mentioned in Scripture as a requirement of *metanoia* and *metanoeo*. The issue again is that we must acknowledge that we are sinners regardless of how we feel and regardless of visible signs of sorrow. In fact, often it is only *after* we trust Christ and begin to walk closely with Him that wrongdoing on our part will have the severity in our eyes that it has in God's eyes. For that reason, the admonition in James 4:8–9 is most pertinent. James addressed believers, exhorting them, "Draw near to God and He will draw near to you. Cleanse your hands, you sinners; and purify your hearts, you double-minded. Lament and mourn and weep! Let your laughter be turned to mourning and your joy to gloom."

Is Changing One's Life a Condition of Repentance?

Once a person has genuinely repented and experienced salvation, he or she certainly should seek to live a life of gratitude to God. The question is, Is the changing of one's life an *element* of repentance—that is, a condition of salvation?

Those who argue that indeed one must change one's life in order to have sincerely repented do so on the basis of verses such as Acts 26:20. Speaking of his own ministry, Paul said that he "declared first to those in Damascus and in Jerusalem, and throughout all the region of Judea, and then to the Gentiles, that they should repent, turn to God, and do works befitting repentance."

A word of caution is needed here. The word *befitting* is the translation of a Greek word meaning "corresponding to" or "worthy of." Paul's admonition to the individuals he mentioned was that they should repent, turn to God, and do the kind of works that demonstrate how highly they value the salvation they have received. But to twist that text, making what ought to be a fruit a *condition* for repentance—making the text in essence say, "If there is no fruit, there has been no repentance"—does not represent an accurate handling of the text. Furthermore, in 1 Corinthians 6 Paul rebuked believers for taking one another to court. Would such actions be considered "works befitting repentance?" Hardly. Yet Paul did not question their salvation. He referred to them as his Christian brothers and to the ones before whom they were appearing in the courtrooms as unbelievers (v. 6).

Instead, in Romans 11:29 Paul declared, "The gifts and the calling of God are irrevocable." Paul's simple statement was that God, in extending mercy to the disobedient (v. 32) and giving the gift of eternal life as He calls people to Himself, never reverses that decision. He never "repents" for doing so. We are indeed to do works befitting repentance and demonstrate on the outside what has taken place on the inside. But we must also recognize that at best good works are fruits of repentance (Matt. 3:8), not a condition for repentance. Otherwise we make God a bargain-maker instead of a gift-giver—a God who in essence says, "If I do this for you, what will you do for me?" We also reduce the simple message of John 6:47—"Most assuredly, I say to you, he who believes in me has everlasting life"—to "Most assuredly, I say to you, he who believes in Me, *and looks and acts as though he does*, has everlasting life." A person who trusts Christ and does not perform works befitting repentance invites God's chastening (Heb. 12:1–11). To sincerely trust Christ and not begin to deal with one's sin is an extremely serious issue in the eyes of God. In addition, those who sincerely trust Christ and do not deal with sin in their lives can expect to be more miserable than they ever were in their non-Christian condition. But good works are, again, fruit—not a condition of repentance.

CONCLUSION

Repentance is inseparable from salvation. When used in a soteriological context, "repentance" means *to change your mind about whatever is keeping you from trusting Christ and trust Him alone to save you.* However, in light of the fact that the gospel of John emphasizes believing in Christ, and the Old Testament as well makes faith the issue in eternal salvation, we too ought to make that our emphasis.

God is asking each sinner to trust in Christ as his or her only means of getting to heaven. As we make this our stress, we ought to be aware that, in order to believe, individuals will have to repent about something, such as their view of their works, recognizing that works cannot save; their view of Christ, recognizing that He is indeed the Son of God; or of some sin, realizing it is what God calls it—sin. However, once individuals have trusted Christ as their only way of salvation, biblical repentance has taken place.[16]

So What?

A proper grasp of the biblical meaning of repentance will avoid some mistakes often made in our presentation of the Gospel. One mistake we will avoid is giving non-Christians the impression that there are "steps" to salvation. I have on occasion seen a rather lengthy list of what one must do to be saved. The list sometimes reads:

1. *Repent* of your sin.
2. *Turn* from your sin.
3. *Recognize* that Jesus Christ died for you.
4. *Accept* Him as your personal Savior.
5. *Invite* Christ into your life.

It is most confusing where faith fits into that formula. One wonders what the difference is between recognizing that Jesus Christ died for you, accepting Him as your Savior, and inviting Him into your life. One also wonders why unbelievers are never admonished to do what the Scriptures exhort—believe in Christ alone for salvation. A proper understanding of saving faith can avoid such confusion as will a proper understanding of the nature of repentance. *Repentance* means to change your mind about whatever is keeping you from trusting Christ and trust Him to save you. There are no steps to salvation. There might be a progression people go through in coming to see their need, but it is wrong to communicate a specific sequence of steps.

The most glaring mistake we will avoid when we understand repentance is that of giving people the impression that they must "change their lives." For example, people living in adultery must stop their adulterous relationship or God will not receive them. Alcoholics must cease drinking. Those who use vulgarity must clean up their language. Such an idea defies the love of God for sinners. He loves us as we are. As we trust Christ and then *grow,* we can experience His strength and help in making important and necessary changes.

Some have said to me, "I want to be sure unbelievers are serious about trusting Christ. If I tell them that they have to change their lives, I'll find out how serious they are." There are several things wrong with this approach. God doesn't hold us responsible to judge how serious unbelievers are. If unbelievers are deceiving anybody, it is themselves. Also, we are told in Scripture that we have a part in helping others live for the Lord. If the apostle Paul helped new believers "as a nursing mother cherishes her own children" (1 Thess. 2:7), we ought to do the same. Sometimes our plea for people to clean up their lives before they come to Christ may be a subtle attempt on our part to avoid helping them grow. As will be seen later, diligent follow-up of new believers often takes more work than evangelism. Most grievous of all, however, in attempting to determine how serious they are, is muddying the Gospel and combined works with grace. If God will accept sinners as they are, why are we telling them to change?

There are those who come to Christ and, for one reason or another, do not go on. As unfortunate and serious a situation as that is due to the consequences of sin in a believer's life, there are very plausible explanations for this, as will be seen in the next chapter. Suppose these people who did not "go on" for Christ were insincere and indeed never truly trusted Christ to save them. Do we now change our message based on such examples? Indeed not. Our message is never-changing.

A comfort we derive from studying repentance is recognizing that we need not apologize for not using the word *repentance* in evangelistic presentations. Repentance is essential to salvation. But when people recognize that they are sinners and trust Christ to save them, biblical faith and repentance have both taken place. Sometimes the danger one faces in using the term *repent* is that it can be so laden with emotional overtones and connotations that lost persons can incorrectly assume that in order to be saved, they must be able to shed buckets of tears for sins and reform their lives. With such a conclusion, the Gospel of the grace of God has been entirely overlooked.

Let us present the Gospel clearly and exhort the lost to trust in Christ alone as their only way to heaven, recognizing that once they do, they have exercised both repentance and faith.

Group Discussion Questions

- In what specific ways does a biblical understanding of repentance contribute to a clear presentation of the Gospel?

- Compare your understanding of your sinful condition prior to coming to Christ with your understanding of it now. How has your concept of sin changed?

- What is the difference between the person who says, "I want to come to Christ, but I don't believe yet that He is the One He said He was," and the person who says, "I want to come to Christ because I'm convinced He died in my place, but I'm not sure I could live the Christian life?" How would you respond to each one?

Chapter Seven

Where Does the Lordship of Christ Fit In?

People may not expect to see perfection, but they do expect to see the gospel make a substantial difference in the character of Christians.
—Francis Schaeffer

Christians want to see individuals who have trusted Christ grow in such a way that their lives reflect their faith in the Savior. But many who have supposedly come to Christ are not living the lives they should be. There is, therefore, much confusion as to whether such people have indeed trusted Christ.

This confusion has expressed itself in different ways, usually centered around a subject referred to as the *lordship of Christ*. This phrase speaks of the control a person allows the Lord to have over his or her life, and according to some, it is a determining factor in deciding whether a person is actually saved. There are differing views on this subject.

To help you understand the problem (since some believers have told me they do not even understand the problem), here are some of the positions arising from this debate over the relationship between salvation and the lordship of Christ:

1. "If He is not Lord of all, He is not Lord at all." This statement basically holds that when people trust Christ, they must immediately give Him control of each area of their lives. If they do not, then they simply are not ready to be saved. For example, one cannot come to Christ and continue living in adultery or being dishonest in business dealings.
2. "When a person comes to Christ, he or she must be *willing* to give God control." This view would claim that the issue is not what an individual does or does not give up on the spot. Instead it is his or her *willingness* to let God work in those areas, even though at the moment he or she may experience difficulty in letting God have control.

3. "If people come to Christ, they must let Him have control of areas of their lives that they are presently aware are not pleasing to Him." Those who hold this view consider that new believers may be unaware of areas of their lives that they must yield to God's control. The issue therefore is not what they have done with those areas, but what they do with the areas they *are* aware of at the moment of salvation.

4. "I don't believe in easy-believism." People holding this view simply say that they refuse to believe that all one has to do is say yes to Christ. I heard one such person say, "I don't believe in decisional regeneration."

5. "When individuals are considering Christ, we must explain to them up front how God is going to expect them to live if they come to the Savior." Those holding this view feel that in so doing they can prevent people from making insincere decisions.

6. "Individuals do not have to do anything else but believe on Christ to be saved. If they do that, they are saved regardless of what they do after that."

7. "I don't know where I stand. I'm not comfortable with saying a person has to give God control of each area of life, but I'm also not comfortable with what is called 'easy believism.'"

Perspectives on other issues can complicate the problem. For example, some believe that a person who comes to Christ and later falls into gross sin has lost his or her salvation. Of that group, some believe that salvation can be regained while others do not.

Still others, because of their convictions on the "perseverance of the saints," want to take the "long view," not the "short view" of a person's life. That is, if someone who has claimed to be a Christian for years displays Christlike fruit, that person is indeed a child of God. If, however, one looks at such a person's life and sees little or no fruit, one has reason to doubt he or she ever met the Savior. "Only time will tell," some would say.

Doctrinal issues are not all that can complicate the problem of lordship. Personal idiosyncrasies can make the issue even more difficult. One person's personality may be such that he likes to "control" others while another's personality is more an "anything goes" attitude. Although those holding any view would claim to base their thoughts on Scripture, it often seems questionable whether the proponents are influenced more by the Scriptures or by their own makeup. With that in mind, we must be sure we are exegeting the Bible and not people. Even though personality enters into almost everything we do, we must come to Scripture submitting our mind and makeup to God's Word, not vice versa. As we do, we must also take care to study a paragraph in its proper context.

When approaching Scripture with that kind of study, care, and concern, several observations can be made.

THERE IS A DISTINCTION BETWEEN
SALVATION AND DISCIPLESHIP

The Scriptures could not be clearer in declaring that salvation is a free gift. When Paul reminded the Ephesians of how they were saved, he said, "For by grace you have been saved through faith, and that not of yourselves; it is the gift of God, not of works, lest anyone should boast" (Eph. 2:8–9). Discipleship, on the other hand, costs something and is available only to those willing to pay the price. In Luke 14:26–27, Christ admonished, "If anyone comes to Me and does not hate his father and mother, wife and children, brothers and sisters, yes, and his own life also, he cannot be My disciple. And whoever does not bear his cross and come after Me cannot be My disciple." He reemphasized, "So likewise, whoever of you does not forsake all that he has cannot be My disciple" (v. 33). We must not confuse salvation and discipleship.[1]

The Scriptures mention those who trusted Christ but hesitated to be recognized as His disciples: "Nevertheless even among the rulers many believed in Him, but because of the Pharisees they did not confess Him, lest they should be put out of the synagogue" (John 12:42). The opposition of the Pharisees was such that if even a highly placed man made known his faith in Christ, he was excommunicated from the synagogue, a costly ostracism in a Jewish society in which certain privileges were connected with synagogue worship. We have no reason to doubt that those John described were Christians. "Believed in Him" is John's most often used construction for trusting Christ as Savior. Nevertheless, fear of persecution kept them from openly testifying of their trust in Christ.

Such situations are still common today. Some people who believe in Christ desire to tell their loved ones what has happened to them but fear rejection and so say nothing. Pressure from family and society can be severe. It sometimes takes time for new converts to find the courage to tell relatives of their conversion.

SALVATION IS CONDITIONED UPON FAITH ALONE

The Scriptures present faith as the sole condition of salvation. What could be plainer than John 6:47, where Christ said, "Most assuredly, I say to you, he who believes in Me has everlasting life"? Similarly, 1 John 5:13 affirms, "These things I have written to you who believe in the name of the Son of God, that you may know that you have eternal life."

When God saves us, does He look back to the cross and accept us on the basis of His Son's performance or does He look ahead at how we are going to live and accept us on the basis of our performance? The answer Scripture gives is that He accepts us based on His Son's performance. Romans 3:24 tells us very clearly that we are "justified freely by His grace through the redemption that is in Christ Jesus." For that reason, our good or bad performance does not alter our salvation. God saves us because of His Son's perfect sacrifice on a cross, not because of our perfect or imperfect behavior afterward. If anyone depends on Christ *plus* the surrendered life he endeavors to life for God to take him to heaven, he is as far from God as the person who has never heard of Christ.[2]

That is why before we can answer the question, Does the Bible teach easy believism? we must first define "easy believism." If what is meant by that is that all a person must do to be saved is recognize he is a sinner, understand that Christ died in his place and arose, and trust in Christ alone to save him, the answer is a definite and dogmatic yes. Christ did the hard part by dying in our place on a cross and taking our punishment (Rom. 5:8). All God asks of us is to receive eternal life as a gift by trusting Christ.

However, if "easy believism" means that anyone who says yes to Jesus, walks an aisle, says a prayer, or "accepts Christ," will go to heaven, even though he has not truly trusted Christ to save him, the answer is no. *The issue is trusting Christ.* Some, no doubt out of zeal and excitement, have begged the lost to believe in Jesus without explaining exactly what that means. Therefore individuals have gone through all kinds of motions and yet not been saved because they have not trusted Christ.

A recognition of the simple truth that salvation is conditioned upon faith alone is what gives significance to the chastisement passages in the Old and New Testaments. If after having trusted Christ we fail to live obedient lives, our walk and fellowship are stunted though our eternal salvation and relationship with the Lord are not affected. God may have to discipline us as a father would his beloved child. For example, Hebrews 12:5–11 says:

> And you have forgotten the exhortation which speaks to you as to sons: "My son, do not despise the chastening of the LORD, nor be discouraged when you are rebuked by Him; for whom the LORD loves He chastens, And scourges every son whom He receives." If you endure chastening, God deals with you as with sons; for what son is there whom a father does not chasten? But if you are without chastening, of which all have become

partakers, then you are illegitimate and not sons. Furthermore, we have had human fathers who corrected us, and we paid them respect. Shall we not much more readily be in subjection to the Father of spirits and live? For they indeed for a few days chastened us as seemed best to them, but He for our profit, that we may be partakers of His holiness. Now no chastening seems to be joyful for the present, but grievous; nevertheless, afterward it yields the peaceable fruit of righteousness to those who have been trained by it.

It is important to notice whom it is God chastens ("God deals with you as with *sons*") and why He chastens (that He might produce "the peaceable fruit of righteousness" in us). When disobeying the heavenly Father who has called us by His grace to His Son, we have every reason to fear God's chastisement; we have no need, however, to fear hellfire and damnation. The fact that we are disobedient does not necessarily mean that we are not Christians. We may very well be saved but simply not living for Him as we ought. During those times, God is very patient, but He may also discipline us to get us back on track—all because He loves us.

THE TERM *LORD* REFERS TO CHRIST'S DEITY AND ROLE IN OUR SALVATION

One might well ask, Does the term *Lord* in the name "Lord Jesus Christ" imply that He must be Lord of a person's life before he or she can be saved? After all, Paul told the Philippian jailer, "Believe on the *Lord* Jesus Christ" (Acts 16:31). The name *Lord* in such texts, however, does not refer to Christ's control of each area in an individual's life but to His deity and unique mediatorial role in salvation. In Acts 2:36, we are told, "Therefore let all the house of Israel know assuredly that God has made this Jesus, whom you crucified, both Lord and Christ." These and other texts emphasize that Christ alone has the ability and authority to punish sin or pardon the sinner. God is asking each person to recognize that not through his or her own merit, but only through Christ can the gift of eternal life be received. He is the divine giver of salvation.

The question that invariably arises on the practical level is, Can a person trust Christ if he or she is not willing to give up a particular sin? Theologically, the answer is yes. God attaches no condition to His free offer of life eternal. "Whosoever will" may come. But what a person is not prevented from doing theologically, he or she will find difficult to do psychologically. To trust the One who died on a cross for one's sin while having decided that one is not, under any circumstances, going to give up a particular sin, is most difficult, if not impossible, for a person to do. He or she feels torn to shreds inside, and it becomes virtually impossible to throw him- or herself upon the Person of Christ who died for us and trust Him for salvation. The problem is not a scriptural or theological one; it is an internal, psychological one.

For that reason, Christ's words in Matthew 18:7–9 are most pertinent:

> Woe to the world because of offenses! For offenses must come, but woe to that man by whom the offense comes! And if your hand or foot causes you to sin, cut it off and cast it from you. It is better for you to enter into life lame or maimed, rather than having two hands or two feet, to be cast into the everlasting fire. And if your eye causes you to sin, pluck it out and cast it from you. It is better for you to enter into life with one eye, rather than having two eyes, to be cast into hell fire.

Christ was saying that many times what the hand touches, what the eye sees, or where the feet go lead into wrong ambitions and keeps a person from God. For example, touching large sums of money may cause people not to see their greatest need of all. A person can feast his or her eyes on a beautiful, spacious house, and that home on earth can become more important than a home in heaven. Christ plainly said it would be better for such a person to cut off a hand or a foot or pluck out an eye than, having two hands, two feet, and two eyes, to be cast into everlasting fire. Christ certainly did not say people cannot receive the gift of life eternal if their eyes beheld or hands touched certain things or if their feet took them certain places. Nor was He advocating self-mutilation as a requirement for being saved. He addressed the problems that often keep people from coming to Christ. God saves real human beings who have thoughts, emotions, and mental alertness. What is possible theologically may be difficult, if not impossible, psychologically.

THE MEANING OF THE TERM *FRUIT*

The meaning of the term fruit must be determined by its context. *Fruit* in Scripture sometimes refers to the characteristics of Christlikeness that should be increasingly found in the believer. Galatians 5:22–23 explains, "But the fruit of the Spirit is love, joy, peace, longsuffering, kindness, goodness, faithfulness, gentleness, self-control." James used the word *fruit* in a similar way when referring to the wisdom that is God-given: "But the wisdom that is from above is first pure, then peaceable, gentle, willing to yield, full of mercy and good fruits, without partiality and without hypocrisy" (James 3:17).

Matthew 7 speaks of a different kind of fruit: "Therefore by their fruits you will know them" (v. 20). The fruit here is not works, but false doctrine and what it produces. Christ warned, "Beware of false prophets, who come to you in sheep's clothing, but inwardly they are ravenous wolves" (v. 15). In other words, what is false about false prophets may not be their outward works, for they may live, act, and talk like Christians. If these false prophets did not act like Christians— "in sheep's clothing"—what Christian would believe their false messages? Thus, their falsity is found predominantly in their teaching not their actions.

The Jewish audience Matthew addressed would naturally think of two Old Testament passages. One refers to a false prophet whose prophecy actually came to pass (Deut. 13:1–5); the other to a false prophet whose prophecy was not fulfilled (Deut. 18:20–22). In both situations the emphasis is not on how the prophet lived, but on what he said.

Matthew 7:20 is not the only passage in which fruit is used to refer to a person's words and doctrine. Examine Matthew 12:33–37. As Christ rebuked the Pharisees, He warned:

> Either make the tree good and its fruit good, or else make the tree bad and its fruit bad; for a tree is known by its fruit. Brood of vipers! How can you, being evil, speak good things? For out of the abundance of the heart the mouth speaks. A good man out of the good treasure of his heart brings forth good things, and an evil man out of the evil treasure brings forth evil things. But I say to you that for every idle word men may speak, they will give account of it in the day of judgment. For by your words you will be justified, and by your words you will be condemned.

The Pharisees were guilty of attributing to Satan the miracles done by the Holy Spirit. As Christ spoke of the good and bad fruit that comes from a person's heart, He was referring to the good or bad words a person speaks: "For out of the abundance of the heart the mouth speaks" (v. 34).

With that in mind, notice how Christ continued in Matthew 7: "Not everyone who says to Me, 'Lord, Lord,' shall enter the kingdom of heaven, but he who does the will of My Father in heaven" (v. 21).[3] The false prophets, some of whom were the Pharisees of Christ's day, taught that one must rely not upon Christ, but on good works for salvation.

For that reason, Christ continued: "Many will say to Me in that day, 'Lord, Lord, have we not prophesied in Your name, cast out demons in Your name, and done many wonders in Your name?' And then I will declare to them, 'I never knew you; depart from Me, you who practice lawlessness!'" (vv. 22–23). False prophets produce false professions, as well as individuals who do not understand the gospel message. Therefore, He said, "I will declare to them, 'I never knew you; depart from Me, you who practice lawlessness!'" He was quoting Psalm 6:8. As King David had spoken of vanquishing his enemies, so Christ will purge from His presence those who trust their works (and therefore have practiced "lawlessness") to give them a just standing with God.

Cultists are modern-day examples of these false prophets. Many of these people are quite good, moral, and zealous. I have even heard it said of one group, "These people are so good, they must be Christians." Some cultists have put their arms around me and said, "The important thing is that we are all headed to the same place." Yet their message reveals that they are not headed to heaven. I asked one cultist, "Is Christ the way to heaven?" He promptly answered, "Yes." I continued, "If one does not make it through Christ, could he make it another way?" He replied, "Yes." By his own confession, he had proven himself to be a false prophet—a man perhaps moral or noble, but with a wrong message.

It is the will of God that a Christian do good works. But Scripture indicates that the will of God is not for the lost to attempt to save themselves by their own good works. Christ alone is the narrow gate and the way that leads to life. Regarding eternal salvation (the context of Matthew 7:13–23), the will of the Father (v. 21) is defined in John 6:40. Jesus said, "This is the will of Him who sent Me, that everyone who sees the Son and believes in Him may have everlasting life; and I will raise him up at the last day."

The importance of a passage such as Matthew 7 to the discussion of this chapter cannot be overemphasized. The text does not say that if a person does not *look* like a Christian, he or she is not one. Rather, it says, "By their fruits"—that is, their message—one can determine if prophets are false or true.

BELIEVERS WHO DON'T ALWAYS LIVE FOR THE LORD

The New Testament is candid in saying there will be various degrees of fruitfulness among believers. Speaking of ministers and the quality of their works, Paul told the Corinthians:

> According to the grace of God which was given to me, as a wise master builder I have laid the foundation, and another builds on it. But let each one take heed how he builds on it. For no other

foundation can anyone lay than that which is laid, which is Jesus Christ. Now if anyone builds on this foundation with gold, silver, precious stones, wood, hay, straw, each one's work will become manifest; for the Day will declare it, because it will be revealed by fire; and the fire will test each one's work, of what sort it is. If anyone's work which he has built on it endures, he will receive a reward. If anyone's work is burned, he will suffer loss; but he himself will be saved, yet so as through fire (1 Cor. 3:10–15).

Should believers' works suffer such a fate, their eternal destiny is not affected. Paul did not question such people's salvation. Although the quality of their work leaves much to be desired, what such ministers have lost is their reward, not their salvation. Whether it was observable by others, there were many times when believers' actions and motives were far from what the Lord desired. Several passages illustrate such less-than-honorable behavior among Christians.

In 1 Corinthians 5:3–5, Paul referred to one church member's fornication while not denying his salvation:

> For I indeed, as absent in body but present in spirit, have already judged, as though I were present, concerning him who has so done this deed. In the name of our Lord Jesus Christ, when you are gathered together, along with my spirit, with the power of our Lord Jesus Christ, deliver such a one to Satan for the destruction of the flesh, that his spirit may be saved in the day of the Lord Jesus.

Paul stated that the one committing the fornication was under divine discipline in which Satan would be the instrument for executing the discipline. Paul later rebuked the same believers for taking one another to court (1 Cor. 6:1–8). Still later, he told the Corinthians that the sickness and even death of some of their number was the result of God's discipline for the sinful way they were conducting themselves at the Lord's table (1 Cor. 11:27–34). So although some of Paul's readers at Corinth were not living godly lives, he nevertheless addressed them as Christians.

When Paul wrote his second epistle to the Christians at Thessalonica, he confronted those who, thinking the world was about to end, had ceased working and were living on the charity of others. His words were pointed:

> We command you, brethren, in the name of our Lord Jesus Christ, that you withdraw from every brother who walks

disorderly and not according to the tradition which he received from us. For you yourselves know how you ought to follow us, for we were not disorderly among you; nor did we eat anyone's bread free of charge, but worked with labor and toil night and day, that we might not be a burden to any of you, not because we do not have authority, but to make ourselves an example of how you should follow us. For even when we were with you, we commanded you this: If anyone will not work, neither shall he eat. For we hear that there are some who walk among you in a disorderly manner, not working at all, but are busybodies. Now those who are such we command and exhort through our Lord Jesus Christ that they work in quietness and eat their own bread. But as for you, brethren, do not grow weary in doing good (2 Thess. 3:6–13).

At the same time, Paul realized his letter of rebuke might not be well received. How were the Thessalonians to treat those believers who did not respond well to his letter? We read, "If anyone does not obey our word in this epistle, note that person and do not keep company with him, that he may be ashamed. Yet do not count him as an enemy, but admonish him as a brother" (2 Thess. 3:14–15). Paul did not argue about whether such persons were indeed Christians. In this context, he took them at their word that they were. He encouraged the fellow believers to separate themselves from such people that they might be shamed into changing their behavior. That treatment of disapproval was a serious and shameful thing for believers. The heathen society about them would certainly take note and so the punishment received from the believing community presented considerable embarrassment. At the same time, the church's goal was to restore such people, not to regard them as enemies. The ostracism was to have a positive effect.

Another passage that should be mentioned is Hebrews 5:11–12:

> You have become dull of hearing. For though by this time you ought to be teachers, you need someone to teach you again the first principles of the oracles of God; and you have come to need milk and not solid food.

It is clear that the writer looked upon these readers as lacking growth, as babies who have difficulty discerning between good and evil; yet, again, their salvation was not questioned. It was their need for growth as Christians that was stressed.

Why do some professing Christians not go on for the Lord? There are at least three possible explanations.

First, they know the language, not the Lord. The Gospel was not made clear to them, and they have gone through all sorts of motions without ever having trusted Christ to save them. Many have the notion that because they attend church, were baptized, walked an aisle, or said a prayer, they are right with God. Rather than relying on Christ and what He did for them on the cross to get them to heaven, they are relying upon something *they* did. They are lost and facing eternal separation from God.

Second, a category of professing Christians who do not go on for the Lord are actual converts who simply have not been followed up correctly. Regrettably, those who are diligent in "fishing for men" are often deficient in following up new believers, giving them only meager help in their new lives. Paul spoke of the care and concern he gave new believers as being like that of a nursing mother cherishing her own children (1 Thess. 2:7), adding, "You know how we exhorted, and comforted, and charged every one of you, as a father does his own children" (v. 11). When a new believer does not go on for the Lord, the finger of blame often should be pointed at the believers surrounding him or her. The growth of new believers is not simply their own responsibility; it is ours as well.

Third, Christians are saved sinners. People coming to Christ today are as human as they were in the days of the Old and New Testaments. Their lack of growth, as in Hebrews 5:11–12; attraction to worldly appeals, as with Demas in 2 Timothy 4:10; or their tolerance of their own unconfessed sin, as in 1 Corinthians 5:3–5 and 2 Samuel 11 (David's acts of adultery and murder) keep them from progressing as they should in their walk with the Lord.

Acts 19 contains an example of believers who had not immediately dealt with a particular sin in their lives. Concerning Paul's ministry in Ephesus, we read in verses 8–10:

> He went into the synagogue and spoke boldly for three months, reasoning and persuading concerning the things of the kingdom of God. But when some were hardened and did not believe, but spoke evil of the Way before the multitude, he departed from them and withdrew the disciples, reasoning daily in the school of Tyrannus. And this continued for two years.

We are then told of "unusual miracles" (v. 11) done by Paul through the power of God. So extensive were the miracles that "even handkerchiefs or aprons were brought from his body to the sick, and the diseases left them and the evil spirits went out of them" (v. 12). So awesome was the power of God working in their midst that it had a cleansing effect upon those who had come to know the Lord. The account continues, "And many who had believed came confessing and telling their deeds. Also, many of those who had practiced magic brought their books together and burned them in the sight of all" (vv. 18–19). Some, although apparently having been Christians for some time, only now were confessing that to use such books of magic was sin.

Sometimes part of the reason believers have not dealt with sin in their lives is that they have not heard enough preaching and teaching centered on the truth that Christ died for sinners and arose on the third day. That truth, as will be seen later, lays a tremendous obligation upon us. When presented clearly, it has a way of making us, as believers, deal with known sin and causing us to desire to live for Christ. As one Christian said to me after a series of evangelistic outreaches in his community, "Each night you spoke to the lost about their soul and God spoke to me about my life." Paul testified in 2 Corinthians 5:15, "He died for all, that those who live should live no longer for themselves, but for Him who died for them and rose again."

Before salvation, we were most selfish individuals. Christ's death has made it possible for us to live no longer for ourselves, but for Him. The more we reflect upon His unselfish death on our behalf, the more our lives are affected. But if we do not reflect on the objective truth of the Gospel by which we are saved, we all too easily forget. It is my conviction that one reason many who have trusted Christ are not living for Him is that many churches fail to announce often and loudly enough the objective truth of the Gospel—Christ died for you and arose. When a person hears that clearly proclaimed, he has reason to examine his life and ask, "Am I living for the One who died for me?"

As Paul did, we should present the Gospel of grace clearly, exhort new believers to grow in that grace, and be an example and encouragement to them.

CONCLUSION

God does not say to a lost person, "You must give Me control of your life or I will not save you." He is asking, "May I give you eternal life?" Once they have trusted Christ, we should then exhort new believers to respond to that grace by living a "thank-you" life for God. As Peter exhorted the saints in Asia Minor, we should exhort new believers to "grow in the grace and knowledge of our Lord and Savior Jesus Christ" (2 Pet. 3:18). We are seldom aware of all the areas of our lives that need to be under His control. Each of us can recall times when God has had to tap us on the shoulder and ask us to move over and let Him have control. As we respond to His Spirit, He will then help us take out of our lives what should not be there and put in what should be.

So What?

Observing the varying views relating to the lordship of Christ raises the question, Could this be simply a problem of semantics in which two people mean the same thing but express it in different words? The answer is, Perhaps yes, but in most cases no.

We ought to be alarmed that we can confuse the Gospel and lead a person to believe that only through faith *and surrender* are they saved. Many on that basis can graduate from trusting their good deeds to save them to trusting Christ *and* their good deeds to save them. Yet all are not saved until they have trusted Christ alone to save them. At the same time, if we are convinced that only if people give God control are they indeed Christians, our tendency will be to stand on the sidelines until we determine if the new converts "mean business." As a result, those who have indeed trusted Christ have our help the least at a time when they need it the most. We may stand by, expecting new believers to achieve within five months a spiritual level that we have not achieved in five years.

In summary, such an attitude toward new believers is critical instead of caring. Quite frankly, it is often far easier for us to criticize new believers for their lack of growth than it is to pour everything we are and have into helping them grow.

Someone once observed, "We always see in others the faults that are not in ourselves so that we do not have to face in ouselves the faults that are not in others." When one approaches evangelism holding to a view that before one can be saved, he must be willing to give God complete control of his life, the question naturally emerges, In what areas must God be given control? Often when we begin to tell people that God must be Lord over certain areas of their lives before they can be saved, the areas we list are simply ones in which we happen to be strong, while they are weak. We somehow never mention our own areas of weakness. Sexual immorality has always been expressed to me as one of the "top five." I have never heard the area of overeating addressed. This once prompted me to say to an overweight acquaintance who adhered to the idea that God must have control of all areas of life before one could be saved: "It's rather interesting that a person can't get to heaven if God is not in control of the person's sex life, but he can get there if God is not in control of his belly and his appetite." I then continued, "I don't mind your presenting that as your standard, but I grieve when you present it as the standard of my loving Lord and Savior."

If we believe that God must be lord of our lives for us to be saved, we begin to look at people's lives to determine if they indeed are saved.

That becomes most confusing. One day we are inclined to say a person is saved. The next day we might think he or she is lost. When the Corinthians were giving of their own resources to help needy brothers and sisters (1 Cor. 16:1–4), one would have been inclined to say, "They are saved." At the same time, when their relations with one another were so strained that they were taking each other to court (6:1–8), one would have been inclined to say, "They are lost."

James 1:22 reminds us that if we have not done what the Word says, whether in trusting Christ for salvation or growing as a Christian, we deceive ourselves. For that reason, as an evangelist I have found it helpful to have the person with whom I am talking determine just where he or she is. I make *him or her* decide. I have often said to a person about whose salvation I was unsure, "There are two possibilities. One is that you are not saved—you know the language, but not the Lord. The other possibility is that indeed you are saved, but you are not growing. Neither is the best situation to be in. Where are you?"

To assess just where a minister of the Gospel is, I have found it helpful to sit down and talk with him or her. I often begin by asking, "If a person had only five minutes to live and wanted to know, 'What must I do to get to heaven?' what would you tell him?" If they express anything other than the need to trust Christ alone, such a person is subject to God's discipline. If they answer, "One needs to trust in Christ alone," I then ask, "Now suppose a person had five years to live instead of five minutes, and that person wanted to know 'What must I do to get to heaven?' What would you tell him or her?" If the answer changes to the need to surrender one's life, do additional good works, and so on in order to be saved, such a person is in danger of the discipline of God. If, however, they reply once again, "Trust Christ alone," and I have heard him or her stress good works as a requirement of salvation, I ask, "Then why did you earlier say . . . ?"

We must discern whether witnesses are simply being sloppy (and unfaithful) in their presentation of the Gospel, whether they tend to be critical of others, or whether they purposely desire to pervert the Gospel of the grace of God. Most of all, we need to let the lesson of Galatians 1:6–9 teach *us* concerning the danger *we* face of "turning away so soon from Him who called you in the grace of Christ, to a different gospel."

One more thought might be mentioned. One of the reasons many struggle when a person sincerely trusts Christ but does not always grow and live for Him as he should is that we feel God has been cheated. "I don't believe in cheap grace," people sometimes exclaim. Because we feel a disobedient person is an embarrassment to God, we would prefer to consider such a person an unbeliever. Bear in mind again that when I meet a person who testifies to being saved but is living in disobedience, I often discover that he or she has missed completely the beauty of the salvation freely provided through Christ's death and resurrection. Could it be, though, that we have missed the very message and depth of the grace of God? Based on what His Son did on the cross, God the Father offers the free gift of life eternal with no conditions attached.

Group Discussion Questions

- Is it easier now for you to let Christ have control of your life than it was when you first came to Him? How should a person's growth in the Lord contribute to his or her willingness to let Christ have control of their life? What do you now understand about Him that you didn't then?

- In talking with someone who is unsure of their salvation, how can you help him or her clearly determine whether they are in need of being saved or if they are already saved and in need of growth?

- It is often easy for us to put demands on a lost person we did not put upon ourselves when we came to Christ. Why do you think we have a tendency to do that?

- Examine your attitude toward new believers. In what ways can you be caring and encouraging toward them?

Chapter Eight

If I Don't Confess Him, Do I Possess Him?

Now Peter sat outside in the courtyard. And a servant girl came to him, saying, "You also were with Jesus of Galilee." But he denied it before them all, saying, "I do not know what you are saying."
—Matthew 26:69–70

Is there such a thing as a silent Christian? If an individual does not confess Christ publicly, is he or she genuinely saved? What part does confession play in salvation?

Romans 10:9–10 is a passage often used to support the argument that if we do not confess the Lord neither do we possess Him. Paul said, "If you confess with your mouth the Lord Jesus and believe in your heart that God has raised Him from the dead, you will be saved. For with the heart one believes to righteousness, and with the mouth confession is made to salvation." A quick glance at these two verses seem to indicate two conditions for salvation: believing and confessing.

GLARING CONTRADICTIONS

Two striking contradictions arise. One is with the opening chapters of the book of Romans. As Paul discussed justification by grace through faith in Romans 2–5, nowhere did he allude to a need for confession. Instead, he made clear that faith in the Person of Christ is the only requirement for salvation: "But now the righteousness of God apart from the law is revealed, being witnessed by the Law and the Prophets, even the righteousness of God which is through faith in Jesus Christ to all and on all who believe" (Rom. 3:21–22). Just as clearly he also said, "But to him who does not work but believes on Him who justifies the ungodly, his faith is accounted for righteousness" (4:5). We might ask, If confession should be a requirement for salvation, why did Paul wait until over halfway through his letter to mention it?

A second contradiction concerns the theme of the entire gospel of

John. On the one hand, there are literally dozens of verses that stress *believing* but say nothing about a need for confession (e.g., John 3:18). On the other hand, John also wrote that of those who did not confess and yet had put their faith in Christ. In the latter part of chapter 12, for example, John discussed the refusal of the Jewish people to believe in Christ despite the many miracles He did among them. At the same time he was careful to point out that there were those among the leaders who "believed in Him, but because of the Pharisees they did not confess Him, lest they should be put out of the synagogue; for they loved the praise of men more than the praise of God" (12:42–43).

The construction, "believed in Him," is *episteusan eis auton* in Greek (John 12:42). This phrase is rarely found outside John and is not found at all in secular material.[1]

Pisteuon eis (believe in) is the construction used in John 3:16: "For God so loved the world that He gave His only begotten Son, that whoever believes in Him should not perish but have everlasting life." (Other verses that use this phrase include John 3:18; 3:36; 5:24; 6:35; 6:40; and 6:47.) In only about three of the thirty-six usages, John 12:42 being one of these, Bible teachers differ as to whether genuine salvation is in view.[2] However, if thirty-three unmistakably refer to genuine conversion, there is little if any reason to dispute the other three. Our first assumption should be that they, too, refer to genuine faith. This is particularly true when, upon examining the texts and contexts of these three usages, there is good reason for concluding that they refer to genuine faith.

Leon Morris comments on John 12:42:

> John does not want to leave us with the impression that none of the leaders believed. On the contrary many from among them did just this. They "believed in Him," where the construction points to a genuine faith. Nicodemus and Joseph of Arimathea are the only ones of whom we have knowledge, but evidently they were but two of a much greater number. The ministry of Jesus was not without its effect even in the highest circles. But by now the opposition of Jesus on the part of the Pharisees was so great that it meant excommunication to confess Him. So they were silent.[3]

EXAMINING ROMANS 10:9–10

If the gospel of John and Romans 2–5 present a supposed contradiction, could it be that some have misunderstood what Paul meant by "saved" in Romans 10:9? After all, as noted earlier, when the word *saved* appears in Scripture, it does not always mean salvation from damnation, even when used elsewhere by the same writer to mean salvation from damnation. For example, in Ephesians 2:8 Paul wrote, "For by grace you have been saved through faith, and that not of yourselves; it is the gift of God." Salvation from hell is clearly in view here. The context and content of the chapter make that clear. Paul was recounting the conversion of the Ephesians. He reminded them that they had been dead in trespasses and sins (v. 1), but were made alive by God's grace (v. 5). However, in 1 Timothy 2, Paul used the word *saved* in what is obviously a different sense when he said concerning the woman, "Nevertheless she will be saved in childbearing if they continue in faith, love, and holiness, with self-control" (v. 15).

The words translated "salvation" or "saved" are seen to have a wide range of application in the Scriptures, depending on the context. A careful study of its usage reveals that salvation is basically thought of as "deliverance" and the context determines from what one has been delivered. In the Greek translation of the Old Testament, salvation often refers to God's delivering His people from hardships and difficulties. In Psalm 18:3 we read, "I will call upon the Lord, who is worthy to be praised; so shall I be saved from my enemies." (See also Psalm 33:16, 1 Samuel 23:5.)

In the New Testament, *salvation* still carries the meaning of deliverance, but is again used in varying ways. Luke, when recounting the voyage and shipwreck en route to Italy, said, "Now when neither sun nor stars appeared for many days, and no small tempest beat on us, all hope that we would be saved was finally given up" (Acts 27:20). The fact that a physical deliverance is in view is seen unmistakably two verses later where Luke recorded Paul saying, "I urge you to take heart, for there will be no loss of life among you, but only of the ship." In another passage, when a storm arose at sea, the disciples woke the Lord with the words, "Lord, save us! We are perishing!" (Matt. 8:25). As Christ was hanging on the cross, the soldiers mocked Him, saying, "If You are the King of the Jews, save Yourself!" (Luke 23:37).

A careful study of what Paul said in his letter to the Romans leads us to conclude that although justification is part and parcel of Romans 10:9–10, by the terms *saved* and *salvation* in those two verses, Paul was referring to something more than simply justification—something that affects the life of a believer, not that of an unbeliever. Consider Romans 5:9 where Paul said, "Much more then, having now been justified by His blood, we shall be saved from wrath through Him." Note the tenses: "*having now been* justified, we *shall be* saved." What in the world was Paul saying?

THE THEME AND FLOW OF THOUGHT IN ROMANS

Look carefully at Romans 1:16–17, which is considered by many Bible teachers to state the theme of this epistle. There Paul said, "I am not ashamed of the gospel of Christ, for it is the power of God to salvation for everyone who believes, for the Jew first and also for the Greek. For in it the righteousness of God is revealed from faith to faith; as it is written, 'The just shall live by faith.'" Paul clearly was saying that the Gospel is the power of God to deliverance for everyone who believes. Deliverance from what? Paul continued, "For the wrath of God is revealed from heaven against all ungodliness and unrighteousness of men, who suppress the truth in unrighteousness." We are delivered from the wrath of God. Heaven has revealed God's anger, specifically upon the unrighteous. As a result of His anger, the unrighteous sink deeper and deeper into the degradation of sin as seen by their actions, specified in Romans 1:21–32. In this paragraph there is a progression downward: repeatedly the text says, "And God gave them up" or "God gave them over." His anger is expressed in unbelievers sinking deeper and deeper into the degradation of their sin.

So the salvation of which Paul was speaking is deliverance from the wrath of God. With that in mind, it must be observed that the next time the word "saved" appears is in Romans 5:9, where Paul said, "Much more then, having now been justified by His blood, we shall be saved from wrath through Him." Just how is this salvation from wrath accomplished? The next verse explains, "For if when we were enemies we were reconciled to God through the death of His Son, much more, having been reconciled, we shall be saved by His life." Notice again Paul said, "*Much more*, having been reconciled, *we shall be* . . . ,*" making it very clear that the salvation from wrath he was stressing is something subsequent to conversion and having to do with sanctification, not salvation from damnation.[4]

Because a holy God is repulsed by sin, in order for us to be delivered from His wrath upon sin, our first need is for justification. As unrighteous people put their faith in Christ and His atoning work on the cross, and God declares them righteous. By Paul's own declaration in Romans 5:9, the blood of Christ has secured that justification for us—the justification discussed from Romans 2:1 to 5:1. That justification rescues us from the damnation we would otherwise receive.

After discussing the benefits of that justification in the early part of chapter 5, Paul then continued, "We shall be saved from wrath" (5:9). Paul explained that this salvation is accomplished through Christ's life: "We shall be saved by His life" (v. 10). His point is that not only did the atoning death of Christ and His resurrection secure our justification, His victory over the grave secures salvation from His wrath; it secures our sanctification.[5] It gives us the deliverance we need from present-day sin and the perverted way of life Paul discussed in chapter 1 so that we may experience the victorious Christian life expounded from 5:9 through 8:39. In this widely recognized section, Paul dealt with the struggle we all undergo to do what is right when faced with the possibility of doing wrong. He explained that only through our identification with Christ do we have victory. He pleaded, "For the death that He died, He died to sin once for all; but the life that He lives, He lives to God. Likewise you also, reckon yourselves to be dead indeed to sin, but alive to God in Christ Jesus our Lord" (Rom. 6:10–11).

From 9:1 to 11:36, Paul discussed the relationship between Jews and Gentiles, the Jews being vessels of His wrath and the Gentiles vessels of His mercy. Paul wrestled with the problem that God, through His prophets, had promised that Israel would be a blessing to all nations. This blessing would consist not merely in giving the world the Messiah, but in Israel's own acceptance of and fellowship with Him. Israel, however, rejected this Messiah, and Gentiles were receiving this blessing of justification. How could what God predicted be reconciled with Israel's unbelief and their being temporarily set aside?

Romans 9 through 11 provides the answer. Paul explained that the promises of God were intended for all who were true children of God by faith, not for those who were simply Israelites by birth. He explained that those who are truly God's people from among Jews and Gentiles alike were receiving the greatest gift there is—the righteousness God provides at the moment of faith. In chapter 10, Paul affirmed that Israel as a nation is accountable to God for rejecting Christ through stubborn unbelief. Their rejection was their doing, not His. Paul gave encouragement in chapter 11 that a time would come when Israel as a nation would trust the Messiah and be a blessing to the nations, as He desires.

As in other epistles, such as Ephesians, after expounding theological doctrine in Romans 1–11, Paul began a very practical exhortatory section of his epistle. Romans 12:1–2 is the key to everything he is about to say:

> I beseech you therefore, brethren, by the mercies of God, that you present your bodies a living sacrifice, holy, acceptable to God, which is your reasonable service. And do not be conformed to this world, but be transformed by the renewing of your mind, that you may prove what is that good and acceptable and perfect will of God.

In Romans 12 through 15, Paul then specified what is the good, acceptable, and perfect will of God. He discussed everything from spiritual gifts to submission to the government to character qualities. Obedience in these areas represents the present-day lifestyle of those saved from the wrath of God.

HOW ROMANS 10:9–10 FITS INTO PAUL'S ARGUMENT

As we return to Romans 10, Paul discussed the relevance of justification by faith to the Jewish need. Speaking of those who are not only unregenerate but also in violent opposition to God, he said in Romans 10:1, "Brethren, my heart's desire and prayer to God for Israel is that they may be saved." Bear in mind that the "salvation" Paul had discussed in Romans is salvation from God's wrath, something subsequent to conversion and related to sanctification. How could the Jews be saved from His wrath and experience the sanctification in which God wants all believers to live?

They, of course, needed to be justified by Christ's blood. Paul warned them about seeking justification any other way. He said:

> For I bear them witness that they have a zeal for God, but not according to knowledge. For they being ignorant of God's righteousness, and seeking to establish their own righteousness, have not submitted to the righteousness of God. For Christ is the end of the law for righteousness to everyone who believes (Rom. 10:2–4).

He then contrasted the two methods of justification—one by works and the other by faith. Quoting Leviticus 18:5, he pointed out that the law required perfection: "Moses writes about the righteousness which is of the law, 'The man who does those things shall live by them'" (v. 5). Perfection, though, was impossible. No one is able to keep the entire law. Paul therefore continued by speaking of the righteousness that is by faith. Making use of the familiar language of Deuteronomy 30:12–14, where Moses spoke of Israel's need to accept God's clear revelation, Paul said:

> But the righteousness of faith speaks in this way, "Do not say in your heart, 'Who will ascend into heaven?'" (that is, to bring Christ down from above) or, "'Who will descend into the abyss?'" (that is, to bring Christ up from the dead). But what does it say? "The word is near you, even in your mouth and in your heart" (that is, the word of faith which we preach) (Rom. 10:6–8).

Righteousness by faith centers around the work of the Messiah, the One the Jews had rejected. A righteousness by faith does not say, "Who will ascend into heaven to bring Christ down?" because He has already come (v. 6). Nor does it ask, "Who will descend into the deep to bring Christ up?" because He has already risen (v. 7). Instead, the righteousness that is by faith speaks of a word from God with which the Jews were completely familiar (v. 8) and which they must now simply believe. That word is, "If you confess with your mouth the Lord Jesus and believe in your heart that God has raised Him from the dead, you will be saved" (v. 9).

Note that in order to be saved from God's wrath they needed to confess Him openly before men. Obviously one cannot confess someone one does not know. Justification must precede sanctification and confession. With that in mind, Paul continued, "For with the heart one believes to righteousness, and with the mouth confession is made to salvation" (v. 10).

No verse in the Scriptures could make it clearer that God's act of justification and our act of confession are two distinct ideas. In this one passage, Romans 10:9, Paul referred to justification ("believing to righteousness") as something that goes on in the heart. The word translated "righteousness" is the noun form of the verb translated "justifies" in Romans 4:5: "To him who does not work but believes on Him who justifies the ungodly, his faith is accounted for righteousness." The moment we exercise faith, trusting Christ alone for a right standing with God, we are justified. His righteousness is placed on our account—"with the heart one believes to righteousness" (10:10). But confession is something done with the mouth. In order to avoid the wrath of God on present-day sin, Paul told them, they must be willing to confess openly their faith in Jesus Christ. No sanctification or victorious Christian living is possible apart from that.

Paul's point in Romans 10:9–10 is very clear. Just as faith in the heart justifies, confession from the mouth saves, not from damnation (our justification has already secured freedom from eternal condemnation), but from the wrath of God on present-day sin.

WHAT IMMEDIATELY FOLLOWS

Continuing the theme of publicly confessing Christ, Paul explained why a person could safely confess Christ: "For the Scripture says, 'Whoever believes on Him will not be put to shame'" (10:11). Paul most likely was referring to Isaiah 28:16, already cited by him in Romans 9:33. God said through His prophet Isaiah, "Behold, I lay in Zion a stone for a foundation, A tried stone, a precious cornerstone, a sure foundation; whoever believes will not act hastily." God emphasized that because the Messiah is a sure foundation for our faith, one who puts faith in Him can be calm.

The parallel Paul made was that one who has trusted Christ will not be disappointed in his hope. He will not be ashamed. Therefore, he ought to have no embarrassment about acknowledging that faith.

What should encourage making that confession? Paul continued, "For there is no distinction between Jew and Greek, for the same Lord over all is rich to all who call upon Him. For 'whoever *calls* upon the name of the LORD shall be saved'" (vv. 12–13).

The phrase "calls upon the name of the Lord" is an interesting one, frequently used as a legal term in the New Testament. For example, in Acts 26:32 we are told, "Then Agrippa said to Festus, 'This man [Paul] might have been set free if he had not appealed to Caesar.'" Paul knew he had done nothing deserving of death or imprisonment. He was completely innocent in the eyes of Roman law. As King Agrippa said, he might have been set free right then. But because Paul had appealed to Caesar—that is, called upon him—the decision of his innocence or guilt lay with the authorities in Rome.[6]

The phrase "calls upon the name of the Lord" was also used of Christians who invoked the assistance of God and therefore publicly identified with the name of Christ. Ananias spoke of Paul's actions prior to his conversion by saying, "Lord, I have heard from many about this man, how much harm he has done to Your saints in Jerusalem. And here he has authority from the chief priests to bind all who *call* on Your name" (Acts 9:13–14). Simple logic tells us those Paul arrested were Christians who openly acknowledged faith in Him and asked for His help as it was needed. In 2 Timothy 2:22 Paul exhorted, "Flee also youthful lusts; but pursue righteousness, faith, love, peace with those who call on the Lord out of a pure heart."

These various usages of "calling upon the name of the Lord" convey that a onetime confession is not in view. Instead, it is a continual confession in which believers invoke the Lord's assistance.

For that reason, it is appropriate that Paul took his quote from Joel 2:32: "Whoever calls on the name of the LORD shall be saved." After predicting the dreadful calamities to come upon Israel, Joel stressed that after those judgments would come a time of great blessing. Whoever among Israel's believing remnant would call upon the name of the Lord, invoking His assistance, would be delivered. Believers were the ones being addressed. Paul's point was that although the circumstances differed, just as the Jewish remnant could invoke the Lord's name for assistance in their day, according to Joel's prophecy, so present-day believers, both Jew and Gentile, could call upon the Lord for deliverance from His wrath.[7]

To "call on the name of the Lord" has the idea of worshiping God and invoking His assistance. It is understandable that we need God's assistance to live the victorious Christian life He has for us, a life in which we openly acknowledge our faith in Him. Paul encouraged believers to invoke His help continually. Whoever calls upon His name will experience deliverance from His wrath and the ability to live a life set apart unto Him.

What clinches this understanding of Romans 10:9–10 are verses 14 and 15:

> How then shall they call on Him in whom they have not believed? And how shall they believe in Him of whom they have not heard? And how shall they hear without a preacher? And how shall they preach unless they are sent? As it is written: "How beautiful are the feet of those who preach the gospel of peace, who bring glad tidings of good things!"

Working from the end backward, one can see the logical progression. A person cannot invoke the Lord's assistance until he or she has trusted Him as Savior. One cannot trust Him until one has heard about Him. One cannot hear unless someone tells him or her. The backward and forward sequence looks like this:

Backward	Forward
step 5: call	step 1: send
step 4: believe	step 2: preach
step 3: hear	step 3: hear
step 2: preach	step 4: believe
step 1: send	step 5: call

The sequence demonstrates that to "call upon the name of the Lord" is different from "believe." Only those who have believed can call.

CONCLUSION

Whether or not one confesses Christ does not determine whether or not one possesses Christ. One possesses Christ the moment one has trusted Him as personal Savior. Deliverance from hell is not on the basis of faith plus confession, but faith plus nothing. At the same time, if an individual wants to experience deliverance from the wrath of God upon present-day sin—the "salvation" spoken of in Romans—if he or she wants to experience a victorious Christian life, there is no way they can do so without openly acknowledging faith in Christ. If we need His assistance to acknowledge continually and openly our relationship to Him, He is most willing to give it.[8]

So What?

A study of confession as it relates to salvation reveals a note of encouragement as well as a note of warning. The encouragement stems from the fact that the apostle Paul in no way contradicted Christ's simple promise in John 6:47: "Most assuredly, I say to you, he who believes in Me has everlasting life." Justification before God by which one secures the gift of eternal life is not based on two conditions; it is based on one—faith in Christ. Romans would discourage us from adding anything to faith. Therefore, we may take comfort in the fact that whenever we have not openly acknowledged our faith, we have in no way forfeited the free gift of life eternal. Eternal life is based on our faith in Christ, not on public and open confession of Christ. God throughout Scripture never adds anything to faith as a requirement for becoming His eternal child.

At the same time, however, we dare not make our open and public acknowledgment of Christ a trivial matter. Though not crucial to our relationship with Him, it is extremely crucial to our walk with Him. One simply cannot be a growing, vibrant, victorious believer without being one who unashamedly lets others know he or she is a Christian.

This acknowledgment is not merely a onetime walking the aisle, signing a response card, attending a new converts' class, or participating in a church's visitation team. All of these may encourage our public confession when done for the right reasons and in the right circumstances. What Paul spoke of, though, concerns something repeated and something that is part of our daily practice, not merely a church's weekly program. It is the way that we refuse to be silent about our knowledge of Him through our daily lives. Calling upon Him for His assistance, we delight to acknowledge openly our faith in Him through our lips and lifestyles. While those without Christ sink deeper and deeper into the degradation of sin, we escape God's wrath and live lives that are set apart. The atoning death of Christ and His resurrection made possible our justification. His victory over the grave and the life of Christ being lived in us and through us are now making possible our sanctification.

I have observed firsthand the truth of which Paul spoke. I have met those who trusted Christ, and because of fear of ridicule or fear that others would expect to see changes in their lives that they were uncertain they had the strength to make, they do not acknowledge publicly their faith in Christ. Should they find themselves completely surrounded by believers, they may publicly acknowledge Christ. Other times, however, their lips are sealed. I have *never* seen one such fearful person whose life truly demonstrated the victory experienced by one who walks closely with God, invoking His help in being outspoken for the Lord. Instead of experiencing victorious Christian living, the life of a silent believer reflects a continual struggle in which sin often has the upper hand. Sometimes such a life degenerates to the point that there is little outwardly that reflects the fact that he or she is indeed born again.

On the other hand, I have met those who desire to acknowledge their relationship to Christ in any way they can. Whether in the neighborhood or on the job, they are quick to state unashamedly through life and lips that they have a relationship with Him. Such people do not always find it easy, particularly in the midst of ridicule, to make such a confession. Nor are their lives completely free of temptation and sin. But they invoke God's help to speak on behalf of the Savior and be an open witness to what God has done in their lives. Such people experience in a personal and dynamic way the strength they need to live a life set apart from sin. Their walks and testimonies for the Savior are marked by victory far more than by defeat. In "calling upon the name of the Lord," they experience a solution for the daily and dangerous influences of sin.

Suppose we know those whom we have reason to believe came to Christ but appear reluctant to tell others about their newfound faith. How do we proceed? We must interact with them to determine if they clearly understand the Gospel and have trusted Christ for their salvation. If they have, we should encourage them to unashamedly speak His name to others.

Suppose we meet those who deny having trusted Christ when years earlier the testimony from their lives and lips was so exciting. Do we assume they are believers? No, we ought not make that assumption but instead question them as to their understanding of the Gospel. They are most likely people who, as mentioned earlier, know the language but not the Lord. We all ought to be warned, though, that upon trusting Christ, we could so stray from the Savior and mess up our lives and minds so severely that we deny the One who redeemed us. Although still recipients of eternal life, we need to return to Him quickly before the damaging consequences of sin take their toll.

Group Discussion Questions

- How could examining Scripture in context prevent us from making very dangerous and misleading assertions?

- Interact with the statement, "There is no such thing as secret discipleship. Either the secrecy destroys the discipleship or the discipleship destroys the secrecy." Why can this be considered a biblical truth?

- Considering your own job or vocation, how has a willingness or unwillingness to publicly acknowledge your relationship to Christ affected your Christian walk?

Chapter Nine

Is Baptism Essential to Salvation?

At best, the teaching that baptism is necessary to be saved is based on passages with debatable meanings.

—Charles C. Ryrie
Understanding Bible Doctrine

If a person has not been under the water, will they ever go above the clouds? That may be a humorous way of putting it, but the question is a serious one. Is baptism essential to salvation? Let's look at the historical significance of baptism in the Bible.

BAPTISM IN THE BIBLE

The New Testament recognizes that there were different kinds of baptism. Paul, having come to Ephesus, asked the disciples, "Into what then were you baptized?" (Acts 19:3). That was another way of asking, What kind of baptism did you have?

It is important to realize that baptism did not originate with the New Testament. Converts in the first century, whether Jew or Gentile, found the practice of baptism familiar. One author comments, "Water is the element naturally used for cleansing the body and its symbolical use entered into almost every cult [every system of religious ritual]; and into none more completely than the Jewish, whose ceremonial washings were proverbial."[1] First Corinthians 15:29 indicates that there was even a group that baptized on behalf of dead people who had not been baptized, similar to that done by a postapostolic heretical sect called the Marcionites.[2] We know from passages such as Leviticus 15:16 that the Mosaic regulations required bathing the whole body for certain uncleannesses. Some early writers stated that the Jews required almost daily washing.[3]

F. F. Bruce comments on what excavations have revealed about the prominence of Jewish baths:

> The excavations carried out from 1963 to 1965 at Masada, where the zealots held out against the Romans to the end in A.D. 73, have given us a silent but impressive picture of their courage and devotion. Far from being the godless miscreants of Josephus' account, the defenders of Masada were scrupulously observant Jews. Amid the splendors of Herod's palace they installed the apparatus of worship. Two rooms of zealot construction have been identified with some probability as a synagogue and school respectively, while there is no room for doubt about two baths for their ritual ablutions which have also been uncovered, and which have been certified as kosher by rabbinical experts of the present day.[4]

More recent digs have uncovered many baths outside the entrance to the temple mount.[5]

The concept of proselyte baptism was particularly known among Jews. Scholars are divided concerning how deeply proselyte baptism influenced the baptism practiced by John the Baptist or Christian baptism. Some feel the earliest references to proselyte baptism belong to the latter half of the first century and others to the beginning of the third century—a difference of well over one hundred years. The Jews, however, made three demands of those who declared themselves to be converts to the Law of Moses: circumcision, baptism, and the offering of sacrifices.[6] Concerning this baptism, J. B. Lightfoot comments:

> As soon as he grows whole of the wound of circumcision, they bring him to baptism, and being placed in the water they again instruct him in some weightier and in some lighter commands of the Law. Which being heard, he plunges himself and comes up, and, behold, he is an Israelite in all things.[7]

In light of how readily the Jews accepted John's baptism (John 4:1), some form of proselyte baptism was undoubtedly known. It was an initiation rite. Those who responded to John's preaching "were baptized by him in the Jordan, confessing their sins" (Matt. 3:6). These were Jews who realized their own need, sinfulness, and inability to save themselves. Having accepted the testimony of John the Baptist concerning Jesus, their baptism identified them as having believed John's message and represented an initiation into that community of people who were looking for the Messiah. It had no saving value. Paul characterized baptism through John's ministry as preparatory: "John indeed baptized with a baptism of repentance, saying to the people that they should believe on Him who would come after him, that is, on Christ Jesus" (Acts 19:4). It would be impossible to prove that all who were baptized had truly trusted John's Messiah as their Messiah. But there undoubtedly was a tremendous openness on their part as represented by their baptism. Their "baptism of repentance for the remission of sins" (Luke 3:3) through John the Baptist made them part of those anticipating the Messiah, the only One who could save them from their sins. It symbolized their preparation to receive the kingdom of God that John heralded.

Why is it important to understand these observations before we look at some verses that appear to require baptism for salvation? Simply because it is inconsistent with history that first-century Jews familiar with baptism as an initiatory rite and a part of regular worship would suddenly view it as a means of attaining justification.

A PROBLEM OF HARMONIZATION

Six verses appear to confirm the assertion that baptism is essential for salvation. Yet if baptism is essential to salvation, we have a severe problem. How does such a notion harmonize with the clear teaching that faith is the only requirement for salvation?

For example, Paul in Titus 3:5 said, "Not by works of righteousness which we have done, but according to His mercy He saved us, through the washing of regeneration and renewing of the Holy Spirit." If "washing" here refers to baptism, how does that reconcile with Ephesians 2:8–9, where Paul said, "For by grace you have been saved through faith, and that not of yourselves; it is the gift of God, not of works, lest anyone should boast"? If we say, "It is a gift, but baptism is required in order to receive it," why did Paul not say, "For by grace you are saved through baptism and faith"? Is a gift that requires an act of obedience a genuine gift, or is it, instead, something that is earned?

Likewise, if baptism saves, we have a difficult passage to explain in 1 Corinthians 1:17. In the Corinthian church some individuals engaged in personality contests. Identifying with well-known Christian figures in a divisive spirit, one would claim loyalty to Paul, one to Apollos, one to Cephas—something the leaders themselves denounced. When Paul rebuked them, he pointed out that no one can divide Christ and it was in His name that they had been baptized, not the name of any church leader. Paul stated his gratitude that he himself had baptized very few individuals (1:16). Then he explained, "Christ did not send me to baptize, but to preach the gospel" (1 Cor. 1:17). Paul

acknowledged that the Gospel is the means by which a person is saved
(1 Cor. 15:1–2). Since he said, "Christ did not send me to baptize, *but
to preach the gospel*," we know that baptizing is one thing; preaching
the Gospel, the Good News of salvation, is another. Baptism, by Paul
the apostle's own confession, has nothing to do with one's eternal
damnation or salvation.[8]

While six verses appear to teach that baptism saves, over sixty verses
in the New Testament clearly tell us we are saved through faith alone.
Many of those verses are in the one book God specifically wrote to tell
us how to be saved—the gospel of John. In light of the admonition in
2 Timothy 2:15, "Be diligent to present yourself approved to God, a
worker who does not need to be ashamed, rightly dividing the word
of truth," what do we do? Being told that the Scriptures must be
handled with accuracy and integrity, do we let the sixty verses interpret
the six, or the six interpret the sixty? The answer is obvious. To do
anything other than let the sixty interpret the six would be a
mishandling of Scripture.

Yet those six verses are still there! If they do not in any way contradict
the statement that one is saved by faith alone, just what are they saying?

Here we should be encouraged. If these six verses did not have
alternative, sensible explanations, we would have reason for concern.
But the fact that these six verses can be explained in a way that makes
biblical sense—a way that reads out of the text what it says—should
be most encouraging. Each of these verses has a sensible explanation
that in no way adds to faith another requirement for salvation.

THE EXPLANATION OF THOSE SIX VERSES

We can safely conclude that whatever these six verses are stressing,
it is not baptism as a requirement for eternal salvation. What then are
they stressing?

Acts 2:38

Of the verses that appear to teach that baptism saves, this one is
perhaps the most alarming. It reads, "Repent, and let every one of you
be baptized in the name of Jesus Christ for the remission of sins; and
you shall receive the gift of the Holy Spirit."

To understand this verse, as well as not become confused with other
verses of Scripture, we must clearly understand regeneration and
forgiveness. Although these come to the believer at the point of faith,
they are not identical.

Regeneration refers to the impartation of new life and is conditioned
on faith alone. In 1 John 5:1 we are told, "Whoever believes that Jesus
is the Christ is born of God." John 1:11–13 says:

He came to His own, and His own did not receive Him. But as many as received Him, to them He gave the right to become children of God, even to those who believe in His name; who were born, not of blood, nor of the will of the flesh, nor of the will of man, but of God.

Regeneration, therefore, concerns something that happens on a judicial level, which nothing can change. The one who has trusted Christ is immediately and forever a child of God.

Forgiveness is on a fellowship level and relates to the restoration of harmony between God and believers. Whereas nothing can change a believer's fundamental union and life forever with God, experiential harmony with Him can be broken. That is one reason Christ, as He taught His disciples to pray, admonished them to ask for forgiveness of sins. He told them to pray, "Forgive us our sins, for we also forgive everyone who is indebted to us" (Luke 11:4). He reminded them, "Judge not, and you shall not be judged. Condemn not, and you shall not be condemned. Forgive, and you will be forgiven" (Luke 6:37). Regeneration and forgiveness are seen in Scripture as two different issues.

There is a parallel on the human family level. A child born into a family will always be the child of his parent, but the fellowship with the parent can be broken through disobedience. This broken fellowship presents the need for forgiveness. Similarly, while union with God can never be broken, communion with Him can be, resulting in the need for forgiveness. For that reason, when John addressed the subject of broken fellowship with the Father (1 John 1:3), he spoke of the need for confession and forgiveness: "If we confess our sins, He is faithful and just to forgive us our sins and to cleanse us from all unrighteousness" (v. 9).

This is not to deny that a "positional" forgiveness is given to us at the moment of regeneration. Speaking in terms of our redemption, Paul said, "In [Christ] we have redemption through His blood, the forgiveness of sins" (Col. 1:14). He echoed the same truth to the church at Ephesus: "In Him we have redemption through His blood, the forgiveness of sins, according to the riches of His grace" (Eph. 1:7). These verses show that at the moment we trust Christ, positionally we are forgiven of all our sins—past, present, and future. The forgiveness is complete and permanent, never to be revoked. Though our closeness or communion with God *is* marred by sin, our eternal relationship with God remains unchanged. Whereas a positional forgiveness is referred to, there is also that forgiveness which enters into the life of a believer and affects his closeness or fellowhip with the Savior.

The setting of Acts 2:38 is quite meaningful. Peter explained to the people that they had crucified their only hope—that Jesus, whom they had nailed to a cross. Now faced with what they had done, they were so "cut to the heart" that they asked, "What shall we do?" (v. 37). Peter answered, "Repent, and let every one of you be baptized in the name of Jesus Christ for the remission of sins; and you shall receive the gift of the Holy Spirit."

As addressed in chapter 6, when repentance is used in the context of salvation, it means changing your mind about whatever is keeping you from trusting Christ and trusting Him to save you. By calling the people to repentance, Peter was commanding them to trust the One they had rejected. Since, as was noted earlier, there is no evidence that first-century Jews looked at baptism as a means of attaining justification, there is no reason to suspect that they would have so viewed it here.

As Peter spoke of Christ, whom they had crucified, as their only hope, they would have understood that faith in Christ is the only requirement for justification. This is confirmed by the fact that verse 41 says, they "received his word." Verse 44 expands by saying, "all who believed." Peter did not stop there. Besides telling them how to be justified ("repent"), he told them what is essential to experience a closeness or fellowship with Christ: "Be baptized for the remission of sins." The particular people who had crucified the Messiah were called upon to be baptized if they were to experience a closeness with the Savior. To put it another way, to be close to the Messiah they had rejected and know that nothing was standing in the way of fellowship with Him, they first had to repent. One cannot be close to someone he does not know. Then, since they were the ones who had crucified Christ, Peter also called upon them to be baptized as an open confession of their faith in Christ.

Bear in mind that the book of Acts is highly transitional, as numerous Bible scholars have acknowledged. The situation in Acts 2 is not meant to be normative for Christians today. In Acts 2, before a Jewish audience charged with the crucifixion of Christ, fellowship or communion with God was given upon baptism, at which time the gift of the Holy Spirit was given, a gift not bestowed before Pentecost. For this unique group of Jews, baptism resulted in the forgiveness of sins; without baptism there was regeneration, but no fellowship. The fellowship resulted in the gift of the Holy Spirit being granted.[9]

The situation in Acts 2 is not even normative in the book of Acts, much less today. Other than the ministry of John the Baptist (Acts 19:3–4 and Luke 3:3), baptism for forgiveness of sins is mentioned only in Acts 2:38 and Acts 22:16, a passage to be observed next. Luke was simply showing how God dealt with the generation of Jewish people who had rejected both John the Baptist and Christ Himself. Twice in the portions of the sermon recorded in Acts 2, Peter told the people that this Jesus was the one *they* had crucified (vv. 23, 36). Immediately after giving them the requirement of Acts 2:38, "with many other words he testified and exhorted them, saying, 'Be saved from this perverse generation'" (v. 40). A particular group is in mind here—those who had rejected both John the Baptist and Christ. A particular issue in addition to salvation is at hand—closeness with God and the bestowal of the Holy Spirit. A particular requirement is made—repent (or change your mind from where it has been concerning Christ and trust Him to save you) and be baptized for the remission of sins.

Therefore, Acts 2:38 is not setting forth baptism as a requirement for entering an eternal relationship with God. Entering into that relationship required repentance concerning the Person and work of Christ. Addressing the Jewish audience who had been charged with crucifying Christ, Peter told those who repented that baptism was essential for fellowship with God and the bestowal of the Holy Spirit.

Acts 22:16

With an awareness of what happened in Acts 2, Acts 22:16 becomes equally understandable. The requirement for Paul's conversion was the same as that in Acts 2:38. He was in the same position as the people addressed there. As he recounted the circumstances surrounding his conversion, Paul explained that Ananias, as commanded by God, had asked him, "And now why are you waiting? Arise and be baptized, and wash away your sins, calling on the name of the Lord."

Scripture indicates that Paul had been regenerated on the road to Damascus three days earlier. Paul stated that he did not receive the Gospel from men, but Christ (Gal. 1:12). His conversion, therefore, must have been on the road to Damascus because this is where Christ spoke to him personally (Acts 9:3–9), as confirmed by Barnabas later (v. 27). As Jesus made Himself real to him (vv. 3–5), Paul acknowledged who He was and asked, "Lord, what do You want me to do?" (v. 6).[10] The Lord directed him to go to Damascus. He went there and fasted and prayed for three days (vv. 6–9). It was in Damascus as Ananias was sent to baptize and commission him (vv. 15–17) that Paul received the full answer to his question, "What do You want me to do?" Interestingly enough, as soon as Ananias saw Paul he addressed him as "Brother Saul," indicating he was already aware of Paul's regeneration.

Paul was regenerated on the road to Damascus, but received forgiveness three days later upon being baptized by Ananias (22:16; 9:17). This was a forgiveness not related to his salvation but to his closeness to the One whom he had just trusted to save him. Having received the gift of eternal life, he was now introduced to a close fellowship with the One whom earlier he had persecuted (9:4).

It cannot be emphasized enough that these two accounts—that of Acts 2 and the conversion of Paul—are exceptional, not normative. The baptism resulted in a close communion with God, an experience totally apart from and subsequent to the regeneration experience. The same demand as a condition for forgiveness is not made elsewhere in the New Testament epistles or, as noted earlier, elsewhere in the book of Acts to a Gentile audience.[11] Again, this was a condition imposed upon the Palestinians who had so openly rejected Christ and His forerunner. Although admittedly unusual, in light of the historical situation involved it is not difficult to comprehend why such a requirement should be made.

Mark 16:16

At a casual glance, Mark 16:16 appears to conclude that in order to be saved, one must be baptized: "He who believes and is baptized will be saved; but he who does not believe will be condemned."

In order to handle the verse accurately, an important question must be answered: "In what sense is the term *saved* being used?"

When Paul used the term *saved* in reference to eternal damnation, he was often referring to those who received eternal life, were regenerated, and were baptized by the Holy Spirit. All who trust Christ are supernaturally and instantly baptized into the body of believers at the moment of faith. We read, "For by one Spirit we were all baptized into one body—whether Jews or Greeks, whether slaves or free—and have all been made to drink into one Spirit" (1 Cor. 12:13).

One place where the Spirit of God is seen to come upon the people at the moment of conversion is Acts 10:44–45:

> While Peter was still speaking these words, the Holy Spirit fell upon all those who heard the word. And those of the circumcision who believed were astonished, as many as came with Peter, because the gift of the Holy Spirit had been poured out on the Gentiles also.

The baptism of the Spirit is not an additional act following conversion. God supernaturally and of His own volition baptizes us into His family the moment we trust Christ to save us. We are thereafter forever His. We are told, "If anyone does not have the Spirit of Christ, he is not His" (Rom. 8:9).

There is reason to believe that the baptism of the Holy Spirit is in view in Mark 16:16. Jesus was using the term *saved* in the same sense it was sometimes used by Paul—to describe ones who were both regenerated and baptized with the Holy Spirit. Mark, when he began his gospel, recorded John the Baptist's words, "I indeed baptized you with water, but He will baptize you with the Holy Spirit" (1:8). The signs spoken of immediately following Mark 16:16 presuppose the gift of the Spirit:

> These signs will follow those who believe: In My name they will cast out demons; they will speak with new tongues; they will take up serpents; and if they drink anything deadly, it will by no means hurt them; they will lay hands on the sick, and they will recover.

It follows that Christ, referring to all individuals after Pentecost, was simply saying, "He who believes and is baptized [by the Holy Spirit] will be saved." But keep reading! He continued, "But he who does not believe will be condemned." It is extremely important to note that condemnation in Mark 16:16 rests only on the failure to believe and is in keeping with the gospel of John (John 3:18). The context leads us to believe that spiritual baptism is in view here, not water baptism. But even if water baptism were in view, if one does not believe, regardless of whether he has been baptized by water or not, he will never see eternal life. In regard to salvation from condemnation, even in Mark 16:16, faith alone is the issue.

With the proper understanding of the word *saved* as it is used in Mark 16:16, one sees that Christ in no way stressed water baptism as being essential to receiving eternal life. To the contrary, He stresses the failure to believe as the only thing that will condemn.

John 3:5

Had you been in Nicodemus's shoes, you probably would have been alarmed to be told by Christ that you must be born again because of how seemingly impossible such a thing was. Nicodemus admitted this frustration when he asked Christ, "How can a man be born when he is old? Can he enter a second time into his mother's womb and be born?" (John 3:4). The absurdity as well as the impossibility of the idea must have puzzled him. Christ, though understanding his perplexity, did not sidestep the requirement: "Unless one is born of water and the Spirit, he cannot enter the kingdom of God" (v. 5).

Christ was trying to take Nicodemus from the physical birth of which he was thinking to the second birth Christ was talking about. Water is a integral part of the physical birthing process. It stands to reason that Christ was referring to the water of natural birth in this verse. He was saying to Nicodemus that one is born of water in order to have life. But one must be born again in the Holy Spirit to enter the eternal kingdom of God.

John 3:6 supports such an interpretation as Christ says, "That which is born of the flesh is flesh, and that which is born of the Spirit is spirit." Christ was explaining to Nicodemus that the first time he were born, he was born of water to begin a natural life. If he was going to enter the kingdom of God, he must be born a second time of the Holy Spirit to begin a spiritual life.

Jesus was simply explaining that physical birth was one of water. To enter into God's kingdom Nicodemus needed a second birth made possible only through the Holy Spirit. As Jesus explained to Nicodemus several moments later, if he would believe in Christ, such a second birth and entrance into eternal life would be his (3:15). This spiritual transformation was predicted in the Old Testament (Ezek. 36:24–27), and as the teacher of Israel (John 3:10), Nicodemus would have understood what Jesus was saying.

Titus 3:5

The apostle Paul was always mindful of the work of grace when God takes a person's life and transforms it into a miracle. In light of that grace, he exhorted his helper Titus to treat the non-Christians around him the way he had been treated by God:

> For we ourselves were also once foolish, disobedient, deceived, serving various lusts and pleasures, living in malice and envy, hateful and hating one another. But when the kindness and the love of God our Savior toward man appeared, not by works of righteousness which we have done, but according to His mercy He saved us, through the washing of regeneration and renewing of the Holy Spirit (Titus 3:3–5).

As we read the phrase *washing of regeneration,* we should bear in mind that Scripture sometimes uses water to portray the Holy Spirit. For example, in John 7:38–39 we read:

> "He who believes in Me, as the Scripture has said, out of his heart will flow rivers of living water." But this He spoke concerning the Spirit, whom those believing in Him would receive; for the Holy Spirit was not yet given, because Jesus was not yet glorified.

It is safe to conclude that water, as found in the idea of washing, is used in this sense in Titus 3:5. Paul used the metaphor to explain the work of the Holy Spirit in imparting new life to us at the moment of conversion. In light of the fact that water symbolized cleansing, a renewing, a refreshing, it is an appropriate metaphor for the work of the Holy Spirit in our lives at the moment of conversion.

Furthermore, the phrases *washing of regeneration* and *renewing of the Holy Spirit* are in the active tense. That is, we do not renew the Holy Spirit, the Holy Spirit renews us. There was no literal water in mind here. Paul was speaking of a spiritual cleansing, which was appropriate since those he wrote to had been saved and justified (vv. 5, 7).

1 Peter 3:21

This verse appears to say that in order to enter heaven, one must be baptized. What else could Peter have meant when he said, "There is also an antitype which now saves us, namely baptism (not the removal of the filth of the flesh, but the answer of a good conscience toward God), through the resurrection of Jesus Christ"?

Once again, the verse's meaning becomes apparent from the context of 1 Peter 3:18–22.

> For Christ also suffered once for sins, the just for the unjust, that He might bring us to God, being put to death in the flesh but made alive by the Spirit, by whom also He went and preached to the spirits in prison, who formerly were disobedient, when once the longsuffering of God waited in the days of Noah, while the ark was being prepared, in which a few, that is, eight souls, were saved through water. There is also an antitype which now saves us, namely baptism (not the removal of the filth of the flesh, but the answer of a good conscience toward God), through the resurrection of Jesus Christ, who has gone into heaven and is at the right hand of God, angels and authorities and powers having been made subject to Him.

Because Christ has already suffered for sins, there is no need for us to do so. The words *suffered once* in verse 18 mean "once at a point in time." Christ suffered once and for all our sins. When He died on a cross, He was the innocent One taking the place of the guilty, the just One dying for the unjust that He might bring us to God. With that purpose in mind, He was put to death in the flesh, but made alive by the Spirit.

At this point, Peter made a digression—a digression to talk not about baptism but about Christ. He said that those who have trusted Christ have shared in His death and resurrection experience. Referring to Christ, Peter said, "He went and preached to the spirits in prison, who formerly were disobedient, when once the longsuffering of God waited in the days of Noah, while the ark was being prepared, in which a few, that is, eight souls, were saved through water" (1 Pet. 3:19–20). Peter was referring to the way Christ by the Holy Spirit and through Noah preached to the unbelievers of Noah's day. The only ones who heeded Noah's preaching were his wife, his three sons, and their wives (Gen. 6:8; 7:7).

Now Peter made his application: "There is also an antitype which now saves us, namely baptism (not the removal of the filth of the flesh, but the answer of a good conscience toward God), through the resurrection of Jesus Christ" (1 Pet. 3:21). Two facts are worth noting. One is that Peter's emphasis in verse 20 is on the ark that was in the water, not the water itself, and understandably so. If there had been no ark, the water would have been the means of drowning for Noah and his family instead of their means of deliverance. It was the ark that was in the water that resulted in their salvation. Second, the word *antitype* in verse 21 recalls that ark. Just as the eight souls escaped the judgment of God by being in the ark, we escape the judgment of God by being in Christ. It is spiritual baptism, not water baptism, that Peter had in view. The moment a person trusts Christ, he or she is spiritually baptized into Christ's body. Galatians 3:26–27 tells us, "For you are all sons of God through faith in Christ Jesus. For as many of you as were baptized in Christ have put on Christ." Being in Him we share in the benefits of His death and resurrection. Just as death no longer has power over Christ, it no longer has power over a believer (Rom. 6:8–11).

The point of Peter's digression is that as Noah entered the ark and escaped judgment, we enter Christ and are safe in Him. For that reason the issue is "not the removal of the filth of the flesh, but the answer of a good conscience toward God." Being spiritually baptized into Christ does not merely divorce us from sin in that we are no longer under its power; it gives us a good conscience regarding the past and enables us to serve Christ in the power of the resurrection.

The problem with supposing that 1 Peter 3:21 supports water baptism as a requirement for salvation is obvious. Not only does that thought clash with the context of the passage, but it also immediately requires one to say that it was through water that the eight souls in Noah's day were saved. If that were true, then everyone should have been saved, because when the flood occurred, water was certainly everywhere! The truth is, water was the problem, not the answer. Had there been no water, the ark would not even have been necessary.

BAPTISM IN A BELIEVER'S LIFE TODAY

Baptism is important. Christ commanded it (Matt. 28:19–20) and the early church and apostles practiced it (Acts 2:41; 8:12; 16:33; 18:8). As the previous study has shown, baptism is not a requirement for entrance into eternal life. What, then, is the biblical place of baptism in a believer's life today?

Bearing in mind the historical significance of baptism as an initiation rite, in the Christian baptism of the New Testament, emphasis fell on the relationship of each new believer to the Savior. Baptism was therefore the first step to discipleship. Christ, as He gave the Great Commission in Matthew 28:19–20, commanded: "Go therefore and make disciples of all the nations, baptizing them in the name of the Father and of the Son and of the Holy Spirit, teaching them to observe all things that I have commanded you."

One example of a new convert taking that first step of discipleship is found in Acts 8. As Philip preached Christ to the Ethiopian eunuch, the eunuch asked, "What hinders me from being baptized?" (v. 36). Philip answered, "If you believe with all your heart, you may" (v. 37). The eunuch responded, "I believe that Jesus Christ is the Son of God."[12] Upon giving that confession and desirous of being considered a follower of Christ, the eunuch was baptized (v. 38). Similarly, when a Philippian jailer found himself the victim of an earthquake and recognized the consequences he would suffer for allowing Paul and the other prisoners to escape, he prepared to kill himself (16:27). Upon receiving Paul's message and trusting Christ, he and his family were baptized—their first step in labeling themselves as Christ's disciples.

Acts 2:41 records an occasion when over three thousand people at once took that step of discipleship. Baptism was the first step of identifying themselves as Christ's disciples and was followed by further acts of living for Him and publicly gathering with others who knew Him: "They continued steadfastly in the apostles' doctrine and fellowship, in the breaking of bread, and in prayers" (v. 42).[13]

Once a person trusts Christ and wishes to make known to others that he considers himself to be a disciple of Christ, the biblical way to publicly testify to that is through water baptism. Since baptism is a public step of discipleship, it is no wonder that Jesus should speak as sternly on the issue of discipleship as He did in Luke 14:26–33:

> If anyone comes to Me and does not hate his father and mother, wife and children, brothers and sisters, yes, and his own life also, he cannot be My disciple. And whoever does not bear his cross and come after Me cannot be My disciple. . . . Whoever of you does not forsake all that he has cannot be my disciple.

Those recognizing the truth surrounding Christ's atoning work on the cross could trust Christ in the privacy of their homes. If they took that public step of declaring themselves to be Christ's disciple through baptism, severe consequences could follow. They could be ostracized by their families and denied societal privileges connected with synagogue worship. There were some who, as mentioned in John 12:42, apparently were not baptized for fear of the consequences. Therefore when Christ spoke about discipleship, He warned that love for Himself must supersede love for any human being, even more than love for one's own life. He also warned of the humiliation and hardship that could be involved. No one within listening distance would have found it difficult to understand the importance of His words. The situation is not unlike times today when someone such as a Hindu comes to faith in Christ. I have known those who, when they were baptized as a means of publicly declaring themselves Christ's disciples, were not allowed back into their homes. Both the Scriptures and the practical experience of many believers show that although eternal life is completely free, discipleship as professed through public baptism may cost a great deal.

So much was baptism practiced upon conversion that the Pharisees were troubled by reports that Jesus had baptized more people than John the Baptist (John 4:1). Through baptism individuals publicly stated, "I have heard the salvation message and trusted Christ and wish you to know that I now consider myself one of His disciples."

CONCLUSION

Baptism is not a requirement for salvation. There are six verses that first appear to say that it is, but there are alternative explanations when the context of each verse is carefully studied.

Baptism was viewed as an initiation rite among first-century Jews. It came to represent the first step of discipleship. Those who had trusted Christ were then called upon to be baptized, outwardly confessing that they were His and wished to follow Him as disciples.

So What?

A careful study of the biblical role of baptism brings many questions to mind. I have had to wrestle with them myself and explore the Scriptures for answers.

ARE THOSE WHO RELY ON THEIR BAPTISM GENUINELY SAVED?

It must be made clear that we are referring to those who are *relying* on baptism to get them to heaven, not to those who *say* they are relying on their baptism. That distinction is important because some are confused about how to verbalize their faith or have become imprecise; thus they can mean one thing and say another.

If, on the other hand, people are indeed *relying* on their baptism to get them to heaven, we must demonstrate from Scripture that they are lost and without eternal life. Acts 4:12 clearly states "there is no other name under heaven given among men by which we must be saved." John in his epistle reminds us, "He Himself is the propitiation for our sins, and not for ours only but also for the whole world" (1 John 2:2). One who attempts to come to Christ relying partially on one's baptism to save them is saying to God, "Your Son's death is a big disappointment. I need to finish what He started—paying for my sins." Such a person does not receive the benefits of Christ's death upon the cross. Refusing to come to God as a sinner with absolutely nothing of one's own to merit salvation, one also refuses to accept salvation on the grounds upon which God gives it—as a free gift.

HOW COULD SO MANY SINCERE PEOPLE BE WRONG?

Many have held onto baptism as a requirement for salvation. In both Christian and non-Christian religions, baptism has been viewed as an act that gives people a right standing with the Supreme Being. In non-Christian religions such a belief might be more understandable. If individuals do not let the Scriptures dictate what and why they believe, the false conclusions at which they can arrive are innumerable.

How can so many sincere people be wrong? First, in order to "rightly divide" the Scriptures (2 Tim. 2:15), one must carefully study them, not casually read them. I remember the day in my teenage years when I came across John 7:38: "He who believes in Me, as the Scripture has said, out of his heart will flow rivers of living water." Having believed in Christ, I was confused about why water was not flowing out of my heart! Had I only studied the verses prior to and following that verse and the context of the whole passage, the confusion would have been eliminated. In the following verse, John made it clear that the water he referred to was the Holy Spirit when he said, "But this He spoke concerning the Spirit." Such a casual reading and lack of careful study too often characterize scriptural examination. Instead, we need to practice care and concern when we read God's Word.

Second, many people cling to baptism because it is our nature to want to *do* something in order to be saved. As humans seek to earn what God only can give, Satan has always had a number of options for them to choose from, not the least of which has been baptism. In so doing, Satan can accomplish one of his primary goals—influencing people to attempt to be like God without being related to God. As Jesus told the Jews of His day, "You are not willing to come to Me that you may have life" (John 5:40).

HOW DO WE HELP PEOPLE WHO ARE MISLED?

An important question to answer is, How do we help people who are misled? The attitude and situation of each individual must be taken into consideration. It is difficult to help individuals see that salvation can occur apart from baptism if they have already made up their mind.

We must never forget, however, that God can get through where we can't. We must pray for individuals who are resting in baptism for salvation, asking God to show them, by His Spirit, their lost condition and need to trust Christ alone. When an openness is there, I have found it helpful to explain what was mentioned in the first part of this chapter concerning the need to let over sixty verses explain six instead of vice versa. It helps to point out Paul's comment in 1 Corinthians 1:17, where he testified, "Christ did not send me to baptize, but to preach the gospel." Many have never been directed to that paragraph and express great surprise at what it says. It also helps to look at the six verses just discussed, showing that there are legitimate explanations for those verses that in no way have to "stretch" the verses to make the explanations fit. Instead, these explanations of what the biblical writer is saying are far easier to support than the notion that one must be baptized to be saved.

I've further found it helpful to direct attention to the thief on the cross. As one of the two thieves crucified with Christ acknowledged Him to be who He claimed, he begged, "Lord, remember me when You come into Your kingdom" (Luke 23:42). Christ's loving response was, "Assuredly I say to you, today you will be with Me in Paradise" (v. 43). If baptism were essential to salvation, Christ could not have made such a promise. If we offer the defense, "That's because the thief died before the Day of Pentecost," that means there are two different means of salvation—faith alone before Pentecost and faith plus baptism afterward—a notion the New Testament does not support.

We have to let the Word be the authority, not personal emotions. Laying the Word before people in a calm, assured way can help. I once had the privilege of leading to Christ the married son of a minister who each Sunday preached that baptism was essential for one's salvation. One of the father's favorite texts was John 3:5. As I explained that passage in context, his son said, "What convinced me was not simply the natural, plausible explanation you gave, but also the way you gave it in such a calm, confident way. Without getting all 'heated up' about it, you could explain that verse in a way that made sense, whereas Dad became quite upset and angry as he explained it in a way that didn't make sense. I never could understand why, if he knew he was right, he had to get so upset about it."

SHOULD BELIEVERS TODAY BE ENCOURAGED IN BAPTISM?

Very definitely! Believers must recognize, though, that baptism has no saving value. One cannot overemphasize to new converts that their eternal life was a free gift the moment they trusted Christ. At the same time, baptism is the way to tell others of that conversion and, in appreciation for what He's done, declare themselves to be His disciples.

Years ago, I was in the West Indies for several evangelistic outreaches. A young man in his late teens from a very devout but non-Christian home came to the services, heard the Gospel, and trusted Christ. So overjoyed was he with what Christ had done for him on the cross, that he desired to be His disciple, willing to follow Him wherever He might lead. When the church announced a baptism service, he wished to declare publicly his decision to follow Christ. When he told his parents of his salvation, they were disturbed. When he then told them of his desire to follow Christ in baptism, they were furious. Not recognizing Christ to be who He said He is, they were not about to entertain the thought of a son who claimed to be His follower. Therefore they promptly told him, "If you are baptized, you can find another place to eat, sleep, drink, and live." It took him one year to think through these consequences, but he did think them through. He was baptized, declaring himself to be Christ's disciple and willing to bear the consequences.

All believers should be encouraged to be Christ's disciples and be baptized. They should also be told of its significance, lest they enter into it lightly and thoughtlessly.

Group Discussion Questions

- If a lost person said to you, "I want to come to Christ but I don't want to be baptized," what would an appropriate response be?

- Why is it important not to merely ask a person what he or she believes but also to ask, "What do you mean by that?"

- How would you respond to a person who says, "It doesn't matter what you believe as long as you're sincere"?

- Why do so many people want to earn eternal life? What in our human experience causes us to think that way?

Chapter Ten

Why, Then, Do Good Works?

The child of God is a creature of eternal destiny. For him no day is without consequence, and no fleeting moment can be called incidental or unimportant. The hours he spends and the decisions he makes have implications that carry on into eternity. What he does today will matter a thousand years from today.

—Dave Breese
Living for Eternity

T he Scriptures are clear that a person's good works have absolutely nothing to do with gaining acceptance by God. Attempting to earn our salvation through good works represents a refusal to accept Christ's finished work on the cross.

Why, then, do good works? A most appropriate question! In fact, when I came to God by faith, that was the first question that came to my mind. I kept asking, "If good works don't save, what good are they?"

It should first be established that although a person's good character or works is unimportant to salvation, it *is* important. Paul instructed Titus, "Remind them to be subject to rulers and authorities, to obey, to be ready for every good work, to speak evil of no one, to be peaceable, gentle, showing all humility to all men" (3:1–2). After noting that such behavior contrasted with the presalvation behavior of Christians, Paul continued, "This is a faithful saying, and these things I want you to affirm constantly, that those who have believed in God should be careful to maintain good works. These things are good and profitable to men" (v. 8).

What did Paul mean by "good and profitable?" In what sense are good works good and why are they profitable? The Scriptures answer those questions from several different angles.

GOOD WORKS—OUR OBLIGATION

Prior to knowing Christ, one must reckon with the cross and the empty tomb. The question each lost person faces is not unlike the question Pilate asked the multitude, "What then shall I do with Jesus who is called Christ?" (Matt. 27:22).

After one trusts Christ, the cross and empty tomb remain the focal point of one's life. Formerly, we looked at the finished work of Christ and saw therein our only hope of a right standing with God. Now, having accepted His sacrificial payment for sins, we see in the finished work of Christ an obligation to live for Him. Throughout the New Testament the motivation for Christian living is the cross. We dare not take what He has done for us lightly. John said it best: "We love Him because He first loved us" (1 John 4:19).

Paul told husbands that they must love their wives because Christ loved them both (Eph. 5:22–25). Believers must put the interests of others before their own because of Christ's death on the cross (Phil. 2:3–8). Christians are told to be kind, forbearing, and forgiving when faced with injuries and abuses because they have experienced God's forgiveness (Col. 3:13). We are admonished to love one another because God loved us enough to pay the debt of our sins (1 John 4:10–11; Eph. 5:2). We must show love to those who differ with us about debatable areas of conduct because God has received all who have come to Him in faith (Rom. 14:3; 15:7). We are told to be subject to authorities over us and be humble toward everyone because of God's grace toward us (Titus 3:1–6). Paul told the Corinthians to walk in holiness because Christ, through His sacrificial death, had cleansed them (1 Cor. 5:1–7).

The surpassing greatness of His grace has placed an obligation upon us to respond accordingly. Peter even stated that a person who does not grow in faith "has forgotten that he was purged from his old sins" (2 Pet. 1:9). Although anything done should be done out of a grateful heart, as will be seen shortly, the obligation to do good remains, regardless of whether our motive is proper or not. In light of everything Christ has gone through that we might be eternally His, we can do no less than seek to fulfill whatever He asks of us. After all, "He died for all, that those who live should live no longer for themselves, but for Him who died for them and rose again" (2 Cor. 5:15).

GOOD WORKS—OUR CHARACTER

No president, while conducting his responsibilities as a national leader, has worn the clothing of a man on death row. Such clothing would not fit his position. It would simply be out of character.

One reason that Scripture gives for the performance of good works by believers is that any other kind of conduct is out of character. It is not fitting. We should not do the things we used to do. Positionally in Christ we are no longer the people we used to be.

Few passages make this any clearer than Romans 6:1–13, where Paul exhorted Christians to present their bodies as instruments of righteousness instead of instruments of unrighteousness. The questions asked and phrases used drive home the message:

> Shall we continue in sin that grace may abound? Certainly not! How shall we who died to sin live any longer in it? . . . just as Christ was raised from the dead by the glory of the Father, even so we also should walk in newness of life. . . . knowing this, that our old man was crucified with Him . . . that we should no longer be slaves of sin. . . . He died to sin once for all; . . . He lives to God. Likewise you also, reckon yourselves to be dead indeed to sin, but alive to God in Christ Jesus our Lord. Therefore do not let sin reign in your mortal body . . . do not present your members as instruments of unrighteousness to sin, but present . . . your members as instruments of righteousness to God.

Paul's admonition to the Thessalonians applies this thought to sexual purity.

> This is the will of God, your sanctification: that you should abstain from sexual immorality; that each of you should know how to possess his own vessel in sanctification and honor, not in passion of lust, like the Gentiles who do not know God; that no one should take advantage of and defraud his brother in this matter, because the Lord is the avenger of all such, as we also forewarned you and testified. For God did not call us to uncleanness, but in holiness (1 Thess. 4:3–7).

Clearly what is expected prior to conversion—conduct characteristic of Gentiles who do not know God—is not appropriate afterward. The previous passion was a passion for lust. The present passion should be for holiness.

Paul approached the same truth from a different angle when he urged the Colossian Christians to look in the direction of their Savior and live accordingly: "If then you were raised with Christ, seek those things which are above, where Christ is, sitting at the right hand of God. Set your mind on things above, not on things on the earth" (Col. 3:1–2). Three verses later he specifically mentioned those activities which had been part of their old lifestyle and should not be part of the new.

Put to death your members which are on the earth: fornication, uncleanness, passion, evil desire, and covetousness, which is idolatry. Because of these things the wrath of God is coming upon the sons of disobedience, in which you also once walked when you lived in them. But now you must also put off all these: anger, wrath, malice, blasphemy, filthy language out of your mouth. Do not lie to one another, since you have put off the old man with his deeds, and have put on the new man who is renewed in knowledge according to the image of Him who created him (vv. 5–10).

In this and other passages is an exhortation to "put to death" and "put off" certain things. It is not that a believer does not have the potential to commit such sins. Otherwise, such exhortations would be unnecessary. Instead, Christians *should not* do them because of how inappropriate and antagonistic they are to the new nature. Paul told the Galatians, "If we live in the Spirit, let us also walk in the Spirit" (Gal. 5:25).

In answering the question, Should a believer continue in sin? Paul urged, "Just as you presented your members as slaves of uncleanness, and of lawlessness leading to more lawlessness, so now present your members as slaves of righteousness for holiness" (Rom. 6:19). The Person who called us is holy. The lifestyle He calls us to is holy. This holiness is so important that Paul spoke of disobedience, such as sexual misconduct, being punished (1 Thess. 4:6). Hebrews and Revelation warn that God will chasten His children if necessary to produce in them the holiness He desires and deserves (Heb. 12:3–11; Rev. 3:19). The new nature He gives us is His. Not to live and work in a way honoring to Him is to live in the past, not the present, and to follow old standards instead of new ones. If we were the people we used to be positionally, we could do the things we used to do. But we are not. Anything other than good works is out of character.

GOOD WORKS—OUR TESTIMONY

Faith alone guarantees salvation (John 5:24) and understandably so. A person with faith but little growth may display little evidence of a new birth. Or a believer may be in such a state of disobedience as to incur the chastening hand of God (1 Cor. 11:28–32). On the other hand, it is possible for a person to have many good, moral qualities that appear godly and yet not be saved (Matt. 7:21–23). Nevertheless, good works, when properly emphasized, do serve to testify to others what an individual knows to be true by simple faith.

A significant paragraph on good works is James 2:14–26. As noted earlier, James in this paragraph was speaking to believers (2:14). He was not in any way doubting their eternal standing with God. He simply stressed the ever-present need for faith to be manifested in works. In terms of our justification before people, it does as little good to tell a person we have faith if we do not have works as it does to say to a person in need, "Depart in peace, be warmed and filled," and yet offer no food or clothing (v. 16). As James says, "What does it profit?" (v. 14). Indeed, we are saved if we have trusted Christ alone as our only hope of heaven, but we ought to show others how alive our faith is by the works that we do. The example from the life of Abraham that James used could hardly be any more pertinent. James is clear that Abraham was justified before God on the basis of faith alone (v. 23.) But he was justified before men and known as God's friend through a life of obedience that included offering Isaac upon the altar. We, too, are God's friends when we do as He has commanded. Jesus told His disciples in John 15:14, "You are My friends if you do whatever I command you." Our faith may be very genuine, whether others see the results of it or not. But in no way can others see our faith, and in no way can we experience victorious Christian living without a life of good works. Through them, after having trusted Christ, we earn the reputation of being a "friend of God."

Equally pertinent in this area is Peter's admonition, "Therefore, brethren, be even more diligent to make your calling and election sure, for if you do these things you will never stumble; for so an entrance will be supplied to you abundantly into the everlasting kingdom of our Lord and Savior Jesus Christ" (2 Pet. 1:10–11). *Sure* is used again in 2 Peter 1:19 where Peter's emphasis is that the Mount of Transfiguration experience gives further evidence to the Old Testament prophecies regarding the second coming of Christ. The certainty of His return did not change; the evidence simply increased. His point in verse 10 when he stresses, "Make your calling and election sure," is that we are to give evidence to others that we are His based on the certainty of Christ's promise to us that we have eternal life (John 5:24). "These things" they were to do refer to the things that pertain to life and godliness that Peter discussed in verses 5–7. His concern was that they not be barren or unfruitful (v. 8). In context, therefore, his desire was that Christians testify to others that they are indeed Christ's. Such a life of obedience helps prevent a person from stumbling into sin or unfruitfulness in his Christian life. It also gives abundant entrance into Christ's kingdom—an entrance, as will be explained in a moment, accompanied by reward.

Simply put, works have a way of testifying to others that we do know God. Without those works, we may indeed be His (2 Thess. 3:6–15), but a life of obedience to Him has a testifying value to others of our salvation.

GOOD WORKS—OUR THANK-YOU

The psalmist called everyone to the praise of God when he said, "Enter into His gates with thanksgiving, And into His courts with praise. Be thankful to Him, and bless His name" (Ps. 100:4). For the Christian, a life of good works becomes a special way to express such thanks. They become his or her thank-you note to God. Underlying a believer's each and every good work is to be an "attitude of gratitude."

After speaking about the righteousness we have in Christ through His atoning work on the cross, Paul begged, "I beseech you therefore, brethren, by the mercies of God, that you present your bodies a living sacrifice, holy, acceptable to God, which is your reasonable service" (Rom. 12:1). Since Christ sacrificed His life for us, our thank offering to Him is to be a life turned over to Him, dedicated to whatever use He wishes.

Paul prayed that the new Colossian believers would be characterized by "giving thanks to the Father who has qualified us to be partakers of the inheritance of the saints in the light. He has delivered us from the power of darkness and translated us into the kingdom of the Son of His love, in whom we have redemption through His blood, the forgiveness of sins" (Col. 1:12–14). A walk exhibiting thanksgiving was so connected with what Christ had done for them in delivering them from darkness and translating them into His kingdom that giving thanks was to be a continual pattern in their lives.

Another example of how specific good works as an expression of our thanks is seen in 2 Corinthians 9:7: "God loves a cheerful giver." He commended them for their own generosity and exclaimed, "Thanks be to God for His indescribable gift!" (v. 15). Paul's reference one sentence earlier to the grace of God implies that the gift of eternal life in Christ is the gift he had in mind. Monetary giving is to be a response of thanks for God's indescribable gift.

We dare not be like nine of the ten lepers described in Luke 17:11–19. After Jesus healed the ten of that torturous and humiliating disease, only one, a Samaritan, returned and "fell down on his face at His feet, giving Him thanks" (v. 16). In light of the tremendous rift that existed between the Jews and Samaritans, his gratitude was most significant. Christ asked, "Were there not ten cleansed? But where are the nine? Were there not any found who returned to give glory to God except this foreigner?" (vv. 17–18). As objects of God's grace, we must determine that we will be like the Samaritan and not the other nine.

The way to "fall down at His feet, giving Him thanks" is with a life abundant in good works.

GOOD WORKS—WHILE WE AWAIT HIS RETURN

Good works look both ways—to the past and the future. We are motivated to do them as we look back to what Christ did for us on the cross. But we are also motivated as we look forward to His return.

> And now, little children, abide in Him, that when He appears, we may have confidence and not be ashamed before Him at His coming. . . . Beloved, now we are children of God; and it has not yet been revealed what we shall be, but we know that when He is revealed, we shall be like Him, for we shall see Him as He is. And everyone who has this hope in Him purifies himself, just as He is pure (1 John 2:28–3:3).

James wrote to believers who were going through trials. He recognized the impact the return of Christ should have in causing them to respond in patience and endurance. He admonished them, "You also be patient. Establish your hearts, for the coming of the Lord is at hand. Do not grumble against one another, brethren, lest you be condemned. Behold, the Judge is standing at the door!" (James 5:8–9). When Peter assured his readers that the Lord is not slack concerning His promise to return (2 Pet. 3:4–9), he charged them, "Therefore, beloved, looking forward to these things, be diligent to be found by Him in peace, without spot and blameless" (v. 14).

Christ, as He spoke of the need for faithfulness, mentioned servants who waited for their master's return, not certain which hour it would be:

> Let your waist be girded and your lamps burning; and you yourselves be like men who wait for their master, when he will return from the wedding, that when he comes and knocks they may open to him immediately. Blessed are those servants whom the master, when he comes, will find watching. Assuredly, I say to you that he will gird himself and have them sit down to eat, and will come and serve them. And if he should come in the second watch, or come in the third watch, and find them so, blessed are those servants. But know this, that if the master of the house had known what hour the thief would come, he would have watched and not allowed his house to be broken into. Therefore you also be ready, for the Son of Man is coming at an hour you do not expect (Luke 12:35–40).

As the servants waited, they worked. When Peter asked the appropriate question, "Lord, do You speak this parable only to us, or to all people?" (v. 41). Christ responded, "Blessed is that servant whom his master will find so doing when he comes" (v. 43). That is the point of the paragraph. As we await His return, we are to be motivated to a life of obedience seen through our good works. Those who are watching ought to be working. D. L. Moody said, "I have felt like working three times as hard since I came to understand that my Lord is coming again."[1]

GOOD WORKS REAP REWARDS

Just as the first and second appearances of Christ, His Cross and His coming again flow together as a motivation for godly living, so, too, do the idea of His return and the distribution of rewards.

John recorded the angel's message concerning Christ, "And behold, I am coming quickly, and My reward is with Me, to give to every one according to his work" (Rev. 22:12). The context of this verse reveals that when Christ returns, the opportunity for people to change their destiny will be gone (v. 11). Therefore, His return will be a day of grief for some, but for those who have trusted Him and lived for Him, it will be a day of gladness. He will reward them for their labor.

Paul addressed the subject of rewards as he instructed the Corinthians:

> No other foundation can anyone lay than that which is laid, which is Jesus Christ. Now if anyone builds on this foundation with gold, silver, precious stones, wood, hay, straw, each one's work will become manifest; for the Day will declare it, because it will be revealed by fire; and the fire will test each one's work, of what sort it is. If anyone's work which he has built on it endures, he will receive a reward. If anyone's work is burned, he will suffer loss; but he himself will be saved, yet so as through fire (1 Cor. 3:11–15).

Gold, silver, and precious stones—which are durable—and wood, hay, and straw—which are perishable—represent works, some of which are worthy of reward and some of which are not. Since fire in the day of the New Testament was used to test the quality of particular metals, it was a fitting analogy. A simple reading of the passage makes clear two things. Reward awaits those whose work endures. For those whose life has little or nothing to show, reward is lost, though salvation is not—"but he himself will be saved" (v. 15). Although all saved people go to heaven, all saved people are not equally rewarded. Good works are the means by which reward is laid up as one builds upon the foundation one is resting on as the only means of salvation—the Person of Christ. Peter sounded the same theme. When he urged a proper response to trials, he spoke of a faith that "may be found to praise, honor, and glory at the revelation of Jesus Christ" (1 Pet. 1:7). He told church leaders who were faithful in their task that "when the Chief Shepherd appears, you will receive the crown of glory that does not fade away" (1 Pet. 5:4). When he exhorted them to be diligent in demonstrating their salvation to others, he reminded them, "For so an entrance will be supplied to you abundantly into the everlasting kingdom of our Lord and Savior Jesus Christ" (2 Pet. 1:11). All saved people have entrance into heaven. Those who are faithful to Him will find their entrance followed by rewards.

It is not surprising that John, Paul, and Peter all spoke of rewards. Even Christ emphasized them. When He admonished His disciples to endure persecution, He told them, "Blessed are you when men hate you, And when they exclude you, And revile you, and cast out your name as evil, For the Son of Man's sake. Rejoice in that day and leap for joy! For indeed your reward is great in heaven, For in like manner their fathers did to the prophets" (Luke 6:22–23).

Probably the most thought-provoking admonition Jesus ever gave concerning works and, interestingly enough, one connected with His return, is in Luke 19:11–27. He told of a nobleman who went into a far country to "receive for himself a kingdom" and later returned. Delivering ten minas to three of his servants, he instructed them to "do business till I come." When he was gone, his enemies decided that they wanted no part of his rule over them. When he returned, he called his servants to him for an accounting of what each man had done with his mina. The first one, having turned his one mina into ten minas, was given authority over ten cities. The second servant, having turned one mina into five, was given authority over five cities. The third, having done nothing with his mina, offered the excuse, "I feared you, because you are an austere man. You collect what you did not deposit, and reap what you did not sow" (v. 21). The master, after rebuking the third servant, gave his mina to the servant who had earned ten, explaining, "Everyone who has will be given; and from him who does not have, even what he has will be taken away from him" (v. 26). He then instructed the servants to kill his enemies who had wanted nothing to do with him.

This passage follows the conversion of Zacchaeus. Having come to faith in Christ (Luke 19:9), Zacchaeus was shown a new way to invest money—a way that honors God.

The nobleman in the passage represents Christ Himself. Much to the disciples' surprise and disappointment, it was not the time for Christ to establish His rule on earth (v. 12). There is no mistake that the parable speaks of rewards for those servants who, having trusted Him as Savior, were admonished to invest their lives and time wisely. In verse 27, the enemies of the nobleman are killed, but not the servants. The issue for each servant is the issue of reward.

Each servant is given a mina—the amount the normal working man was paid for three months labor. Though we all have differing abilities and potential, we are all alike in having one life to live for God. All that began well for the servants, however, did not end well. Each started with a mina, but when the nobleman returned and an accounting took place, the three servants had varying amounts.

The first servant is the most praised and the most rewarded. He had invested his mina in such a way that it earned ten minas. The nobleman told him, "Well done, good servant; because you were faithful in a very little, have authority over ten cities" (v. 17). His reward was directly connected to his work and resulted in a high position of authority in the nobleman's kingdom. The second servant was not as highly rewarded, suggesting that he did not use his abilities to the extent the first man did. There is no commendation mentioned, but there is reward. His mina having earned five minas, he heard the nobleman say, "You also be over five cities" (v. 19).

It is the last servant who does not fare so well. Why not? As he confessed, "Master, here is your mina, which I have kept put away in a handkerchief. For I feared you, because you are an austere man. You collect what you did not deposit, and reap what you did not sow" (vv. 20–21). The nobleman's response is sobering. Regarding him as a servant, but a most irresponsible one, he said, "Take the mina from him, and give it to him who has ten minas" (v. 24). The faithful servant is rewarded even further, while the unfaithful servant has nothing. He was afraid to launch out into service for his master and paid the consequences.

Put yourself in the shoes of each servant. For either of the first two, there must have been a deep sense of satisfaction in having used what they were given and been appropriately rewarded. The first must have sensed the greatest satisfaction of all. But for the third, there was only regret. With no time to make amends, he was forced to look into the face of his master, having wasted his opportunity.

The rewards available to be earned ought to motivate each one of us to a life of good works. According to this parable, the rewards given are specifically in the area of reigning with Christ, as one servant is given authority over ten cities and one over five. This is not the only place this kind of stress is made. In Revelation we are told, "He who overcomes, and keeps My works until the end, to him I will give power over the nations" (2:26). One chapter later we read, "To him who overcomes I will grant to sit with Me on My throne, as I also overcame and sat down with My Father on His throne" (3:21).

The importance of works to future reward is a prominent theme of Scripture. If we wish to share in the glory of reigning with Christ, we must live a life of obedience and good works here on earth. Christ ties together His second coming and the reward of reigning with Him as motivation for good works when He says:

> Who then is a faithful and wise servant, whom his master made ruler over his household, to give them food in due season? Blessed is that servant whom his master, when he comes, will find so doing. Assuredly, I say to you that he will make him ruler over all his goods (Matt. 24:45–47).

GOOD WORKS GLORIFY GOD

Christians do not exist to draw attention to themselves. They exist to draw attention to the One who both made them and died for them.

Good works do just that. Although done by a human instrument, they glorify the One who made it possible for the human instrument to do them. As He spoke of righteous living, Christ exhorted, "Let your light so shine before men, that they may see your good works and glorify your Father in heaven" (Matt. 5:16). Good works cause onlookers to praise God.

Christ reemphasized this when He spoke of His special relationship to the disciples—He as the vine and believers as the branches. He told His disciples, "By this My Father is glorified, that you bear much fruit; so you will be My disciples" (John 15:8). Those who trust Christ as Savior are eternal objects of His grace. Ephesians 2:7 indicates that He is looking forward to that day when He will make a showcase out of us. When as His disciples we produce good works, we glorify Him now.

Along the same line, the apostle Paul told his much loved converts at Philippi:

> This I pray, that your love may abound still more and more in knowledge and all discernment, that you may approve the things that are excellent, that you may be sincere and without offense till the day of Christ, being filled with the fruits of righteousness which are by Jesus Christ, to the glory and praise of God (Phil. 1:9–11).

As others saw the kindnesses extended to Paul by the Philippians and the unity and love that existed among them, their attention would be focused on the One who brought them to Himself.

Even when it comes to the use of our spiritual gifts, why are we told to be faithful in the use of whatever gift God has given us? The goal is "that in all things God may be glorified through Jesus Christ, to whom belong the glory and the dominion forever and ever" (1 Pet. 4:11).

In a paragraph in which Paul exhorted believers to flee sexual immorality, he explained, "For you were bought at a price; therefore glorify God in your body and in your spirit, which are God's" (1 Cor. 6:20). Good works, actions that are aligned with the character and holiness of God, are a means by which we glorify God. Since we belong to Him, each good work lifts up His name before people and gives Him the recognition He desires and deserves.

CONCLUSION

If heaven is assured to those who have trusted Christ, aren't good works a waste? No! Although good works are of no value in meriting acceptance with God, they are of great value subsequent to salvation. As Paul told Titus, they are "good and profitable." Why? We have an obligation to the God of grace who saves us; anything else is out of character. Good works have a testifying value and are an expression of our gratitude. The imminence of the return of Christ demands that we be found faithful in doing good. There are rewards to be earned, and they are the means by which we glorify God. In short, a person who knows the Savior cannot afford to be without them and, properly understood, neither can he or she indulge too heavily in them. As objects of God's grace, we must take seriously Paul's admonition to Titus:

> For the grace of God that brings salvation has appeared to all men, teaching us that, denying ungodliness and worldly lusts, we should live soberly, righteously, and godly in the present age, looking for the blessed hope and glorious appearing of our great God and Savior Jesus Christ, who gave Himself for us, that He might redeem us from every lawless deed and purify for Himself His own special people, zealous for good works (Titus 2:11–14).

So What?

The middle-aged man I was talking to was from a moral, religious background. It was safe to assume that he lived one of the most Christlike lives, humanly observed, that one could live. As I presented the Gospel to him, he came to see that goodness would not secure eternal life. As I saw him struggling with that concept, I thought at first that he might be struggling with pride. I have noticed that many who come from a good background, when confronted with the Gospel of grace, find it difficult to humble themselves and come to God the way a murderer, thief, or rapist comes—as a sinner. But that was not this man's problem. He had come to understand the Gospel of grace so well that it made sense to him why God can receive us only on the basis of what Christ did for us on a cross. His frustration became evident when he asked, "But then, why not trust Christ and immediately go out and 'paint the town red'?" When I presented him with the biblical perspective on good works, the picture came together. He saw that although good works couldn't mean less before he was saved, they could not mean more afterward.

Understanding how and where good works fit into God's plan helps us deal with lost people who struggle in this area. A businessman once said to me, "If I understand what you are saying, a teenager who wants to go to heaven has simply to trust Christ. A murderer with a lifetime of evil works who trusts Christ on his deathbed will also be saved. That hardly seems fair. Why should God accept a dying murderer who has not lived for Him and a teenager on the same basis?" At the same time, he admitted that Scripture did say that salvation by grace through faith was the only basis for life eternal.

I replied, "Let me explain something I am not sure you understand." I directed him to 1 Corinthians 3:11–15, going through the paragraph with him. I then explained that the murderer who trusted Christ on his deathbed both won and lost. He won because, having trusted Christ, eternal life was his. But he lost in the sense that there was now no life to live for Him, whereas the person who trusted Christ in his youth had, under God's good hand, an entire lifetime to glorify God and earn reward. In that way, God is both loving and fair. He is loving because whosoever will may come. But He is fair in that only those who trust Christ and then live for Him will be rewarded. I'll never forget the expression on his face as he said, "I've never understood that before." His tension resolved, he trusted Christ and today is an exciting testimony of a transformed life.

A biblical perspective on good works also shows us why we need not feel guilty if we desire to be rewarded when we stand before the King. Indeed, we should examine ourselves carefully if that desire is not present and seek to determine why it is not there. The idea that one should not labor for reward, as though that were a selfish and unjust motive, is foreign to the New Testament. All we do should be done with a grateful heart, but we should continually have on our minds that day when we will stand before the Lord and be appropriately rewarded. If Christ means anything to us, we should desire to hear Him say, "Well done, thou good and faithful servant." Imagine for a moment the president of the United States choosing you as his ambassador to a foreign country. After discussing your responsibilities and assuring you of reward for good service upon his return, he then leaves. What would honor the president more than an ambassador who labors looking forward to that day of reward? Similarly, we also ought to labor looking forward to the day when we will be rewarded.

One might well ask, "What if one who comes to Christ is not motivated by reward? He doesn't care whether or not he will receive a reward. He feels just getting into heaven will be enough." It must be noted that this is the outlook of a person who has not looked at his Savior face-to-face. The very fact that John spoke of not being ashamed before Him at His coming (1 John 2:28) would indicate that looking into His face is going to cause us much remorse if we have not lived for Him. The believer who has not thought of that has not done much thinking at all. Furthermore, seeing what reward he could have had is going to cause him to wish he could make amends. But there will be no time for that.

Appropriating and appreciating what a God of grace has done in our lives should make us the hardest workers of all. As a friend of mine was telling about two cultists going door-to-door in his neighborhood, undaunted by rejection or the heat of the day. He remarked, "Unfortunately, they believe that by doing so they can earn eternal life. Since I know what it means to be saved by grace, I ought to work harder than they in simple appreciation." He was right! Those who have obtained heaven as a free gift have a more pressing obligation upon them than those wrongly seeking to obtain heaven by good works and religious efforts. Furthermore, as they seek to earn heaven, their efforts are in vain. We who are saved and respond in thanks with a life of good works will find our efforts are not in vain. Paul affirms that when he says, "Therefore, my beloved brethren, be steadfast, immovable, always abounding in the work of the Lord, knowing that your labor is not in vain in the Lord" (1 Cor. 15:58).

One might ask, "But isn't the line between working in order to be saved and working because we are saved awfully thin?" The answer is,

"That line could not be any wider." When one works in order to be saved, he or she casts away the atoning work of Christ on the cross and looks to his or her own efforts as the basis for an eternal standing with God. Such people do not see themselves as God sees them nor see the cross as God sees it. When individuals work because they are saved, they recognize the depth of God's love in sending a perfect Son to die in their place. The eternal standing with God they have through faith causes them to desire that all they do will glorify Him. At the same time they are keenly aware that when they fail or for however long they fail, they have not forfeited heaven. Eternal life is based on Christ's work on the cross, which believers appropriate by faith.

Group Discussion Questions

- How will a believer's reason for performing good works affect his or her attitude in doing them? Be specific.

- Thinking of areas where you have resisted God in your Christian life. Which of the reasons for doing good works in this chapter would have been most helpful to you?

- Suppose a lost person said to you, "If I understand what you have told me about heaven being free, that means I can trust Christ and then go out and live any way I want to." How would you respond?

- Review the reasons for doing good works. How should each of those reasons affect your attitude toward doing the work of evangelism?

Chapter Eleven

What Is New Testament Evangelism?

Father, make of me a crisis man. Bring those I contact to decision. Let me not be a milepost on a single road; make me a fork, that men must turn one way or another on facing Christ in me.

—Jim Elliot
The Shadow of the Almighty

The word *evangelism* means different things to different people. It has been used for everything from winning lost people to Christ to making society a better place to live. Everything from being neighborly and praying for non-Christians to leaving a tract or opening up the Scriptures is considered evangelism.

THREE PREDOMINANT VIEWS

There are three understandings of evangelism, which are commonly referred to as proclamation, presence, and persuasion evangelism. Let's summarize each of the three views.

According to the *proclamation evangelism* view, as long as you announce the Gospel, you have evangelized. Regardless of the outcome, evangelism has taken place when the Gospel has been announced. It should be announced in an intelligent and understandable way, but as long as the Gospel has been proclaimed, the hearer has been evangelized.

The *presence evangelism* view considers that as long as you live the Christian life around the non-Christian, you have evangelized even if you say nothing. This view has been particularly appealing to those who sense the need for Christians to be involved in social action. To live the Christian life and help one's fellow man is considered evangelism, regardless of whether the news of eternal salvation is proclaimed. Feeding the hungry, helping the homeless, aiding a neighbor, and doing a favor for a friend are all considered evangelism.

Persuasion evangelism differs from the above two in that its proponents say that if you do not convince, you have not evangelized. The measurement this view then uses to determine who and how many have been evangelized is whether or not they have become members of a church. One author states:

> Persuasion evangelism is measured by the number of disciples becoming members of the church. This is a valid measurement. It must be done by the effective presentation of the gospel, communicating Christ in the power of the Holy Spirit; "He communicated Himself in the person of His Son, in whom the Word became flesh," . . . and then persuading the people to become disciples.[1]

ARRIVING AT A BIBLICAL DEFINITION OF EVANGELISM

Which of these views is accurate? How do we arrive at a biblical definition of evangelism? The word *evangelism* does not appear in the New Testament. Thus it is impossible to study *evangelism* in the Scriptures and draw appropriate conclusions. One cannot study a word that is not there. So how do we arrive at a biblical definition of evangelism?

Examine the New Testament for the Basis for Our Word Evangelism

Since the word *evangelism* is not found in the New Testament, we must examine two words that are used and do address the subject.

The first is the Greek word, *euangelion*, from which we get *evangel*, meaning *good news*. In the New Testament, it refers to the specific Good News about Christ and is translated *gospel*. As we saw in chapter 1, Paul gave the historical data of the Gospel in 1 Corinthians 15: Christ died for our sins and arose from the dead.

The second word to examine is *euangelizō*, from which we derive our word *evangelize*. This is simply the verb form of the above noun. Since *euangelion* means "good news," *euangelizō* means "to announce good news." As we saw earlier, in the New Testament the term is usually translated "preach the gospel" and refers specifically to the Gospel of Jesus Christ, as in Acts 14:21: "When they had preached the gospel to that city and made many disciples, they returned to Lystra, Iconium, and Antioch."

At this point, we know two things. The first is that *evangel* means "good news." The second is that *evangelize* means "to announce good news." Thus, evangelism would simply be the announcement of good news.

Our definition cannot stop here, though. If evangelism meant only to announce good news, an atheist would be evangelizing if he stood before people and said, "Christ died for your sins and arose," even though he proceeded to call that whole declaration nothing but foolishness. A cultist would be evangelizing if he simply announced the Gospel, even though his next statement was to the effect that anyone who believes should consider himself a fool. Evangelism in the New Testament must mean more than simply the announcement of good news.[2]

It is not enough to study the meanings of these New Testament words. One must also study the *environment* or *atmosphere* in which, in the New Testament, a person engages in the activity.

Such a study reveals that there must be intent or purpose behind the proclamation. Paul acknowledged his intent when he told the people of Lystra, "We also are men with the same nature as you, and preach to you that you should turn from these vain things to the living God, who made the heaven, the earth, the sea, and all things that are in them" (Acts 14:15). Peter also acknowledged a purpose behind the proclamation: "For this reason the gospel was preached also to those who are dead, that they might be judged according to men in the flesh, but live according to God in the spirit" (1 Pet. 4:6). The Gospel was preached so that people who are dead in trespasses and sins (Eph. 2:1) might, by trusting Christ, live in the Spirit.

At other times, although the intent or purpose is not stated, it is certainly implied, as in Romans 10:14–15:

> How then shall they call on Him in whom they have not believed? And how shall they believe in Him of whom they have not heard? And how shall they hear without a preacher? And how shall they preach unless they are sent? As it is written: "How beautiful are the feet of those who preach the gospel of peace, Who bring glad tidings of good things!"

The stance of one who evangelizes in the New Testament is that of a persuader. He recognizes that God is ultimately responsible for the results, but he endeavors to be used of God in persuading the lost of the truth of the Gospel and their need to trust Christ.

Examine Evangelism-Related Activities and Commands in the New Testament

This implied purpose is also seen in other words and commands used in the New Testament in reference to evangelism. These show that the men making the announcement were not simply seeking to give information; they were hoping to see the hearer come to faith in Christ. An attempt was made to persuade men concerning the truth of the Gospel. Examine the following that I've listed for you.

Acts 18:4	"And he reasoned in the synagogue every Sabbath, and persuaded both Jews and Greeks." (As a result of this persuasion the church of Corinth was started.)
Acts 18:13	"This fellow persuades men to worship God contrary to the law." (This is how the Jews assessed the ministry of Paul as they brought him before the governmental judgment seat.)
Acts 26:18	"To open their eyes and to turn them from darkness to light, and from the power of Satan to God, that they may receive forgiveness of sins and an inheritance among those who are sanctified by faith in Me." (In sending Paul, God's purpose was to persuade people.)
Luke 5:10	"Do not be afraid. From now on you will catch men." (Christ made it clear that as His disciples presented the Gospel, their goal was to draw the net and win people.)
2 Corinthians 5:20	"Therefore we are ambassadors for Christ, as though God were pleading through us: we implore you on Christ's behalf, be reconciled to God." (As Paul spoke of his responsibility as an ambassador of Christ, the terms he used indicate that he understood the need not only to preach, but also to persuade.)

A DEFINITION

Evangelism in the New Testament is not simply proclaiming the Good News about Christ. It is doing so with the intent of seeing the hearer come to faith in Christ. Whether or not the hearer trusts Christ is not the speaker's responsibility. As Jesus declared, "No one can come to Me unless the Father who sent Me draws him" (John 6:44). We must, however, have that purpose or intent behind our proclamation. If we announce but do not invite, we have given information, but we have not evangelized. If we invite without giving information, we have encouraged and exhorted, but we have not evangelized. Evangelism is presenting the Gospel of Jesus Christ with the intent of seeing the unbeliever place faith in Christ.

CONCLUSION

The three views stated at the beginning of this chapter are all seen to be misconceptions of the biblical definition. Proclamation evangelism does not go far enough. There must be the *intent* to persuade. Even if the person presenting the Gospel knows the person is in no way ready to trust Christ, what he says must still be said with the intent that the person will indeed decide to trust Christ—whenever that may be. Presence evangelism misses it altogether. Simply living the Christian life around an unbeliever is not evangelizing him or her.[3] This is not to say that the testimony of one's life is unimportant—it certainly is important! However, in order for individuals to be saved, somebody must *tell* them the Good News and invite them to trust Christ. Persuasion evangelism goes too far. If one presents the Gospel and *invites* the lost person to trust Christ, one has done the work of evangelism, regardless of whether the individual trusts Christ. God does not expect us to bring the lost person to Christ. Only the Holy Spirit can do that. He expects us to bring Christ to the lost with the intent that they will receive the gift of life eternal.

Giving information alone is not evangelism. An invitation alone is not evangelism. The New Testament definition of evangelism includes both information and invitation. *Evangelism is presenting the Good News of Christ with the intent of seeing the hearer come to faith in Christ.*

So What?

Having in mind a biblical definition of evangelism helps us to better understand what we are attempting with a lost person. Regardless of who the individuals may be or the circumstances through which we meet them, our desire should always be to see the lost come to Christ. That means they must be evangelized. As Romans 10:14 puts it, "How shall they hear without a preacher?" We observed, though, that they have not been evangelized unless the Gospel of the grace of God has been shared with the intent of seeing them come to faith in Christ. As God gives us opportunity to interact with the lost, that should therefore be the goal we have in mind.

The questions then that naturally arise are, Is a person wrong in not talking about Christ to every lost person he meets? What if the time or opportunity just is not there? If someone circulates leaflets in preparation for an evangelistic outreach, is he not being faithful to the Lord? What about the person who distributes tracts in order to win the lost? Is he evangelizing?

To answer these questions, keep in mind that we are not talking about a matter of faithfulness; we are simply and strictly defining evangelism. No one can speak about Christ to *every* lost person he or she meets. The simple physical limitations of time, a job, family responsibilities, as well as the logistics of the situation prevent that. For example, if one were to present the Gospel to a bank teller while making a deposit, the bank teller's employer as well as the line of people waiting may not appreciate it. It may do more to harm than help the cause of Christ. We also all meet individuals who, for whatever reason, are not in a mood to talk at all.

I once sat in a plane next to a man in his mid-thirties. I attempted to speak to him only to discover he preferred to sleep, not talk. I discerned very quickly that to pursue conversation would irritate him. Two hours later he awoke, looked at me, and said, "I want to apologize for not wanting to talk, but I'm flying back from my buddy's wedding. The guys stayed up almost all night last night and I only had one hour of sleep. I just couldn't keep my eyes open." I assured him that I completely understood and for the next ten minutes before the plane landed, we had a delightful talk. The most I could do was introduce myself, explain that I was a speaker, and give him a booklet to read. To that example could be added countless others.

We should in each situation do the most we can. That may mean expressing a kind word to a grieving widow who is an unbeliever, living a life of example before an atheist who has been "turned off" to religion, participating in preparation for an evangelistic outreach, or praying for a lost friend a Christian neighbor of yours is attempting to reach. All of this amounts to faithfulness to the Savior. What I am suggesting is that, strictly speaking, all actions and activities short of presenting the Gospel and inviting the person to trust Christ could more accurately be called "pre-evangelism." Unless the Gospel has been presented and the person invited to trust Christ, evangelism has not occurred.

Whatever one does, the importance of pre-evangelism cannot be overlooked. I often say to individuals I lead to Christ, "A year from now you will be able to look back and see even more clearly all the people, circumstances, and events God used to bring you to Christ." Each one had his part and each circumstance was used by the Lord. For example, a former atheist attributed his salvation to a timid Christian neighbor. When the neighbor received that compliment, he responded to the new believer, "I never spoke to you about Christ the way I should have." The former atheist responded, "No, you didn't. But you lived me to death. I could refute others' arguments and upset their logic, but I could not refute the way you lived."

A proper understanding of a biblical definition of evangelism does not mean it is wrong ever to present the Gospel to a lost person without inviting him to trust Christ. Whenever possible we should inform and invite. In certain circumstances, however, informing the lost person may take place one week and inviting him or her to trust Christ some time later. To lack patience at that point may hinder. That's one reason why, as we set out to evangelize, we need to do so with a sensitivity to both the lost and the Holy Spirit as He desires to use us.

We must also bear in mind that given the definition of evangelism at which we have arrived, we are not talking about the *means* of evangelism. If on the radio a preacher presents the Gospel and invites the hearer to trust Christ, each unbeliever who hears his voice has at that point been evangelized, even though it has not been done one-to-one. If a person distributes tracts that clearly present the Gospel and invite the reader to trust Christ, a lost person has been evangelized when he has read that tract. The means or method by which the Gospel has been presented is not the issue.

Evangelism involves information and invitation. People have been evangelized for the first time when the Good News of the Gospel has been explained to them and they have been asked to trust Christ. Up to that point, although they have not been evangelized, pre-evangelism has taken place—the kind of pre-evangelism that may play a big part in their coming to the Savior.

Group Discussion Questions

- As you think of opportunities you have had to evangelize, in what situations have you put more pressure upon yourself than necessary? How?

- Are there times, on the other hand, when you did what could properly be called pre-evangelism but could probably have gone further and actually presented the Gospel? What held you back?

- Some believers are so tactful that they never actually confront someone with the Gospel. Others get to the issue of asking a person to trust Christ but lack tact. How can a believer develop a proper balance between being too aggressive and not aggressive enough?

Chapter Twelve

What Is the Best Way to Evangelize?

"There are two great dangers in evangelism," said an astute observer. "One is to change the message; the other is to refuse to change the methods."

—Leighton Ford
The Christian Persuader

A message breeds the need for a method. If there is a message people need to know, that immediately raises the question, How do we get the message to them?

Methods are many—a fact to which anyone can attest—and many times the questions arises, What is the *best* way to evangelize?

A NEW TESTAMENT OBSERVATION

What is the best way to evangelize? Both Christ and His disciples used any and all ways possible to evangelize: open-air speaking in the temple (John 10:22–39), speaking by the seashore (Luke 5:1–3), speaking in homes (Mark 2:1–2), presenting the Gospel one-to-one (Acts 8:26–39), home visitation (Acts 5:42), literature (the entire book of John—cf. John 20:30–31), and speaking in the synagogue (Acts 17:1–4). There does not even seem to be a distinction in their minds between home and foreign missions.

WHY IS THE QUESTION OF METHOD NOT PROMINENT?

One reason the question of method is not prominent in the New Testament is that the emphasis in the New Testament is on message, not method. So much is this so that one of the strongest warnings in Scripture is found in Galatians 1:8: "Even if we, or an angel from heaven, preach any other gospel to you than what we have preached to you, let him be accursed." That warning is in no way addressed to those who would change their method, but is in every way addressed to those who would tamper with the message. A second reason appears to be that there was such an excitement about this message and the One at the center of it that the prevailing attitude was, "Let's just get the Word out—anywhere, everywhere, to anybody and everybody." This idea has been summarized well:

> Evangelism never seems to be an "issue" in the New Testament. That is to say, one does not find the apostles urging, exhorting, scolding, planning and organizing for evangelistic programs. In the apostolic church evangelism was somehow "assumed," and it functioned without special meetings, special courses, special training, special techniques or special programs. Evangelism happened! Issuing effortlessly from the community of believers as light does from the sun, it was automatic, spontaneous, continuous, contagious.[1]

> Evangelism in New Testament times was not an eight-day proceeding, a two-week event, or even a two-month affair once or twice a year! Acts 5:42 describes it "and daily in the temple, and in every house, they did not cease teaching and preaching Jesus as the Christ." The early church made evangelism their "daily" business. There was no let up; in season and out of season the ransomed were constantly and consistently about the business of presenting their redeemer to those dead in trespasses and sins.[2]

Is it not true, though, that some ways to evangelize are more successful than others? Undoubtedly! But dare we call those a better way to evangelize when Scripture does not do so? If thousands were reached by Peter's preaching in Acts 2, and only a few by Peter's visit in Acts 10, dare we call preaching a "better" way? The means used to reach one individual many not be as effective in reaching another. Yet each individual needs to be reached.

One might ask, If Christ sent His disciples out two by two (Luke 10:1), isn't that how we should do it? The answer is possibly so. But bear in mind two things. As mentioned earlier, that was not the only way evangelism was done. Second, we must examine whether our situation has enough parallels to a given New Testament situation to make a particular method used in the New Testament possible and practical. If there are enough parallels, we ought to consider the same method. If there are not, we need to bear in mind that both the command and the emphasis surround message not method. The command was, "Go into all the world and preach the gospel to every creature" (Mark 16:15). The means by which that is to be done involves both prayer and careful thought.

CONCLUSION

There is no best way to evangelize. Instead, as one author has stated, "Methods of evangelism are as diverse as those who are to be reached, and those who reach them."[3] The emphasis of Scripture is never on which means we use to talk to a lost person. It is instead that we do talk. As has been observed, "Every method of not evangelizing is wrong—and many methods are right."[4]

So What?

Restrictions set us free and so does the absence of restrictions. When we are restricted by someone we love, we know what we are allowed to do. When we are not restricted, we know the same!

God has restricted our message. If we desire to be faithful to Him, we dare not change the terms of the message. We must extend the message of God's free offer of life eternal to whomever would put their trust in Christ. Tampering in any way with the message is something we dare not do.

God has not restricted the method. That means as believers in Christ desirous of touching our community with the Gospel, we are free to use the tremendous ability God has given each of us to think and brainstorm as to how we might spread the Gospel. There is no one way to do it. In fact, the one who asks, "What is the best way to evangelize?" has missed the thrust of the New Testament. There is no "best way." What may be effective in one community may not work in another. What may be effective one year may not be effective the next.

Any and all methods may be used. True, we each must display integrity in terms of how we approach the lost. We should not approach them in an underhanded, deceptive way. We should also do it out of a genuine love for Christ and concern for the lost. Whether it be on an individual level at our home or a group level at our church, any and all methods can be used.

My wife and I have found mealtimes in our home to be an effective way to present the Gospel to others. More than once we have had the privilege of leading the lost to Christ over the dinner table. Women have enjoyed shopping trips as opportunities to evangelize. Two ladies enjoying a ride to the mall have often had opportunity to converse about spiritual things. Men have taken advantage of a small carpool as a chance to evangelize. A man once said to me, "While going to work on Monday, we got into a discussion about a sermon one of the men heard the day before. They knew I was interested in spiritual things and asked me a lot of questions." Other men have had opportunity at a backyard cookout, a scouting trip with a few boys and their dads, or even through something as simple as helping a neighbor cement his patio. In some of these opportunities, a piece of literature explaining the Gospel was used, and in others a pocket New Testament was the evangelizing tool.

Churches have experienced the same freedom and diversity. One church I know had an evangelistic volleyball game. In order to play, each Christian had to bring a non-Christian friend. The court was delightfully filled half with Christians and half with non-Christians. As a result, some newcomers began attending the church in weeks following. One church had a Friday night dinner once a month cooked by men to reach men. They would have a speaker at each dinner who talked about the secular work in which he was employed, explaining the difference Christ had made in his life on the job and at home. Others have used evangelistic crusades, Bible studies, and films. If there is one thing I have discovered in traveling as an itinerant evangelist, it is that evangelistic churches do not lock themselves in. They use any and all ways they can to get the Word to others.

When contemplating reaching a particular lost person for Christ, a believer should ask himself, "What appears to be the best thing to do for this person, in this situation, at this time?" The answer may be bringing him to a special evangelistic service. Or it may be inviting him to an evangelistic Bible study in your home. It could be that the unbeliever would not be receptive to either of these activities. Instead, he may respond to going on a fishing trip. A day in the middle of God's creation may allow the Christian to talk about the Creator. A woman who is turned off by church may welcome a booklet dealing with the certainty she may have of life after death. With each person and each situation, do what appears to be the best and wisest thing.

D. L. Moody was asked the question, "What is the best way to reach the masses?" His answer was, "Go for them." The New Testament sets us free to do just that—go for the lost using whatever means we might to reach them.

Group Discussion Questions

- What often prompts us to think that there is only one way to evangelize instead of freeing our minds to think and brainstorm? What causes us to be restricted in the ways we seek to reach lost people?

- List five non-Christians you know. What means can you presently think of to evangelize them? Are you going to?

- How many people have you met who were evangelized by the same means you were? What was similar or different about the approach? What do these observations tell you?

- What are some ways you can think of that your church can collectively reach out to non-Christians?

Chapter Thirteen

What Is the Gift of Evangelism?

*The evangelistic gift, like any other gift, may perish through neglect but,
as with other things, it can be developed to a wonderful extent when its
presence is recognized and its powers are exercised.*

—Lionel B. Fletcher
The Effective Evangelist

Y ears ago residents of a wealthy residential section of Richmond, Virginia, complained about the singing from a small Christian church. They contended that the singing was loud and disturbing, and they circulated a petition to have the city council take action. The petition reached a Jewish resident for his signature, but he refused to sign. "I cannot sign it," he said. "If I believed as do those Christians that my Messiah had come, I would shout it from the housetops and on every street in Richmond, and nobody could stop me!"

"Shouting the Good News" is something every believer is privileged to do. God has never declared that only those with a certain amount of formal training can evangelize. He has allowed each of us to speak to whomever we can and simply tell them, "Jesus Christ died for your sins and arose from the dead."

Some, though, have more than opportunity in evangelism; they have special ability. Ephesians 4:11 makes that clear. As Paul spoke of the way God had equipped people within the church, he said that Christ "gave some to be apostles, some prophets, some evangelists, and some pastors and teachers."[1]

What is the gift of evangelism? To answer that question, let's first answer two others. We'll then be able to arrive at an understanding of the gift of evangelism.

WHERE DOES THE TERM *EVANGELIST* COME FROM?

Our English word *evangel* comes from a Greek word *euangelion*, meaning "good news." The verb being related to the noun, our word *evangelize* comes from a Greek word *euangelizō*, meaning "to announce good news." As a result, our English word *evangelist*, the translation of *euangelistes*, means "one who announces good news." In the New Testament, of course, the good news the evangelist announces is the Good News of the Gospel of Christ.

It is important to look not just at the derivation of the word, but also at how it is used. Surprisingly, although the Greek words for gospel and for announcing the gospel are used numerous times, the Greek word translated *evangelist* is used only three times in the New Testament. Those three instances are well worth examining.

> Acts 21:8—On the next day we who were Paul's companions departed and came to Caesarea, and entered the house of Philip the evangelist, who was one of the seven, and stayed with him. [Philip is the only evangelist mentioned in the New Testament. He preached in Samaria (Acts 8:5), presented Christ to the Ethiopian eunuch (vv. 26–39), and continued a traveling ministry along the southern coast of Palestine (v. 40).]

> 2 Timothy 4:5—But you be watchful in all things, endure afflictions, do the work of an evangelist, fulfill your ministry. [Timothy was a gifted pastor-teacher and a member of the Pauline missionary group. Paul exhorted him to do the work of an evangelist. This command would directly apply to pastor-teachers today, whether resident or not.]

> Ephesians 4:11—And He Himself gave some to be apostles, some prophets, some evangelists, and some pastors and teachers. [Here Paul lists the different gifted individuals God has given within the church so that the entire body might be equipped to do the work of the ministry (Eph. 4:12).]

Since the evangelist is seen in Acts 21:8 as one who preaches the Gospel to the non-Christian and in Ephesians 4:11 as one who assists in building up the saved, it can be concluded that the evangelist has a ministry to both unbelievers and believers. It can be assumed, although it is not specifically stated, that because the nature of the gift assumes a special capacity in the area of evangelism, the evangelist's main ministry to believers is to equip them to evangelize. The evangelist thus has a reaching ministry to the non-Christian and a teaching ministry in evangelism to the saved.

We can now arrive at a definition. The gift of evangelism is the special ability to communicate the Gospel to sinners and to equip the saints for evangelism.

WHAT CHARACTERIZES THE GIFT?

Rather disappointingly, the New Testament does not list the characteristics that evidence a gift in evangelism. Such a list would undoubtedly help persons who have wondered if they might have special ability in speaking to the lost about Christ.

Although the New Testament does not give such a list, several things can be safely assumed from the above definition. One is that because of what is at the heart of the gift, the evangelist has an intense longing to announce the Gospel. A person who is gifted in evangelism can often find greater joy in talking to others about Christ than in anything else. Along with this, contacts and conversations with the lost are undoubtedly more enjoyable to this person than to most for the simple reason that they afford an opportunity to exercise the gift of evangelism. Just as a gifted pastor-teacher can be frustrated if he or she is without an audience to teach, a person gifted in evangelism can be frustrated without a lost person to reach.

An evangelist can easily identify with the description given by G. Campbell Morgan:

> A man who received the gift of the evangelist is one to whom there is given a clear understanding of the evangel, a great passion in his heart results from the clear vision, a great optimism fills his soul, born of his confidence in the power of Christ to save every man; and growing out of that passion and that confidence a great constraint seizes him to tell somebody, to tell everybody that glad news of salvation by Jesus Christ.[2]

Then, too, evangelists often are very effective in communicating with unbelievers. Because their gift centers in the Gospel and their audience centers in the ones who are non-Christians, evangelists are often more able than others to sense what unbelievers are asking and thinking. That is one reason evangelists are often effective in bringing non-Christians to a point of decision. Evangelists understand both the stated and unstated objections of non-Christians and are effective in bringing them to a point of seeing their need for Christ.

It should be mentioned, however, that the gift alone is no guarantee of success. Success in reaping can depend on the condition of the soil in which the seed is sown (Luke 8:4–15; John 4:35) and the development of the gift (2 Tim. 1:6).

I should also mention that I have spent much time with many like me who feel convinced they possess a gift in evangelism. Although it cannot be proven from the New Testament, it appears that some gifted in evangelism feel more effective in doing one-to-one evangelism, while others, even though they enjoy that, enjoy as much or more the opportunity to preach the Gospel from the pulpit. Then, too, some feel a special ability in expressing their gift through the writing of materials effective in reaching the unbeliever and building up believers for evangelism. One must be careful not to limit too severely the way the gift of evangelism is used, because there do seem to be differing ways the gift is manifested. The New Testament appears to allow for such variation. When the word *evangelist* comes to mind, we often think immediately of a professional traveling evangelist. However, this spiritual gift, as with others, is not restricted to the pulpit or the road. Lay people in all walks of life may have the gift of evangelism.

I'm often asked if women can have the gift of evangelism. As an expositor of Scripture, I cannot show you a woman in the New Testament who is said to have such a gift. It is my personal opinion, however, that the New Testament would not limit such a gift to men. I have met women who I'm convinced possess such a gift.

CONCLUSION

The gift of evangelism can be defined as the special ability to communicate the Gospel to sinners and to equip the saints for evangelism. Those with this gift intensely desire to see people come to Christ, enjoy their contacts with the lost that they might reach them, and are effective in communicating with them. The body of Christ must do all it can to benefit from those with the gift of evangelism, to encourage them as they seek to win the lost, and to learn from them. Those gifted must do all they can to reach the lost and teach believers how to do the same.

So What?

Believers with the gift of evangelism are peculiar people. (Just ask my friends about me!) One thing that makes them peculiar is that though they, too, have times when they experience fear in evangelism, for the most part they enjoy talking to lost people. In fact, I have discovered in traveling that if a church adds a man to its staff as a minister of evangelism and keeps him so occupied with believers that he has little time to evangelize, they usually have one frustrated staff member on their team.

Because winning the lost gives them such immense satisfaction, evangelists can sometimes be critical of those in the body of Christ who do not enjoy seeing people saved as much as they do. I have heard evangelists say to groups of believers, "If you do not cry when someone gets saved, you had better check your spiritual temperature." If Christians do not enjoy seeing people come to Christ, yes, they have a problem. However, if they do not enjoy it as much as an evangelist does, that is no problem. The nature of the evangelist's gift is to a great degree what contributes to his or her joy in seeing people saved.

My wife and I have experienced the joy of giving and have grown spiritually in that area. We now realize as never before that we are the managers, not the owners, of whatever we possess. It has been a delight to give to the needs of others. I will admit, however, that I do not experience the thrill from giving that I experience from evangelizing. But God did not give me the gift of giving. Instead, He chose to give me the gift of evangelism. Just as those who have the gift of giving should not criticize me if I do not experience the thrill they do in giving, neither should I as an evangelist criticize those who do not enjoy seeing people saved as much as I do.

It is important to note that the ministry of an evangelist centers in the Gospel. I am convinced that throughout church history Christians have made two mistakes as a result of failing to see that clearly.

One is that we have assumed that evangelists and those referred to as "revivalists" have the same gift. That is not necessarily so. A revivalist may have the gift of exhortation and be very effective in stirring Christians out of their slumber. That does not mean a revivalist has the gift of evangelism. In fact, unless revivalists understand that distinction, they may try to function as evangelists and, without knowing why, be frustrated in doing so. Likewise, evangelists will often excite believers about their Savior. Many Christians have felt called to a higher level of service as a result of hearing an evangelist. At the same time, those evangelists should not be critical of themselves if they find more fulfillment in talking to unbelievers than to believers. Because the evangelist's gift centers in the Gospel, that should not be surprising. A prominent radio preacher once said that it was his conviction that one reason an evangelist enjoys talking to different groups is that the variety of settings and people offers even more opportunities to evangelize. I am inclined to agree.

A second mistake we have made from failing to recognize the centrality of the Gospel to the gift of evangelism is confusing the personality of an extrovert with the gift of evangelism. One cannot confuse gift with personality. Because of the nature of their gift, most evangelists I have met are extroverts. But I have also met some gifted in evangelism who struck me as being introverted. Some of them told me, though, that they were convinced they were indeed gifted in evangelism. I had opportunity to observe a few of them and sure enough, in their own quiet way, they were leading many to Jesus Christ.

One must remember that the gift of evangelism, like any other spiritual gift, must be developed. A man came to my office one day spiritually distressed. He said, "I am convinced I have the gift of evangelism but apparently I do not. I witness to at least one person every day, and yet I have never led one to Christ." I answered, "You witness to at least one person every day and have not led *anyone* to Christ?" "Never," he responded. I replied, "Okay, let's suppose I am not a Christian. You lead me to Christ right now." He went through his method of talking to the lost. Something he said at the end of his conversation would have confused them to no end. I have since forgotten what it was. I told him how to change what he was doing to make clearer to the lost what they needed to do. A few weeks later I received a letter from him telling me of several he had led to Christ just since our talk. The gift of evangelism, like any other gift, needs development.

Unfortunately, we have also assumed that if we are ever afraid to talk about Christ, then we must not have the gift of evangelism. Not so! Anyone gifted in evangelism who is honest will admit that there are times they are afraid to evangelize. Also, it may be that the gift simply needs to be developed. I used to dread talking to strangers about Christ. For that reason, when I began my evangelistic ministry, at times I wondered if I had the gift of evangelism—even though many who had observed me were convinced I did and told me so. One day I was traveling with a friend who also was gifted in evangelism and loved talking to strangers. As we headed down the street, we observed a hitchhiker. I sat there in fear and trembling knowing two things. One, my friend would pick the hitchhiker up. The other thing I knew was that once he picked him up, my friend would ask *me* to talk to him about Christ. Sure enough, both my fears were realized. My friend picked up the stranger, introduced him to me and winked at me. I knew what he meant—you are on! After I did a totally botched-up job of speaking to the man about his need of Christ (I think that is who I said he needed), my friend took control of the situation and beautifully explained the Gospel to him. That is the day I learned how to witness to strangers. To this day strangers are some of my favorite people to talk to about Christ.

As I travel and speak, I am often asked, "How does one determine if one has the gift of evangelism?" My answer is, "The same way one discovers any spiritual gift—by experience and exposure." First, people need to become involved doing whatever they can for the Lord. I am convinced God directs moving objects, not still ones. As people become involved, God uses their experiences to develop them and show them where they are spiritually gifted. That may not happen in a few weeks; it may take a few years. Second, people need to have exposure to godly men and women who can observe the Lord using them. During my years in school, I pastored for two summers in two different churches. I would not trade those experiences for anything. In each church, I had a few godly men and women who on occasion pulled me to the side and said, "Has anyone ever told you that you have the gift of evangelism?" Because of the character of these people, I weighed their comments heavily and God greatly used them to confirm my gift.

One characteristic I have personally experienced with the gift of evangelism, and all those without exception who share the gift agree. Those of us with the gift of evangelism have a crying need to proclaim the Gospel—wherever, however. Take away the opportunity to present the Gospel in one way or another, and you have in some respects cut our jugular vein. We live, act, and breathe to the end that the lost might be won. Thank God for people gifted in evangelism, ask Him to use us and, whatever you do, do not hesitate to ask us to help you in your own evangelism.

Group Discussion Questions

- Think of those you have met who in your opinion demonstrate the gift of evangelism. What concrete things should you do to encourage them?

- What struggles do you have in personal evangelism and in what specific ways might someone with the gift of evangelism be of help to you?

- What could hinder someone with the gift of evangelism from realizing it and developing such a gift?

Chapter Fourteen

How Does Prayer Fit In?

Prayer is not overcoming God's reluctance; it is laying hold of His willingness.

—Richard Chenevix Trench
Dictionary of Thoughts

As Christians contemplate the topic of prayer, a host of questions come to mind. Why do some prayers go unanswered? What is the best time to pray? How long should one spend in prayer? What if you feel as though your prayers are not getting through? How do you keep your mind from wandering as you pray? How does prayer actually work?

What about prayer and evangelism? I've known of some who question whether the New Testament even encourages prayer for lost people. They suggest that one pray instead for the believers who are doing the evangelism. Others question the value of prayer altogether because if certain ones are part of the elect and certain others are not, "What will be will be." So why pray?

In order to understand the biblical position on prayer as it relates to evangelism, five questions should be addressed.

WHY PRAY?

An exhaustive treatment of subjects such as the sovereignty of God, predestination, election, and the free will of humankind would entail far more than a single chapter. Volumes have been written on those subjects. Nor are they within the scope and purpose of this book. But lest anyone think that prayer concerning the lost is a meaningless exercise in futility because "What will be will be," certain facts must be noted to help us see the complete picture of why our prayers are needed and that they do play a real part in people coming to Christ.

God Is Sovereign

That God is sovereign in the realm of salvation is so well attested in Scripture that it cannot be denied. For example, Paul told the Ephesian church:

> Blessed be the God and Father of our Lord Jesus Christ, who has blessed us with every spiritual blessing in the heavenly places in Christ, just as He chose us in Him before the foundation of the world, that we should be holy and without blame before Him in love, having predestined us to adoption as sons by Jesus Christ to Himself, according to the good pleasure of His will (Eph. 1:3–5).

The two clauses "chose us in Him before the foundation of the world" and "having predestined us to adoption as sons . . . according to the good pleasure of His will" say clearly that God is in control. With that in mind, there are unquestionably those who are "the elect." Paul began his letter to the Thessalonians by saying:

> We give thanks to God always for you all, making mention of you in our prayers, remembering without ceasing your work of faith, labor of love, and patience of hope in our Lord Jesus Christ in the sight of our God and Father, knowing, beloved brethren, your election by God (1 Thess. 1:2–4).[1]

On what do predestination and election rest? Clearly on His foreknowledge! Paul asserted that when he said:

> As we know that all things work together for good to those who love God, to those who are called according to His purpose. For whom He foreknew, He also predestined to be conformed to the image of His Son, that He might be the firstborn among many brethren. Moreover whom He predestined, these He also called; whom He called, these He also justified; and whom He justified, these He also glorified (Rom. 8:28–30).

The word *foreknew (proginōskō)* means to know beforehand or in advance. The *whom* in the phrase "whom He foreknew" (Rom. 8:29) clearly tells us that people are in view. The issue of what God knew about them is not even addressed; it is the fact that He knew them that is stressed. The verse is therefore simply saying that God knew beforehand those whom He destined to be conformed to the image of

His Son. The verse looks toward the glorious future that lies ahead for believers.

What does God's "knowing beforehand" have to do with His choosing? Although this side of heaven we will never know the details of what went through God's mind, it is clear that His knowing does bear some relationship to His choosing. Paul asserted, "God has not cast away His people whom He foreknew" (Rom. 11:2). Paul was testifying that God has not forgotten the promises He made to His people, the Jews. Examining the corresponding Hebrew word (*yada*) in the Old Testament, we are told, "You only have I known of all the families of the earth; Therefore I will punish you for all your iniquities" (Amos 3:2). Referring to the people He brought up from the land of Egypt (v. 1), it is clear that He chose them to be His people. This did not deliver them from facing the punishment they deserved for their waywardness. He assured them, "I will punish you for all your iniquities." The idea of God's knowing being related to His choosing, not just His mental awareness, is also brought out in His selection of Abraham as the one through whom the nations would be blessed. We read:

> The Lord said, "Shall I hide from Abraham what I am doing, since Abraham shall surely become a great and mighty nation, and all the nations of the earth shall be blessed in him? For I have known him, in order that he may command his children and his household after him, that they keep the way of the Lord, to do righteousness and justice, that the Lord may bring to Abraham what He has spoken to him" (Gen. 18:17–19).

Similarly, concerning the selection of Jeremiah for his prophetic ministry, God declared, "Before I formed you in the womb I knew you; . . . and I ordained you a prophet to the nations" (Jer. 1:5).

God's knowing in ways understood only by Him bears some relationship to His choosing. God is sovereign. He knew us. He chose us. There are those who are elected to be His forever. Before we ever knew Him, He knew us and had already determined ahead of time that which He wanted for us. The existence of such a group of people as the "elect" presents the undeniable biblical picture that God is in control.[2]

God Is in the Process of Populating His Kingdom

Equally prominent in Scripture is the truth that God is in the business of winning the lost. He is populating His kingdom. Again and again it comes through Scripture that the heart of God is a seeking heart—He seeks out those who would respond to His offer of eternal life and welcomes them into His kingdom. Take, for example, Christ's simple words to Zacchaeus, a despicable tax collector for whom other people could not have had less concern. He said to him, "The Son of Man has come to seek and to save that which was lost" (Luke 19:10).

In John 6, Christ placed His offer before the people using the imagery of bread. Desiring that they receive what He had for them, He testified, "I am the bread of life. He who comes to Me shall never hunger, and he who believes in me shall never thirst" (v. 35). However, people do not come to Christ of their own volition. As He would later testify concerning the convicting work of the Holy Spirit, God must work within them (16:8). Christ therefore spoke of God's interest in bringing men to Christ when He said, "All that the Father gives Me will come to Me, and the one who comes to Me I will by no means cast out" (6:37). Can there be any doubt of Christ's own interest in the lost? Does He share His Father's desire? Most certainly! In light of the perfect unity that exists between Christ and the Father, He heartily accepts all the Father gives. He affirmed that even further by stressing that not one whom the Father gives will be lost, but instead each will be raised at the last day. He assured them, "This is the will of the Father who sent Me, that of all He has given Me I should lose nothing, but should raise it up at the last day" (v. 39).

Whatever else might be overlooked in that paragraph, one cannot escape the fact that God is going to bring lost people to Himself. God's plan will not be thwarted. Individuals without Him will come to Him never to be lost again. His unchanging desire is to save and keep. He is determined to populate His kingdom.

Another forceful paragraph regarding God's desire is 2 Peter 3:8–9. Peter refuted those who scoffed at the truth of Christ's return. Asking the question, "Where is the promise of His coming?" their argument was that "as has been will be"—everything continues as it did from creation (v. 4). Peter demonstrated the truthfulness of God's Word with the judgment of the flood during the day of Noah (vv. 5–7). He then spoke of the reason Christ had not yet returned:

> But, beloved, do not forget this one thing, that with the Lord one day is as a thousand years, and a thousand years as one day. The Lord is not slack concerning His promise, as some count slackness, but is longsuffering toward us, not willing that any should perish but that all should come to repentance (vv. 8–9).

There has been no delay; there has been only a vivid display of longsuffering. He is right on time—using His calendar and clock, not

ours. The reason the Lord has not returned is His fervent desire to see
even more come to know Him. His desire, in fact, would be "that all
should come to repentance."

The truth of God does not stop there. A third fact Scripture presents
balances out the picture.

Man Is in Need and Completely Responsible

There are people whom Scripture refers to as elect. God wants to
populate His kingdom. In no way do these truths negate the fact that
man is totally responsible for accepting or declining God's offer of life
eternal.

God expressed His heart in sending His Son: "For God did not send
His Son into the world to condemn the world, but that the world
through Him might be saved" (John 3:17). Who is responsible when
individuals in the world are not saved? To whom does God point the
finger of blame? The next verse continues, "He who believes in Him
is not condemned; but he who does not believe is condemned already,
because he has not believed in the name of the only begotten Son of
God." The one who has rejected the message is clearly held responsible.
As John the Baptist declared, "He who does not believe the Son shall
not see life, but the wrath of God abides on him" (v. 36). The words
of Christ and John the Baptist make evident that God turns only from
those who have turned from trusting His Son. Christ bore the
punishment for our sins. Our refusing His substitutionary act on our
behalf means that God has no choice but to allow us to take the
consequences of rejecting His Son's provision for our sin. Man is
completely responsible.[3]

Although many other passages could be cited showing man's
responsibility, at least one more should be noted—the story Christ told
of a rich man and a beggar named Lazarus. These two were as separated
in death as they had been in life. The rich man, recognizing his eternally
tormented condition, pleaded with Abraham to send Lazarus to his
brothers to warn them of that dreadful place (Luke 16:27–28). Abraham
replied that if they would not listen to Moses and the prophets, then
even one returning from the dead would not persuade them (v. 31).
The rich man and each of his brothers were held responsible for having
rejected the testimony of Moses and the prophets. Each had no one to
blame but himself.

The question that invariably arises at this point is, What about those
who have never heard of Moses and the prophets—those who have
never heard of Christ and the Scriptures? How could God condemn
those? Romans 1, a passage often cited but seldom studied closely
enough, answers that question. Paul declared, "For since the creation

of the world His invisible attributes are clearly seen, being understood by the things that are made, even His eternal power and Godhead, so that they are without excuse" (v. 20). That verse does not merely say that creation testifies to the fact of a Creator. It says much more. Creation testifies to "even His eternal power and Godhead." Looking at creation finds evidence not only that there is a God, but also that there is a God to whom there is no equal. To claim that creation states there is a God and then to fashion a rock and declare that to be God is not a biblical option. The Creator to whom creation testifies is of such magnitude and magnificence that He made us; we could not have made Him. For that reason, a person who has not examined the evidence of creation can be sincere and an atheist in saying, "There is no God"; but one cannot be objective about creation and be an atheist. If a person looks at creation with an open and objective mind, the facts attest to an almighty God.

The evidence God has afforded us in creation is one way He seeks after us, desiring us to come to Him. The implication of Scripture is that if any will receive this evidence and search after Him, God will reward that search with the message of His Son (Acts 17:22–34). He is a rewarder of those who diligently seek Him (Heb. 11:6). Cornelius is a good example. He is described as "a devout man and one who feared God with all his household, who gave alms generously to the people, and prayed to God always" (Acts 10:2). God rewarded that searching by sending Peter to him with the message of the forgiveness offered him through Christ (Acts 10).

Over and over man is seen to be responsible before God. Knighted by the Queen of Belgium for his medical missionary work in the Belgian Congo, Sir Alexander Clarke once asked a group of new converts how they came to Christ. They answered, "We used to be out under the stars at night to worship the God who created us, and to pray for Him to reveal Himself to us."[4]

HOW DO YOU RECONCILE GOD'S SOVEREIGNTY AND MAN'S RESPONSIBILITY?

When examining the above facts of Scripture, some ask "How do you reconcile the fact that God is sovereign and yet man is still responsible?" First, we should discard the word "reconcile." Reconcile carries the idea that these facts do not fit with each other, that they do not go together. Nowhere does Scripture even hint of such a possibility. That something does not "fit" in our minds in no way says it does not "fit" in God's. Scripture does not present God's sovereignty and man's responsibility as contradictions but instead as harmonious facts. Instead of being frustrated by them, we should be comforted by them in that if every way of God were totally understandable to us, He would certainly not be God. Granted, to our human mind these facts may present difficulties. But nowhere are they presented in Scripture as difficulties He felt He had to explain to us—otherwise He most certainly would have done so. Besides that, they are only difficulties until the day we stand before Him and see things from His perspective.

Might it be that in our seemingly endless frustration over something that does not present a conflict to God, we take away from His glory? Whenever God says something, our first need is to take Him at His word, not to understand and most certainly not to feel a need to "reconcile." There are numerous things in the Bible we do not understand, yet there is nothing in the Bible we need to hesitate about believing. Who would have the audacity to claim that the Trinity is entirely understandable? However, does the fact that the explanation of it escapes the human mind prevent us from believing it? Not at all. Similarly, regardless of how difficult God's sovereignty and man's responsibility seem to our human mind, we have no need to hesitate believing them. In God's mind they go together. That's what matters.

WHAT OUGHT WE TO DO?

Mark Twain is reputed to have said, "The parts of the Bible that bother me are not those I don't understand but those I do." Instead of concerning ourselves primarily with what we find difficult to understand, we ought to attend to what we do understand. As will be seen in a moment, Scripture clearly teaches that as we evangelize, we ought to pray. Because God desires to populate His kingdom and because man is responsible, we can pray with a complete awareness that our prayers are not only needed but that they also play a large part in seeing men and women come to Christ.

Christ told His disciples, "In that day you will ask Me nothing. Most assuredly, I say to you, whatever you ask the Father in My name He will give you" (John 16:23). During Christ's life on earth, the disciples asked Him many questions. After His ascension "in that day," they would direct their prayers to the Father, who on the basis of all the Son is and does, would respond to their prayers. Christ's point is that on the basis of His atoning work, people approach God and have answers to their prayers. A woman who saw her alcoholic husband come to know Christ was asked how she prayed. She answered, "I prayed not only knowing God could, but believing that He would."[5]

The well-known account of the results of George Mueller's prayers ought to be an encouragement to us. Regularly he prayed for five of his friends. After many months, one of them came to Christ. Two others were saved ten years later. The fourth came to know Christ after a quarter of a century. Mueller continued to persevere in prayer 52 years for his fifth friend that God in His grace would save him. His prayer was answered. Soon after George Mueller's funeral, the fifth friend came to know Christ.

WHAT DO YOU PRAY FOR?

Do you intercede for the lost or do you intercede for the believers who are witnessing to the lost?

There is no paragraph in Scripture in which the intent of the author is to give a comprehensive list of what we should pray for as we evangelize. We do, however, find scattered exhortation and examples to follow.

Pray for Laborers

Scripture encourages us to pray for laborers in Luke 10:1–2. As Jesus traveled from place to place, He had little time to devote to each location. It was paramount, therefore, that everywhere He went, His arrival be well prepared for. Just as He had sent messengers before Him at other times, He now summoned seventy people and sent them before Him in pairs. We read:

> After these things the Lord appointed seventy others also, and sent them two by two before His face into every city and place where He Himself was about to go. Then He said to them, "The harvest truly is great, but the laborers are few; therefore pray the Lord of the harvest to send out laborers into His harvest."

Evangelism is not done by something; it is done by someone. God has seen fit to use a human mouthpiece to communicate the message. Therefore, as we think of lost people we know, we need to obey the exhortation to pray for someone to be God's instrument in communicating the Gospel of grace to them. If our hearts are in tune with God's heart for the lost, we will want the work to be accomplished more quickly. That necessitates more workers. As we think of communities and areas inside and outside our own country, we need to pray that laborers might be sent to those fields. As we pray for more workers, we need to be aware that we might be the answer to our own prayers. The lips that God might see fit to use may be ours.

Pray for Opportunity

Opportunity is a second thing for which we are encouraged to pray. When Paul wrote to the Colossians, he was a prisoner of the Roman

Empire. He undoubtedly spent many hours chained to Roman soldiers. Being the zealous proclaimer of the Good News that he was, he undoubtedly took advantage of every opportunity to present the Gospel in prison. At the same time, he desired not to be limited by the walls of a prison. So speaking on behalf of himself and his fellow workers, he said, "Meanwhile praying also for us, that God would open to us a door for the word, to speak the mystery of Christ, for which I am also in chains" (Col. 4:3). The phrase "door for the word" speaks of opportunity. As he wrote to his friends in Colosse, Paul most likely thought of the many places he had covered in his missionary journeys and yearned to preach Christ in areas still unreached. He therefore asked the readers of his epistle to pray for such an opportunity. He went on to add, "That I may make it manifest, as I ought to speak" (v. 4). His earnest desire was that he might have the opportunity to make clear to everyone the Good News of the saving grace of Christ. As a lighted billboard in the darkness announces the message contained on it, Paul wanted to make it just as obvious to a dying world that there is a Savior who had died for their sins. He wanted a door of opportunity so that the message of the Gospel could be an exposed truth, not a hidden one.

Paul spoke of such a door for the Gospel. Referring to the situation at Ephesus, he testified, "For a great and effective door has opened to me" (1 Cor. 16:9). He spoke again of such a door when he referred to the situation afforded him at Troas: "Furthermore, when I came to Troas to preach Christ's gospel . . . a door was opened to me by the Lord" (2 Cor. 2:12).

One cannot present the Gospel effectively when the door is closed. The "door" that needs to be opened may include everything from transportation to the area of evangelization to the receptivity of those we are approaching. There must be a way to that person, and the individual must at least be willing to listen to what a servant of the Lord has to say. As we think of lost ones we know, we need to pray that there will be such opportunity. When there is no way, humanly observing the situation, for us to go physically to them, God can provide that way. Those who will not receive us at the moment may open their hearts to our message as we pray for that open door.

Pray for Boldness

Few, if any, will not confess to having moments of fear when considering an opportunity before them to present the Gospel to a lost friend or relative. Many have expressed that fear to others, but not to Christ. In so doing, they overlook a third item for which believers are encouraged to pray as they evangelize—boldness.

The fourth chapter of Acts reveals the disciples in a very tense situation. The governing authorities were in a predicament. They were unable to deny that a lame man had been healed. As the lame man stood with full use of both limbs before the people, the evidence spoke for itself! At the same time, the authorities were unwilling to affirm the truth of what Peter and John were proclaiming. Their only recourse, therefore, was a threat. Bringing Peter and John before them, they commanded them not to utter a word (v. 18). To have spoken then would have incurred the anger of powerful authorities.

What did Peter and John do? We are clearly told that as they rejoined their Christian brothers and sisters, they gave God a simple request. Their request was not that their enemies might be destroyed or that they might be delivered from further attacks. They asked God, "Now, Lord, look on their threats, and grant to Your servants that with all boldness they may speak Your word" (Acts 4:29). Two verses later, Luke records God's answer to their prayer: "When they had prayed, the place where they were assembled together was shaken; and they were all filled with the Holy Spirit, and they spoke the word of God with boldness."

Often opportunity and boldness in Scripture are so united they are almost inseparable. In Ephesians 6, after requesting prayer that there might be an opportunity to speak the Gospel, Paul quickly added, "That I may open my mouth boldly to make known the mystery of the gospel" (v. 19). Opportunities are of little value unless one uses them to proclaim the Gospel boldly.

Fear in evangelism is normal. Even evangelists have moments when they are afraid. At those times we must follow the pattern given in the New Testament and take that need first and foremost to the Lord. His provisions are not restricted to food and finance. He also has a generous supply of boldness if we are willing to admit our need and ask Him for it.

Pray for the Good Success of the Gospel

A fourth prayer item related to evangelism is often overlooked. In 2 Thessalonians 2, Paul told the people in Thessalonica what his prayer request was for them. He then told them what his prayer request was for himself and his fellow workers: "Finally, brethren, pray for us, that the word of the Lord may have free course and be glorified, just as it is with you" (3:1). "The word of the Lord" is in this context another term for the Gospel, the message that had such a powerful impact in Thessalonica. The words "free course" convey the idea of swift advance and triumph and are often translated *run*. Along with the use of the word *glorified*, it conveys the idea of great success. Writing in Corinth, Paul wanted his friends at Thessalonica to pray that the Gospel would have the same success in Corinth that it had experienced in Thessalonica. Acts 17:4 records that success at Thessalonica: "Some of them were persuaded; and a great multitude of the devout Greeks, and not a few of the leading women, joined Paul and Silas" (cf. 1 Thess. 1:5–8). He therefore requested the Thessalonians to pray that as the Gospel was being preached in Corinth, it would meet with similar success.

Many times both our faith and prayer life are too limited. We see only the one for whom we are concerned, but not the neighbor alongside him. Scripture, by the example of Paul, encourages us to pray that as the Gospel is preached, it will be accompanied by good success— that not only will the one whom we know come to Christ, but his neighbors and contacts as well. That kind of "spontaneous explosion" of the Gospel has often occurred. Many in a family, block, or community have come to Christ as a result of one individual being reached. Our prayer request ought to be that the Gospel would "take off" in a community and result in many coming to the Savior.

Pray for Safety and Deliverance

Paul gave the believers in Thessalonica another request related to evangelism. After asking the Thessalonians to pray for the Gospel's good success, he asked them to pray for his safety and deliverance: "That we may be delivered from unreasonable and wicked men; for not all have faith" (2 Thess. 3:2).

Paul was undoubtedly thinking of those enemies who were giving him trouble at the moment. Acts 18:1–7 describes this opposition. Jews in Corinth so opposed his ministry that in their anger, they created a revolt that resulted in bringing Paul before the judgment seat of Gallio. The phrase "for not all have faith" reminded Paul's readers that opposition is not surprising, simply because not all are believers. Recognizing the danger this opposition posed, Paul requested prayer for safety and deliverance.

Those who oppose the Gospel in a particular locality may be few or many, influential or of little authority, and quite varied in circumstances or occupation. It may be a witch doctor on a foreign field, or a city mayor, police chief, or minister on American soil who has no regard for the Scriptures. The opposition at times works behind the scenes while at other times is very open and confrontational. The stress such opposition presents can hinder the work or the health of a servant of the Lord. As the Gospel is preached, it needs to be accompanied by prayer that God will grant safety to the laborers and deliverance from harm.

Pray for the Lost

As we pray in the five areas just mentioned, we are also to pray specifically for lost persons themselves. Paul, as he wrote to Timothy, said:

Therefore I exhort first of all that supplications, prayers, intercessions, and giving of thanks be made for all men, for kings and all who are in authority, that we may lead a quiet and peaceable life in all godliness and reverence (1 Tim. 2:1–2).

Two things are interesting about Paul's exhortation. One is that he stressed prayer for "all men." Nobody is excluded! Second, he particularly stressed, "kings and all who are in authority"—those with governing responsibilities. Only as we pray for them will they be able to govern in such a way that we can lead quiet and peaceable lives in all godliness and reverence. Paul went on to stress that such prayer is "good and acceptable in the sight of God our Savior" (v. 3) because God "desires all men to be saved and to come to the knowledge of the truth" (v. 4). Although we know that not everyone will come to Christ, we are free to pray for any person, knowing that God desires him or her to trust Christ. The clear teaching of 1 Timothy 2:1–2 is that we are to pray for all people. The implication in 1 Timothy 2:4 is that their salvation ought to be heavy on our minds because it is heavy on His mind. Therefore, 1 Timothy 2:1–4 would most definitely encourage prayer for lost people.

WHEN DO YOU PRAY?

Asking when to pray might seem rather foolish. Actually it is not. Churches often engage in visitation programs in the community or follow-up on Sunday morning visitors. As they contemplate prayer as it relates to evangelism, they have reason to wonder, do we pray before we go out or do we first honor God through witnessing, then ask Him to use what we have said?

Two verses drive home the biblical position. As mentioned earlier, in Luke 10:1–2 Christ was about to send out the seventy two-by-two. Prior to doing so, He exhorted them, "The harvest truly is great, but the laborers are few; therefore pray the Lord of the harvest to send out laborers into His harvest." Prior to going, they were exhorted to pray for people who would go. In at least one paragraph in the book of Acts, also referred to earlier, the situation is the opposite. The believers had already evangelized, encountered opposition, and come together for prayer seeking God's help. Their petition to God was, "Now, Lord, look on their threats, and grant to Your servants that with all boldness they may speak Your word" (Acts 4:29). After already having gone out, they sensed the need for boldness and asked God to supply.

Therefore, the emphasis of Scripture is neither go and then pray, nor is it pray and then go. Instead it could be correctly stated: as you go, pray, and as you pray, go. Believers in the New Testament were going as they were praying and praying as they were going.

An illustration might serve to drive home this balance. Two children on their way to school found themselves late. The one said to the other, "Why don't we stop and pray and ask God to get us there on time?" The other answered, "Why don't we run as fast as we can and pray as we run?" That would be the scriptural balance. While going, pray, and while praying, go!

CONCLUSION

As we see from 1 Timothy 2:1–4, Scripture does exhort us to pray for the lost. A careful study of Scripture, however, reveals that the *emphasis* of the New Testament is not on praying for unbelievers. Instead, the emphasis is on praying for the believers as they do the evangelism. We ought to pray for laborers, opportunity, boldness, the Gospel's good success, for safety and deliverance and, at the same time, lost persons themselves.

The reason for this kind of emphasis is most understandable. Much of the New Testament was written by those with evangelistic zeal who knew why they needed prayer as they encountered the lost. Also, it is far easier to pray intelligently for what we know than for what we do not know. For example, it is easier for most people to pray specifically for missionaries they support and their opportunities, boldness, and so forth, than for the people the missionaries confront. The missionaries know what the people are like whom they are confronting, whereas the people praying only know the missionaries.

It is not an "either-or" situation, but a "both-and" one. Although the emphasis in the New Testament is on praying for believers doing evangelism, we pray for both the believers and the unbelievers. Thus, a proper way to approach prayer as it relates to evangelism would be:

Dear Lord, I pray for Joe as he witnesses to his neighbor. Give him the opportunity to present the Gospel to the neighbor. May the neighbor be receptive to what Joe has to say. Help Joe not to be afraid. Protect Joe from any harm Satan would like to inflict on him to hinder him. I pray that the neighbor might come to know You. May the Gospel spread throughout the community. In Jesus' name, Amen.

As we do pray, we ought to pray expectantly, remembering God's ability and promise to answer. We should also make sure that as we pray, we are evangelizing. God desires us to speak to Him about the lost, but He also desires that as we do, we speak to the lost about Him.

So What?

The heart of God is a hungry heart—hungry for the lost. This is probably one reason why those who are consistent in evangelism receive so many ripe opportunities to lead others to Christ. Put yourself in the Lord's shoes. If you had a choice of allowing a lost person you are trying to reach to come across the path of a Christian who regularly looks for opportunities to share the Gospel or a Christian who neglects to tell others of his Savior, whose path would you direct him across?

As we evangelize, we need to bathe our efforts in prayer. Our neglect in praying has undoubtedly hindered us in evangelism. Consider, for example, the matter of praying for a door of opportunity, which could include anything from a means to approach a person to receptivity on the part of the person. Sometimes everything from distance to discouragement stands in our way. We ought to ask, How many times might doors have opened more quickly had we given that request to the Lord?

A situation with a neighbor and his wife might serve as a testimony to what God can do. Developing a friendship with them was rather difficult because our hours never seemed to mesh. Besides that, since they were living rather hectic lives, when they did come home in the evening they preferred to "collapse." Extended conversations were not exactly their delight. The previous weeks I had begun studying Paul's request in Colossians 4 concerning praying for a door of opportunity. I said to my wife, "I don't think we're praying enough for God to give us the opportunity." So we began praying to that end. Several weeks later I came home from a speaking engagement and early the next morning, the neighbor knocked on my door in tears. He informed me that his wife had just left him. To say he was a shattered person would be an understatement. After assuring him of my sympathy and concern for him, I began talking to him about the love and concern God had for him as demonstrated on the cross. I found a most open person—far more open than he had been before when I had simply alluded to spiritual things. It was exciting to see him express a desire to trust Christ and ask for His help in getting his marriage back together.

What if we pray and the door doesn't open? We ought to keep praying. In Luke 18:1–8 Christ told a parable concerning persistence in prayer being rewarded. My biggest burden for twenty-seven years was my own father's salvation. He had a big impact on my life and although he was a good, moral, religious man, I was not certain he knew the Lord. Every time I made any attempt to bring up the subject, he would "clam up." It didn't help any that the church he came from treated religion as a very private matter—your relationship to God is your business and mine is my business. I loved him deeply and kept praying that God would give an open door for the Gospel and even use somebody in addition to me to witness to him. I can honestly say I have never prayed harder or longer for anyone than I did for him. There were nights I would awaken from nightmares over his salvation. As hard as some of those times were, they taught me to lean on the Lord. Being sixteen hundred miles apart didn't help the situation or the communication.

On September 23, 1987, my sister called. I knew something was wrong and expected her to say, "Dad died." We knew he had a bad heart. Instead she said, "Johnny [our forty-six-year-old brother] just died of a massive heart attack." I was comforted by the fact that years earlier when I had spoken to Johnny, he had assured me that he was trusting Christ alone for his salvation. My dad took his passing so badly that two weeks later he suffered a serious heart attack. When I went home to be with him, I met a different dad—a dad who told me for the first time that he came to Christ when he was thirteen years old. More importantly, he also assured me that he understood that his goodness would not get him to heaven, and only through Christ was a person saved. When I was with him several months later, he spoke more about spiritual things in three days than he had in the past forty years. He even told a pastor whom God used during this time (remember, that was the second thing I had asked God for—another voice in addition to mine to speak to him) that if Mom died before he did, he knew she would be in heaven and he also knew he would be there with her. Two weeks later he suffered a second heart attack and went to be with the Lord. Twenty-seven years of praying had been answered in seeing him come to the complete realization that one is saved by Christ alone. He may indeed have settled that when he was thirteen, or he may have settled it during those last five months. The important thing is, as he assured me, it was settled.

Of all the items we have just discussed, none for which to ask God is more meaningful than boldness. The fear many believers have is that relatives or friends will reject them. If at the moment we are afraid we will tell God first, we will often be surprised at the difference it will make. A God who has an abundant storehouse of all we need can also supply boldness. We often tell others that we are afraid, but not Him. They cannot help us the way He can. We need first and foremost to tell Him.

I have found, as have many who travel, that airplanes present good opportunities for witnessing. Usually the rougher the flight, the greater the opportunity! On one flight the man who sat next to me was the epitome of insecurity. He explained how he had "told the stewardess off" on the last flight. He spoke in a loud voice, hoping others would hear and be impressed with what a fearless man he was. I recognized that sooner or later he would ask me what I do, and I would have a chance to tell him that I'm a preacher and explain the Gospel. But I have at least one thing in common with most people— I don't like to be humiliated! I sensed that when he learned I was a preacher, he would probably scorn me in front of those sitting around us.

However, remembering the advice I had given to others, as I sat there without bowing my head or closing my eyes, I asked God for boldness. As I did so, God gave me a conviction that this man's soul was more important than whether or not he would humiliate me. God also filled my mind with thoughts of how good He had been to me, with His ability to break the coldest hearts, and a list of other things. Within the matter of a moment I was sensing the courage I needed. So when he turned to me and said, "Well, we've been talking about me, but what do you do?" I told him. Wow! Instead of reacting as I had anticipated, he confessed his lack of attention to spiritual things, and we talked about the Gospel. He promised to read a booklet I shared with him concerning how he could know he was going to heaven. That encounter taught me much. God is willing to give me all the boldness I need if I am willing to ask Him for it.

When it comes to praying for safety and deliverance, those who live in a free society find that hard to appreciate. But in areas where there is not the same tolerance to the Gospel, one finds how deeply individuals appreciate such prayers. In January of 1987, I held my first crusade in a third world country. Delhi Bible Fellowship invited me to come for an evangelistic outreach. God gave us a tremendous week. Before my visit, there had been a flare-up of terrorist activities in India. When my wife and I arrived in New Delhi and saw barricades outside the airport and soldiers with machine guns, we were very conscious of danger, but also of God's protection. We dare not take lightly what Satan might attempt to do and must always ask God to give safety and deliverance.

When we study the emphasis on prayer as it relates to evangelism, we cannot help but wonder how much more we might see happening if more were taking place in our own prayer lives. It is safe to say that we often give more time to discussion on prayer than we do to praying. We do not need to understand everything concerning the dynamics of how prayer works. It is only necessary that we understand that it does indeed work. A man who has had a great impact on my life said to me, "I once decided I would diagram on a sheet of paper how prayer works. So I did. I had some lines going from me to God and others going from God to me." Then he added, "I found that my prayer life was greatly improved when I stopped diagraming and simply concentrated on praying."

Group Discussion Questions

- Think of those three non-Christians you know. Are you prepared to pray regularly and fervently for them? Why have you sometimes doubted they will come to Christ? What should encourage you to pray in faith?

- Thinking of these same three non-Christians, in what ways can you be more specific in your prayers for them?

- When you have missed opportunities to present the Gospel, how could a failure to pray have resulted in the failure to evangelize?

- In bringing our needs before God, as Philippians 4:6 encourages, why should requests as they relate to evangelism be foremost in our minds? Why are they often not?

- When talking to God about the lost and our need to evangelize them, how will a proper understanding of *His* feelings for the lost affect the way we pray?

Chapter Fifteen

What Part Does Wisdom Play in Evangelism?

God gave us five senses: taste, touch, smell, sight, hearing; but we need two more: common and horse.

—W. A. Criswell
chapel service at Dallas Theological Seminary
February 17, 1971

It is a common tendency to downplay the importance of wisdom and exalt the importance of knowledge. An individual's worth is often determined on the basis of which schools they attended or how many degrees they have. Whether they know how to handle life or apply what they know becomes relatively unimportant. What matters most is the transcript from their alma mater.

In the Scriptures God does the opposite. He does not applaud a man for his native ability or acquisition of information, but instead for his wisdom. The book of Proverbs nearly bursts with admonitions about how to develop wisdom. In Proverbs wisdom is "skill for living"—the ability to live out our lives beautifully, knowing we have made a contribution to God's kingdom. We are admonished: "Happy is the man who finds wisdom, And the man who gains understanding; For her proceeds are better than the profits of silver, And her gain than fine gold. She is more precious than rubies, And all the things you may desire cannot compare with her" (Prov. 3:13–15).

The matter of wisdom becomes equally important when speaking to individuals about the Savior. Knowing how to speak and act wisely can play a big part in bringing others to the Savior. Therefore, we ought to ask, What part does wisdom play in evangelism?

To answer that question, we must first define wisdom as it relates to evangelism. Knowing what wisdom is will then help us see how it is demonstrated in the New Testament.

WHAT IS WISDOM IN EVANGELISM?

Examining Colossians 4:5

One verse commanding wisdom in our relationships with non-Christians says, "Walk in wisdom toward those who are outside, redeeming the time" (Col. 4:5). The Greek word used here for "wisdom" is *sophia*. As the primary word used for "wisdom" in the New Testament, it represents wisdom in its highest and noblest sense. It is used of Christ as well as men like Joseph in the Old Testament and Stephen in the New Testament. An examination of how Paul used the word *sophia* in his epistle to the Colossians reveals that this wisdom is what he asked God to give them after hearing of their conversion.[1] He testified: "For this reason we also, since the day we heard it, do not cease to pray for you, and to ask that you may be filled with the knowledge of His will in all wisdom and spiritual understanding" (1:9). Combined with understanding, wisdom here speaks of a mind that is able to grasp spiritual truth, examine its meaning, and apply it to life.[2]

Bearing these thoughts in mind as we come to Colossians 4:5, we read, "Walk in wisdom toward those who are outside, redeeming the time." The phrase *redeeming the time* has the idea of buying up every opportunity to influence the lost for Christ. This is something Christians can ask God for and is increasingly experienced by those who are maturing in Him and sensitive to His Spirit. It has a noticeable effect on the way we conduct ourselves. It stands to reason, based on how *sophia* is used in Colossians, that the more we grow in knowledge of Christ and the Scriptures, the better we will understand how to practice wisdom in dealing with the unbeliever.

Examining Matthew 10:16

Before we can arrive at a definition of wisdom in evangelism, another significant verse must be examined. Christ, as He prepared to send out His twelve disciples, reminded them that they would be like sheep in the midst of wolves. Therefore, He exhorted them, "Be wise as serpents and harmless as doves" (Matt. 10:16). Here, the word for *wise* is not *sophia* but *phronimos,* meaning "sensible, thoughtful, prudent."[3]

Christ urged the disciples to be "wise as serpents." Serpents are shrewd—they are known for their craftiness. We are told in Genesis 3:1, "Now the serpent was more cunning than any beast of the field which the LORD God had made." The craftiness of serpents can be used for a helpful or harmful end. It is helpful when it aids them in obtaining their next meal. It can be a symbol of harm, though, such as in Genesis 3 when the serpent suggested to Eve that in restricting her from eating of the fruit of one of the trees, God was not kind or fair. Given the kind of persecution the disciples would experience, the exhortation Christ gave in Matthew 10:16 was appropriate. To avoid as much opposition as possible, the disciples needed to know how to boldly but tactfully advance the message of the Gospel. They needed to know how to skillfully approach those who, in their lost condition, were enemies of God (Rom. 5:10). At the same time, when persecuted for righteousness' sake, they needed to know how to use every lawful means possible to protect themselves. They needed discernment.

Hearing this, we may contend, "Wait a minute. I'm not about to be crafty or shrewd in my approach to the unbeliever. That sounds deceitful and manipulative."

Lest you think Christ was encouraging anything of the sort, notice that He did not stop at the serpent analogy. He continued with an analogy of a dove that presented the total picture. He said, "Be wise as serpents *and harmless as doves.*" The Greek word for "harmless" is *akeraios,* meaning "pure, innocent, and unmixed." In a marketplace, if you had asked a wine merchant a question concerning the quality of his wine, he might have replied, "It is *akeraios,*" meaning it had no water mixed with it; it was pure wine. A metal worker could have spoken of his metal as being *akeraios,* meaning it had no alloy in it. The word thus conveys the ideas of purity, innocence, and harmlessness. A dove becomes a fitting image. A dove in anybody's mind conveys innocence and harmlessness, not trickery or deceit.

It is helpful to observe how Paul used *akeraios* in particular contexts. In Romans 16:19, *akeraios* is translated "simple" as Paul exhorted, "Your obedience has become known to all. Therefore I am glad on your behalf; but I want you to be wise in what is good, and simple concerning evil." When faced with the craftiness of false teachers (v. 18), Paul wanted Christians to be wise in following what is good and pure as they abstained from what is evil. In Philippians 2:14–15, *akeraios* is translated "harmless" where Paul said, "Do all things without murmuring and disputing, that you may become blameless and harmless, children of God without fault in the midst of a crooked and perverse generation, among whom you shine as lights in the world." Amidst a society characterized by wickedness of all kinds, believers need to live lives that are blameless and pure.

We can see how the analogies of a snake and a dove balance each other. God wants us to practice the aspects of a serpent's shrewdness that is prudent and intelligent. At the same time, He is encouraging no deceit, manipulativeness, or viciousness of any kind. Instead, we are to be harmless and innocent like a dove.

A DEFINITION

Putting these two passages together, we can arrive at a definition of wisdom in evangelism. Colossians 4:5 teaches the need for common sense whereby we buy up every opportunity to influence the lost for Christ. Matthew 10:16 stresses the need to be both shrewd and harmless. Therefore, wisdom in evangelism could be defined as common sense combined with a disarming purity—a purity that encourages the lost to let down their guard and open up to us. Regardless of the situation, as we interact with non-Christians with a view to winning them to the Savior, we ought to demonstrate common sense.

WHERE AND HOW IS WISDOM DEMONSTRATED?

How do we practice common sense combined with a disarming purity? The New Testament provides several examples.

Identify with People Where They Are

The goal of all evangelism must be to see each person enter into an eternal relationship with the Son of God. That necessitates a certain amount of understanding about who Christ is and what He has done. Bringing others to that understanding will never occur unless we can relate to them in their present frame of mind. "That's common sense," one might say, yet interestingly enough, this is often one of the most difficult areas of evangelism for believers—knowing how to relate to the lost so that the Gospel may be communicated to them. In fact, the longer one is a believer or one is removed from the company of unbelievers, the more frustrating that can become.

At least two ideas come through the pages of the New Testament concerning how one can identify with people where they are. One idea is illustrated by Christ Himself.

Relate to Unbelievers in the Area of Their Need. Christ, by His own example, related to the lost in the area of their needs. As He relaxed by the well and a Samaritan woman came to draw water, He requested, "Give Me a drink" (John 4:7). Since the Jews and Samaritans, due to their differences in background and worship, had a cat-and-dog relationship, the woman was astounded at His request: "'How is it that You, being a Jew, ask a drink from me, a Samaritan woman?' For Jews have no dealings with Samaritans" (v. 9). Immediately Jesus seized the opportunity to take her from the subject of physical water to spiritual water. He said, "If you knew the gift of God, and who it is who says to you, 'Give Me a drink,' you would have asked Him, and He would have given you living water" (v. 10). Immediately that statement raised in her mind the question of how and where to obtain that water. The empty bucket was no longer her focus, her empty life was.

That conversation becomes even more meaningful when we turn back to John 3 and notice how Christ dealt with a person on the other side of the spectrum—religious Nicodemus. He also related to him in the area of his need. Nicodemus was already interested and involved in spiritual things (v. 10). Jesus simply explained his need for the new birth. No sooner had Nicodemus addressed Him as a teacher, than Christ said to him, "Most assuredly, I say to you, unless one is born again, he cannot see the kingdom of God" (v. 3).

Both conversations readily show how Christ used common sense combined with a disarming purity by relating to people in the area of their needs. His motive was to bring each one to Himself. With a Samaritan woman, He approached that need with innocence and shrewdness by discussing her need of water. With a religious Jew, he used the same wisdom by discussing his need for the second birth.

People expose many needs in conversations. They range from the need of forgiveness to the need for fulfillment, from how to handle hardships to how to obtain happiness, from finding meaning in life to meaning in marriage. Their greatest need of all, however, and the need they must ultimately confront, is for an eternal relationship with the Son of God. Other needs become a bridge by which we can communicate to them that the Savior can meet all their spiritual needs when they receive from Him the free gift of eternal life. In so doing we demonstrate common sense with a disarming purity in evangelism.

Relate to Unbelievers in Their Culture and Background. Another way to identify with lost people is in the area of their culture and background. In 1 Corinthians 9:19–23 Paul spelled out his approach to Christian liberty in ministry.

> For though I am free from all men, I have made myself a servant to all, that I might win the more; and to the Jews I became as a Jew, that I might win Jews; to those who are under the law, as under the law, that I might win those who are under the law; to those who are without law, as without law (not being without law toward God, but under law toward Christ), that I might win those who are without law; to the weak I became as weak, that I might win the weak. I have become all things to all men, that I might by all means save some. Now this I do for the gospel's sake, that I may be partaker of it with you.

Paul broke with the law of Moses in terms of recognizing its inability to justify a person before God (Rom. 3:20). He nevertheless recognized that some Jews might feel scandalized (in the sense that he would be a stumbling block to them) if he did not observe some of their customs and practices in accordance with the law. He also recognized that in a real sense, he was under law—the law of Christ, which dictated all that he now did. Having trusted Christ as his only means of eternal salvation, he allowed everything he did to be dictated by what Christ in His holiness would have him do. His earnest desire in actions and attitude was to please God. Therefore, he accommodated himself to the backgrounds of both Jews and Gentiles and in so doing led many to Christ.

Culture and background are rich in affording an opportunity to relate to the lost and introduce them to Christ. Many have had some experience, whether positive or negative, with church or some type of organized religion. Explaining your own frustration with religion, you can introduce them to the One who brought you from religion into a relationship. Farmers see the fingerprints of the Creator wherever they turn. If you have been influenced by His handiwork in creation, you can direct them to the Creator and the expression of His love on the cross. Factory workers can appreciate One who grew up in a carpenter's shop and developed skills requiring the use of His hands. Using your own labor experience, you can refer them to His. Individuals who have been treated as outcasts by family and friends can identify with one who saw in Christ a real friend (Luke 19:1–10). If your family situation has not been the most desirable, you can introduce someone else to the One who is the friend of both of you.

Good common sense combined with a disarming purity is illustrated by Christ and by the apostle Paul as they identified with the lost in the areas of their needs and their background. Both of these areas open up an untold number of doors whereby lost people can be approached with the Gospel.

Needs and the area of culture and background are far from being the only two areas where one can identify with the unbeliever, although they appear to be the two most graphically illustrated in the New Testament. Anything we might have in common with non-Christians in terms of personality factors, victories, and defeats could serve to help us identify with them.

Display a Balance Between Grace and Truth

Conversations about Christ sometimes degenerate into arguments. Should they? If not, when does one confront the lost concerning the error of their thinking?

Common sense would tell us there is a balance in this area. There are some people who need confrontation. Characterized by a selfish and self-righteous attitude and a refusal to see themselves as sinners, they need someone to confront them in love. Others are so covered over by their own sinfulness that they feel hopeless. Their need is not for someone to remind them of what they already know all too well—how sinful they are—but for someone in grace to tell them where and how to find forgiveness.

Interestingly enough, Christ was noted for that balance. John observed that Christ was "full of grace and truth" (John 1:14). He was so gracious that the worst sinner found in Him a friend, and yet so truthful that individuals were often sharply rebuked by what He told them. Both of these characteristics are illustrated superbly by His manner in John 8. As the Pharisees brought Him a woman who had been caught in the midst of an adulterous act, the penalty appeared to them to be both obvious and simple—stoning her. After rebuking them for their own sin (v. 7), Christ said to the woman, "Neither do I condemn you; go and sin no more" (v. 11). Put yourself in her situation. To participate in such a shameful act is one thing; to be caught on the spot makes the shame even greater. What kindness could be any greater than for the Architect of the universe to say, "Neither do I condemn you; go and sin no more"? If ever there was a woman who experienced what we many times refer to as a "new lease on life," it was her.

Some time later, to Pharisees who needed to see their sinful state, Christ said, "I am going away, and you will seek Me, and will die in your sin. Where I go you cannot come" (v. 21). They were confused by His statement, "Where I go you cannot come." Christ endeavored to remove that confusion and again stressed His warning by saying, "You are from beneath; I am from above. You are of this world; I am not of this world. Therefore I said to you that you will die in your sins; for if you do not believe that I am He, you will die in your sins" (vv. 23–24).

Is this the same Christ who earlier spoke with such grace and kindness? Yes, indeed! Was He speaking unkindly here? Not at all. He simply recognized that common sense with disarming purity required that in a spirit of love He had to confront the Pharisees with their lost condition. His earnest desire was that they might come to Him for eternal life (John 8:51). He was well aware that self-righteous people need kindness, but kindness expressed through confrontation of their lost and sinful condition.

Using common sense combined with a disarming purity means that we need to speak with both grace and truth. If we are intelligently and wisely going to reach people for Christ, we must tell the lost what they need to know to see the peril of their own condition. In so doing we do not mean to harm; we mean to help. "Harmless" does not mean we step back from being truthful. It simply means there is no carelessness or ill intent in the way we speak. As we speak, there is a grace about us seen in the One who was a friend of sinners (Luke 15:2). The situations cited from the life of Christ do not illustrate either grace or truth to the exclusion of the other. Although either grace or truth might be more prominent in a particular situation, both are present. Wisdom simply recognizes that people must see their sin and also their need of a Savior. If we are going to use wisdom, we must therefore speak with grace and truth.

Read the Bible and the Newspaper

Wisdom in evangelism requires knowing the language of the Bible. Of what help is a testimony if it presents a means of salvation other than the one presented in the Scriptures? But wisdom also requires being able to relate to where people are living. Christ recognized the importance of current events in relating spiritual truth to the lost. Once again, common sense accompanied by disarming purity is seen as Jesus spoke of two events fresh on the minds of the people:

> There were present at that season some who told Him about the Galileans whose blood Pilate had mingled with their sacrifices. And Jesus answered and said to them, "Do you suppose that these Galileans were worse sinners than all other Galileans, because they suffered such things? I tell you, no; but unless you repent you will all likewise perish. Or those eighteen on whom the tower in Siloam fell and killed them, do you think that they were worse sinners than all other men who dwelt in Jerusalem? I tell you, no; but unless you repent you will all likewise perish" (Luke 13:1–5).

The first current event Christ spoke of concerned pilgrims from Galilee who had come to Jerusalem for one of the feasts. In a most gruesome act, Pilate's soldiers apparently had massacred many of these Galileans as they were sacrificing in the temple courts and mingled their blood with the blood of the slaughtered beasts. The second event concerned eighteen men crushed by the fall of a tower. As they viewed both of these tragedies, the people were tempted to see them as a sign of special sinfulness on the part of the victims, whom God was judging. Instead, Christ said, "Unless you repent you will all likewise perish." It seems that Christ in this context was speaking of the judgment of the nation of Israel through the coming fall of Jerusalem, not of eternal hell. Matthew 23 would indicate that it was their physical destruction through the fall of Jerusalem that he had in mind (note especially verses 34–39). Christ's point, however, is that all sinners face divine justice. By the use of a current event, He very wisely changed their focus from what had happened to others to what could happen to them.

Use Evidences

Trusting Christ is a step of faith. That does not mean Christianity has no intellectual basis. Wisdom in evangelism means there are times a lost person must be shown the intellectual basis upon which Christianity rests.

This, too, was apparently common sense to Paul as he talked to King Agrippa (Acts 26:24–29). Paul's motive was to see King Agrippa come to faith in Christ (v. 29). While Paul gave his testimony and appealed to Agrippa to recognize who Christ is, Festus, the governor, interrupted with: "Much learning is driving you mad!" (v. 24). What did Paul do? Recognizing Agrippa's belief in the Old Testament prophets (v. 27), he appealed to him to compare the prophets' descriptions of the Messiah with Jesus Christ. Paul recognized that the ultimate end of such a study, if done in sincerity and integrity, would be that Agrippa would need to acknowledge the facts and believe. He shrewdly used evidence from a source Agrippa did know to convince him of the One he did not know.

Various estimates claim that from forty to sixty people have at some time or another walked the surface of the earth claiming to be the Messiah. Two things distinguish Jesus Christ from all of these. Foremost is the empty tomb the third day. None other arose from the dead. Second, Jesus was pre-announced. The others simply showed up! Christ alone fulfilled over three hundred prophecies of the Old Testament. Common sense means sometimes individuals who are lost must be directed to this compelling evidence and asked to believe. In using such evidence to convince them of Christ, we are being wise as a serpent and harmless as a dove. Fulfilled prophecy as well as the resurrection of Christ can be effective evidence to wisely present to the non-Christian.

When confronted with idol worship, Paul also used creation, pointing to what respected poets testified concerning the creation:

> For in Him we live and move and have our being, as also some of your own poets have said, "For we are also His offspring." Therefore, since we are the offspring of God, we ought not to think that the Divine Nature is like gold or silver or stone, something shaped by art and man's devising. Truly, these times of ignorance God overlooked, but now commands all men everywhere to repent (Acts 17:28–30).

Put yourself in Paul's sandals. Common sense tells anyone that God has to be Someone who has made us, not something we have made (Ps. 115:2–8; Jer. 10:14–15). Therefore, if one in a sincere desire to reach the lost wants to shrewdly appeal to them, what better way than to argue from creation to the Creator to Christ?

Speaking of his own experience prior to his salvation, Josh McDowell made a comment that sums up the opinion of many unbelievers: "I figured every Christian had two brains; one was lost and the other was looking for it."[4] God used historical facts and evidences about Christ to later bring Josh to the Savior. On behalf of Christ, we can wisely use whatever evidence is available and pertinent to the person and the situation to appeal to the lost.

Learn the Value of a Compliment

There is not a person alive who does not enjoy a compliment. Sincere compliments serve a variety of purposes in evangelism. On the one hand, by complimenting people in an area where they deserve to be complimented, we are able to speak to their need without their thinking that we regard them as worthless individuals. Compliments have a way of reminding people that although there are some things wrong about them, there are also some things right about them. Compliments also help tear down defenses. They can have a warming effect upon someone who tends to justify his actions or attitude instead of coming face-to-face with his need of Christ. Nobody seeking to reach an acquaintance for Christ wishes to come across as "holier than thou." Sometimes just by virtue of the fact that we have settled our eternal destiny and we are asking them to settle theirs, it can *appear* that we feel superior. Compliments have a way of destroying that false notion simply because compliments focus the attention on them instead of on us.

When conversing with the Samaritan woman mentioned in John 4, Christ recognized that before she could receive what he had to offer, she first had to see herself as a sinner. So He said to her, "Go, call your husband, and come here." She answered, "I have no husband" (vv. 16–17). At that point, Christ commended her for her honesty—a quality for which she needed to be commended. He responded, "You have well said, 'I have no husband,' for you have had five husbands, and the one whom you now have is not your husband; in that you spoke truly" (vv. 17–18). In so doing, He did not discount the severity of any past sin or her present sin of living with a man who was not her husband, but neither did He distract from the care and concern He had for her.

The apostle Paul was no stranger to the wise use of compliments, either. When he arrived in Athens, he was provoked as he looked at a city whose people thrived on the worship of idols. As he proclaimed

Christ and His resurrection, he met with much resistance. Called both a babbler and a proclaimer of foreign gods, he was brought to the hill where the council that decided religious and educational matters met, and these leaders asked Paul to defend himself (Acts 17:16–21). Paul, having both common sense and shrewdness, along with a sincere concern for their lost condition, knew that to rebuke them immediately for their idol worship would do little good. But he also knew of an area where he could commend them and then go from there to speak to them about Christ. We are told:

> Then Paul stood in the midst of the Areopagus and said, "Men of Athens, I perceive that in all things you are very religious; for as I was passing through and considering the objects of your worship, I even found an altar with this inscription: TO THE UNKNOWN GOD. Therefore, the One whom you worship without knowing, Him I proclaim to you" (vv. 22–23).

Paul proceeded to speak of Christ and His resurrection. His message did not reach everyone, but it did reach some. Concerning the results, we read: "However, some men joined him and believed, among them Dionysius the Areopagite, a woman named Damaris, and others with them" (v. 34).

Preaching was not Paul's only arena in which to use a compliment. When given an opportunity to answer for himself before King Agrippa, he not only expressed his gratitude, but applauded Agrippa publicly for his knowledge of Jewish matters and customs. No one is grieved to be called an expert in an area where indeed he is one. Paul said:

> I think myself happy, King Agrippa, because today I shall answer for myself before you concerning all the things of which I am accused by the Jews, especially because you are expert in all customs and questions which have to do with the Jews. Therefore I beg you to hear me patiently (Acts 26:2–3).

Moments later, Paul paid Agrippa a second compliment for his belief in the Old Testament prophets (v. 27). His shrewd handling of the situation and tactful use of compliments played a definite part in helping to defuse the opposition. Determining that Paul had done nothing worthy of death, Agrippa commented to Festus: "This man might have been set free if he had not appealed to Caesar" (v. 32).

Common sense combined with a disarming purity tells us that we must first win the lost to ourselves if we are to win them to our message. Compliments help us do just that.

CONCLUSION

Wisdom in evangelism is good common sense combined with disarming purity.
Although there are undoubtedly many ways such wisdom is illustrated
in the New Testament, five examples stand out.

- Identify with the needs and background of the lost, using that as
  a bridge to share the message of the Savior.
- Display a balance between grace and truth, knowing both when
  to confront and when and how to permeate that confrontation
  with grace.
- Use current events to show how the Bible relates to life as people
  are experiencing it.
- Use evidences to give the truth concerning Christ an intellectual
  and objective basis.
- Learn the tremendous value a compliment can have in
  overcoming a non-Christian's defensiveness and causing him or
  her to open up to your message.

As noted at the beginning of this chapter, W. A. Criswell, former
pastor of First Baptist Church in Dallas, once said: "God has given us
five senses. We need two more—common and horse." Indeed, he was
right. It is that good common sense in our dealings with the non-
Christian that we need and, as we walk in sensitivity to God's Spirit
and the lost, we will have.

So What?

A biblical understanding of wisdom as it relates to evangelism has both a thought-provoking and freeing effect upon our witness for the Savior. Several examples will clarify what I mean.

One of the areas where believers struggle the most in evangelism is knowing how to take a normal conversation and turn it to spiritual things. They recognize how crucial it is to be able to do that. Few lost people are going to walk up to a believer and say, "Could I speak to you about my eternal destiny?" At the same time, Christians are not sure *how* to turn a conversation to spiritual matters. The mistake they often make is assuming that there is a "set" way to do it. Sometimes they even go to the point of memorizing five different ways to turn a conversation. Their frustration is only increased when they prepare to witness to a friend and discover that none of the five ways works.

Following the definition of wisdom at which we have arrived, however, we can simply relax and practice common sense combined with a disarming purity. Common sense means that before we can get unbelievers talking about spiritual things, we must get them talking. As they talk, we can think of a way to direct the conversation to Christ. As we use our common sense, we realize that three areas where people most easily talk with one another are family, job, and background. These three areas, therefore, become great places to relate to the lost.

With that in mind, as I have advised many, I simply "plow and pursue." I plow into the conversation, enjoying it immensely, and pursue any way possible to turn it to spiritual things. Until we have been talking a while, I do not know how I am going to direct the conversation to Christ. What happens or does not happen as we are talking will dictate that. You will discover that there are as many ways to direct a conversation to spiritual things as there are people to whom you will speak. You will also discover how free your mind is to think if you "free up" instead of "freeze up."

I love the outdoors and am an enthusiastic runner as well. I was once speaking to a non-Christian introduced to me by a mutual friend. As we were talking, he mentioned that he enjoyed golf. He explained that one of the reasons was that as he stood on a golf course and admired nature, everything seemed so peaceful. Not only did I agree, but I told him that was one of the reasons I enjoy running. I told him of some of the trails and parks in traveling I had been privileged to use. I even added that having time in the outdoors has greatly affected me spiritually. His immediate response was, "Yes, being in the outdoors really helps you feel close to God, doesn't it?" That comment gave me a choice opportunity to explain the part creation had in bringing me to Christ. He listened with great interest as I explained the Gospel and how a person could be certain of life everlasting. He did not trust Christ that day but our conversation could not have been a more splendid one. When we parted, I gave him a booklet to read that further explained the Gospel and God's offer of life eternal.

Many people have a religious background, whether it be negative or positive. It is absolutely amazing how often as one talks to the lost the subject of "church" comes up. It may be only a passing reference as when someone says, "After church last Sunday . . ." and then proceeds to talk about the Sunday afternoon activity. Or it may be a more direct reference as a man speaks of his and his wife's conflict in that area or mentions a comment a preacher made on a pertinent subject. Frankly, regardless of how the subject of church arises, it allows the opportunity to return to that point later and say, "Moments ago you mentioned going to church. Where do you and your wife attend?" After he responds, you can then ask, "How long have you been interested in spiritual things?" Questions such as that and the resulting reply offer you the opportunity to go from there and say, "Has anyone ever taken a Bible and shown you how you can know that you are going to heaven?"

While walking in our neighborhood, my wife met a woman who was also getting her exercise, so they decided to walk together. As they did, the woman asked, "What does your husband do?" (Notice—the subject that arose was occupation.) After my wife said that I was a preacher, the woman immediately asked, "What church?" Tammy explained that I am an evangelistic speaker who speaks in many churches and communities. She then said to the woman, "Why did you ask?" The woman then began to talk about the struggle she and her husband were having in the area of attending church. As my wife encouraged her to share a bit more about those struggles, she related that most of them centered around the question, Was Christ who He said He was? Needless to say, that gave my wife the opportunity to talk freely about Christ and the Gospel and even continue those talks in further walks together. Was the fact that Tammy is a preacher's wife crucial to that conversation? It was helpful but by no means crucial. Anyone who had engaged in conversation with this woman and even hinted at church or some area of spiritual things would have found a woman most ready to talk.

A believer once said to me, "I can't get over how many hurting people there are." He is right. People are hurting. As you begin speaking to them in the area of family, job, and background, and demonstrate a sincere and caring heart, often those hurts are revealed. Their marriage is in trouble, a good friend has a terminal disease, their job is not working out as well as they had hoped, their parents are separated, or they have gotten into trouble with a good friend or with the law. Whatever the hurt is, I have met very few people with whom I could not tactfully proceed to get into spiritual things and the One who offers whatever they need—peace, forgiveness, happiness, a friend, hope— whatever it may be. Every time I explain that a person's first and foremost need is the assurance of life eternal. Until the matter of their eternal destiny is settled, a person cannot know the many other benefits Christ has to give.

As I took my assigned seat on a plane, I engaged in conversation with the woman next to me. She soon revealed that things were not going well. As we talked, she exclaimed, "My husband is leaving me after thirty-eight years and I can't handle it." At that point, she began to cry. That gave me the opportunity to explain that being married for many years, I could empathize somewhat with her. As we talked, she unfolded the details of a husband who apparently was going through a mid-life crisis. I was able to ask her warmly, "May I ask you a personal question? I don't know how you feel about spiritual things, but I'm convinced God cares for you and wants to help you. Have you thought much about that?" She confessed that this experience was making her think more about spiritual things than she ever had before. An hour later I had the privilege of leading her to the Lord. I then obtained her address to send her some information that would help her grow.

Let your mind do what God created it to do—think freely. As you use common sense, you will be surprised at the many ways you can move a conversation from the general to the specific, and from the secular to the spiritual. In fact, the more people you speak with, the more abundant the ways to turn conversations to spiritual things will become.

Recognizing that wisdom is seen in a balance between grace and truth also gives a great sense of freedom. I am many times asked by people contemplating discussions about Christ with their friends, "How can I keep from offending someone?" My answer is almost always, "Don't worry about it!" I have discovered that the people who ask that question are not the ones who are offensive in the way they come across. The very fact that the question is on their minds indicates their desire to be sensitive and tactful—and that is usually what they are. The people who offend seldom ask such a question. Furthermore, we have to be careful how far we carry concern about offending someone. Wisdom means we have a balance between grace and truth. Sometimes the truth that a person cannot get to heaven on his own merit but must trust Christ to save him is terribly offensive. If we shrink from saying that out of a concern not to offend, we will not tell the lost what they need to know and we end up pleasing men, not God (Gal. 1:10). We should feel completely free to tell people the truth of the Gospel as the opportunity presents itself and we should package it in a gracious spirit. Common sense then tells us that we have explained what they need to hear and have done it shrewdly so as to win them to the Savior.

Christians can become very narrow-minded. They see what the Scriptures are saying but often fail to see how events in life can be used to make Scripture relevant to a lost person. Wisdom tells us that lost persons often understand life. They see it happening in front of them every day. What they do not understand is the Bible and how it relates to life. One who is wise in evangelism recognizes how helpful it is to tie the events of life to the Scriptures and vice versa. Common sense combined with a disarming purity shows how to make those correlations.

A Dallas newspaper once told of a school crossing guard who was killed as she pushed a child out of the way of an oncoming car. In so doing, the guard died but the child lived. An illustration such as that can serve to drive home in a lost person's mind the substitutionary nature of Christ's death and the love that was behind it. When a popular musician was assassinated, his son, who was always told that he could do anything he wanted and that anything was within his grasp, remarked to his mother, "There is one thing we cannot do. We can't bring Daddy back." That comment was on the radio throughout Dallas at that time. It gave me the opportunity to say to many lost people, "That boy understood a simple truth of Scripture. You cannot bring Daddy back. Whatever agreement you want with God then, has to be made now." From reading the paper and listening to the news on radio and TV, I have picked up scores of comments and illustrations about life, death, loneliness, happiness, boredom, heaven, hell, Christ, God, religion, friends, and countless other subjects. Many have been extremely helpful to me. Even as I wrote this book, I read of a professional coach who spoke of his son and his good character and life. He then remarked, "He has a one-way ticket to heaven." A comment such as that helps me in conversing with lost people who mistakenly feel the same way—that goodness will get one to heaven. Common sense tells us that we need to know our Bible but we also need to have our eyes and ears open to current events. As Christ demonstrated, current events can be effectively used in imparting spiritual truth to the lost.

We have seen that one way wisdom is demonstrated in Scripture is with the use of evidence. It helps us to realize matters such as the empty tomb and fulfilled prophecy were not merely matters of coincidence. Therefore, they become most weighty in talking to the lost. Josh McDowell in *More Than a Carpenter* mentions an analysis done by Peter W. Stoner that shows the credibility of something like fulfilled prophecy. Suppose there were only eight prophecies fulfilled by Christ instead of the actual number of over three hundred. By using the science of probability in reference to eight prophecies, we learn that the chance that any man might have lived down to the present time and fulfilled all eight prophecies is 1 in 10^{17}. That would be 1 in 100,000,000,000,000,000. Stoner illustrates that staggering statistic and its ramifications by imagining that 10^{17} silver dollars were placed on the face of Texas. The entire state would be covered to a depth of two feet. He then imagines that one of these silver dollars was marked and then the entire mass stirred. If a man were then blindfolded and told to travel as he liked but that he must pick out the marked silver dollar—his chance of finding the right one would be the same as the prophets of writing eight prophecies and having them all come true in one person, if they wrote with only their own wisdom.[5]

One sometimes asks, "What about the evidence of changed lives? Can that not be wisely used in evangelism?" Most definitely. More than one person has testified of how Christ took his life and made a miracle out of a mess. Also, those disciples who were martyred for what they believed attested to who He was. Intelligent men do not die for what they know to be a lie. It helps to tie these evidences, though, with the objective facts of Christ's resurrection and fulfilled prophecy. Those who would argue against the validity of changed lives or the disciples' experiences find it very difficult, if they are honest, to refute the historical facts concerning Christ.

This helps one see the place of apologetics. In the Scriptures apologetics support evangelism. We go out with the message of Christ's death and resurrection. Should we find the lost unwilling to accept that message or demanding proof, we use whatever evidence is appropriate and needed. I might mention that there are two books I have used repeatedly. By the way, I lend them to non-Christian friends, rather than giving the books to them to keep. That way I can solicit a response. I say, "Let me lend you this book to read. I think you will find it very helpful. In a couple of weeks I'd be interested in knowing what your thoughts are."

One book I've used repeatedly is *Evidence That Demands a Verdict*, by Josh McDowell. McDowell has compiled the secular, historical, and prophetic proof that Jesus Christ was the One He claimed to be. McDowell argues that Christ could have been only Lord, liar, or lunatic and shows the evidence for His being Lord to be absolutely overwhelming. It is an excellent book to give to a skeptic. Another one I've used is *Who Moved the Stone?* by Frank Morison. As noted in an earlier chapter, Morison was an English journalist who set out to prove that the story of the resurrection of Christ was nothing but myth. He describes how his probings and studies led him instead to a full conviction that the resurrection of Christ and events surrounding it rest on a historical basis. Particularly valuable is his examination of the six alternative explanations to the empty tomb, all of which lack logic and support. Whereas McDowell's book is more on an academic level, Morison's book is geared to a popular audience. The circumstances of the person I'm speaking to determines which book I use and recommend.

Along with the other items I've discussed, compliments are also freeing as we seek to be wise in evangelism. Often as we talk to the lost we will notice that they are threatened by what we are saying. That is undoubtedly one reason most come to Christ prior to age thirty instead of afterward. The older a person gets, the harder it is to admit in the most important area of life—the spiritual—that he or she has missed something extremely important. As was noted, we may be accused of harboring a superior attitude. The non-Christian can even be threatened by our "audacity" to believe that we know beyond the shadow of any doubt that we are going to heaven when we die.

Compliments often help us get through these defenses. I have used compliments in advance of presenting the Gospel, throughout a gospel presentation, and at the close. I have commended everything from a person's interests to his or her intelligence, background, occupation, family, appearance, mate, children, goals, questions, comments, and numerous other things. I have never met a person who could not handle a compliment. Who does not like to hear something good about him- or herself? Will Rogers is reported to have said, "I always like to hear a man talk about himself. I usually hear nothing but good." To honor God, compliments must be sincere, but there is no reason they should not be.

I like to take non-Christian men to lunch. I have discovered that men will open up with me about spiritual things in a restaurant when they would not do so in front of their own wife and family. As I begin to discuss spiritual things with him, I sometimes sense that he feels threatened. A compliment will often defuse the situation.

Here is an example of what I mean. On one occasion, a non-Christian school principal attended our outreach and afterward asked to talk to me in his office the next day. In this particular case we were at a lunch table in the privacy of his office. I knew he was struggling with spiritual things and, because he and I come from the same religious background, I knew what he was going through. I was brought up not to talk of spiritual things openly. When I went to see him again the next day, I sensed that the struggle had only intensified. In addition, he appeared concerned that I recognize the stature he had in his community and how that made it difficult to be vocal for Christ. I even remember him saying, "In my position, I have to be careful how far I go." I complimented him for not only his position, but also for the good job I had heard he was doing. That had a way of putting us on the same level and he recognized that regardless of what he did with Christ, I did not think any less of him. Did that ever help the situation! I could now say to him, "I am not concerned at this point about how vocal you are for Christ; my concern is that you trust Christ alone to save you." A few nights later he responded at the end of an evangelistic service to tell me he wished to trust Christ. He then became active in a Bible-believing church in the area.

Compliments can be particularly helpful in reaching relatives. Sometimes the hardest ones to reach are those in one's own family. In interacting with many people about their situations every year, I have discovered the hardest situation is trying to reach parents. No doubt the reason is that it does not matter how lovingly we present the Gospel, we are nonetheless saying, "In the most important area of life, you have blown it." That is tough for a conscientious parent to take. With that in mind, I have often suggested that whether through verbal conversation or letter, children should applaud their parents for all they did right. Just the fact that you have made it into adulthood says something. Those compliments help tell parents that your respect for them has not changed. You are simply concerned that the family will be together in heaven. I have even used compliments children have given me about their parents to lead the parents to Christ. I have had parents who came to hear me speak just to satisfy their children whom they loved. When I have been able to talk alone with them, I have sometimes been able to say (because of compliments their children paid them), "I hope one day my boy talks as highly about me as your children do about you." Numerous times I have seen God use that to break down the barrier and bring them to Christ.

As we note that wisdom is common sense with a disarming purity, we dare not forget that inherent in that biblical definition are the elements of honesty, sincerity, and purity of motive. For that reason, some ask, "Is it proper to go door-to-door in a neighborhood, explain that we are conducting a religious survey, and use that as an opener to present the Gospel?" My answer is yes, if indeed a survey is being done. I would even suggest you offer to mail them the results of the survey. Otherwise, no. Bear in mind that visiting a total of twenty homes hardly represents a survey. Instead, use an approach that has integrity. If a survey is not being done, an honest approach such as, "We are from (name of church) and are attempting to get to know some of the people in our community. Would you have a little time to talk?" would honor God more.

When God saves us, He does not take away our common sense. If anything, He gives us more of it. As individuals directed by His Spirit, we can use common sense and shrewdness in approaching the lost and interacting with them. When acting with sincerity and integrity, we demonstrate a wisdom God used in the New Testament and is using today in appealing to the lost on behalf of His Son.

Group Discussion Questions

- Evangelism is not easy. It involves work. How, though, do we often make it harder than it is, and how can common sense help us? Be specific.

- Think of news-making events that have occurred in your community within the last year. How may they have served as opportunities or bridges to present the Gospel?

- Think about conversations you have had with lost people within the last month. Using the "plow and pursue" principle, how might you have turned the conversations to spiritual things?

- In what ways will increased experience and consistency in evangelism affect the development and use of common sense with a discerning purity?

- How does being effective in evangelism necessitate being a good listener?

Chapter Sixteen

What Is Boldness, and How Does One Obtain It?

Sometimes I am almost afraid to ask the Lord to give me a soul, because I know that if I ask Him, I am going to have to get busy. I have been a Christian for twenty-nine years, and it still frightens me to talk to a man about his need of salvation.

—Dawson Trotman

Few Christians would not admit to being fearful in talking to others about Christ, myself included. One individual commented, "I'm never afraid to witness as long as the person I plan to talk to is not at home!" Fear so grips the average Christian that even when faced with a prime opportunity to speak about Christ, he tends to clam up instead of speak up. The noted preacher Charles Spurgeon said:

> I often envy those of my brethren who can go up to individuals, and talk to them with freedom about their souls. I do not always find myself able to do so, though, when I have been Divinely aided in such service, I have had a large reward.[1]

Many Christians have asked, "How can I get rid of my fear in evangelism? What do you have to do to stop being afraid?"

The New Testament responds to the problem of fear by talking about boldness. For example, when the prominent men of Jerusalem "saw the boldness of Peter and John, and perceived that they were uneducated and untrained men, they marveled" (Acts 4:13). When contemplating our need to be bold as Peter and John were, questions immediately arise.

WHAT IS BOLDNESS?

The first and most obvious question is, What is boldness from a New Testament perspective? When the Scriptures speak of the boldness of Peter and John, what exactly does that mean?

221

The predominant word used in speaking of boldness or courage in evangelism is *parrēsia* and the corresponding verb *parrēsiazomai.* Together, these are used a total of forty times; all except fourteen are in a context lending itself to evangelism.

Perhaps the best way to determine the basic idea conveyed by these two words is to examine several representative uses. Consider the following:

John 7:12–13—"There was much murmuring among the people concerning Him. Some said, 'He is good'; others said, 'No, on the contrary, He deceives the people.' However, no one spoke *openly* of Him for fear of the Jews." [Opinion about Jesus was divided, some considering Him a trustworthy teacher and others a deceiver. Because of that, people were afraid to speak "openly"—meaning publicly—of Him, fearful of the opposition they might encounter.]

Acts 4:13—"Now when they saw the *boldness* of Peter and John, and perceived that they were uneducated and untrained men, they marveled. And they realized that they had been with Jesus." [This statement concerning Peter's and John's boldness is found in the context of the first persecutions recorded in the book of Acts. Having healed a lame man, the apostles had been brought into the custody of the highest Jewish court (4:5–7). Peter, instead of accepting the accusations concerning what he had done, accused the rulers of crucifying the One who was the long-promised Messiah (4:8–12). Since Peter and John were not trained in the rabbinic schools, the rulers were amazed that they would speak with such courage before a court of such high authority.]

Acts 4:29–31—The believers prayed, "Now, Lord, look on their threats, and grant to Your servants that with all *boldness* they may speak Your word . . . . And when they had prayed, the place where they were assembled together was shaken; and they were all filled with the Holy Spirit, and they spoke the word of God with *boldness.*" [Having been commanded not to utter a word (4:18), the disciples knew that to speak would go against the highest Jewish authority in the land. They instantly gathered for prayer, asking God for His supply of boldness, and they received what they needed.]

Acts 13:46—"Then Paul and Barnabas grew *bold* and said, 'It was necessary that the word of God should be spoken to you first; but since you reject it, and judge yourselves unworthy of everlasting life, behold, we turn to the Gentiles.'" [Paul and Barnabas faced strong opposition to the message of the Gospel, opposition that eventually resulted in their being expelled from the area (v. 50).]

Acts 26:26–27—"For the king, before whom I also speak *freely*, knows these things; for I am convinced that none of these things escape his attention, since this thing was not done in a corner. King Agrippa, do you believe the prophets? I know that you do believe." [Paul stood before King Agrippa with the possibility of imprisonment or death hanging over his head. He attempted to use Agrippa's acceptance of the Old Testament prophets to convince him of the identity of Jesus Christ and his need of Him.]

What do these reveal? The fundamental notion in the words *parrēsia* and *parrēsiazomai* as used in evangelistic contexts is that of courage. This is quite in keeping with the meaning these words originally had in Greek of the right or courage to appear in public, freedom of speech, or openness.[2]

The issue is not the absence of circumstances that could make one fearful. In fact, when these two words occur in the context of evangelism, there is always a risk of personal harm or injury. Boldness resulted, therefore, not from the absence of fear or fearful circumstances, but from the conquest of it. Boldness overtook fear and created a state of mind from which freedom of speech flowed instead of silence. Boldness gave Christians a freedom to speak the Gospel publicly to convince their hearers of the Person of Christ and their need of Him. When believers ask, "How can I avoid fear in evangelism?" they are asking the wrong question. The need is not to be unafraid—the need is for courage even though we may be scared.

A news reporter listened as an evangelist was being interviewed by the press. Upon returning, she mentioned to a friend, "I was overwhelmed by his boldness in talking about Christ. He even told all of us as reporters that he was hopeful it wouldn't be long before each one of us came to know the Savior." That illustrates well the New Testament thrust of boldness—a courage to announce the Savior regardless of the consequences.

Boldness may therefore be appropriately defined as the courage to speak with freedom, plainness, and confidence about the Lord regardless of the circumstances. That courage is what enables one to speak up, not clam up.

HOW DOES ONE OBTAIN BOLDNESS?

After studying what boldness is, the next question that naturally arises is, How does one obtain it? Although no paragraph of the Bible gives a precise formula for boldness, several things come to light through a careful study of the Scriptures.

Boldness Is Something for Which to Ask God

To begin, it must not be overlooked that boldness in Scripture does not always come naturally. Even the apostle Paul knew fear in the midst of evangelism. He testified concerning his ministry in Corinth, "I was with you in weakness, in fear, and in much trembling" (1 Cor. 2:3). The reason individuals in the New Testament are often said to be bold is that they asked God for boldness—and He gave it! Paul further testified that it was in the context of his relationship with Jesus Christ that he found the boldness he needed. He explained, "We were bold *in our God*" (1 Thess. 2:2). Paul asked God for boldness and asked others to pray with him to that end (Eph. 6:19–20).

Return to the first persecutions recorded in the book of Acts. The early part of Acts 3 tells us that in the name of Christ, whom the Sanhedrin had recently crucified, Peter and John healed a lame man who always sat at the gate of the temple. Peter used the amazement surrounding that miracle to speak to people about their need of the crucified One. Unable to refute the miracle and yet unwilling to believe in Christ, the rulers decided the only alternative was to command Peter and John "not to speak at all nor teach in the name of Jesus" (4:18). Dismissed from the presence of the rulers, what did Peter and John do? Returning to their own company, they prayed that God would grant boldness (v. 29), and God answered that prayer: "They were all filled with the Holy Spirit, and they spoke the word of God with boldness" (v. 31).

The urging of Scripture is that if we are afraid, we are to ask God for boldness. We ought not tell everyone else we are afraid and neglect to tell Him. Knowing His desire that we speak to the lost, we can claim the promise "that if we ask anything according to His will, He hears us. And if we know that he hears us, whatever we ask, we know that we have the petitions that we have asked of Him" (1 John 5:14–15).

We should ask God for boldness *while* evangelizing. That is, we need not and ought not sit around and wait for it. As disciples in obedience to Him (Luke 5:1–11), we ought to step out to evangelize, asking Him for boldness as we do so. It is exciting to know that we can say a silent prayer for boldness to present the Gospel even as we begin conversing with the lost.

Boldness Results from Confidence in the Message and from Concern for People

A second source for obtaining boldness results from Paul's testimony about his evangelistic labor in Thessalonica. To his friends at Thessalonica, Paul said, "But even after we had suffered before and were spitefully treated at Philippi, as you know, we were bold in our God to speak to you the gospel of God in much conflict" (1 Thess. 2:2). As Paul entered Thessalonica he encountered, as he had in Philippi, opposition from those who desired to slander his ministry by accusing him of having the wrong message or the wrong motives. His opponents said that he and his associates were misguided in their preaching and that they ministered for selfish reasons. As Paul answered these accusations, he reminded them of how he and his associates had conducted themselves in Thessalonica.

What made him bold in such adverse circumstances? Paul first pointed to his confidence in the message: "For our exhortation did not come from deceit or uncleanness, nor was it in guile. But as we have been approved by God to be entrusted with the gospel, even so we speak, not as pleasing men, but God who tests our hearts" (vv. 3–4). Deceit, uncleanness, and guile were all accusations leveled against Paul's ministry. Those attempting to slander his name and work wished for the opportunity to say his message was in error, his preaching of grace encouraged sexual immorality, and his methods were underhanded. In fact, his accusers' message, not Paul's, had the components of deceit, uncleanness, and guile. In some of the religions of Paul's day, prostitution was even part of the worship service.[3] In contrast to this, Paul stated that God had examined him before entrusting him with the message of the Gospel and still examined him (v. 4). He spoke as one entrusted with that message. His boldness, therefore, resulted from his own confidence that he had the right message, was entrusted by God with it, and had to speak as one being examined by God in his handling of it. The message of the Gospel of grace enhanced his boldness.

Continuing from there, Paul spoke of his concern for people: "For neither at any time did we use flattering words, as you know, nor a cloak of covetousness—God is witness. Nor did we seek glory from men, either from you or from others, when we might have made demands as apostles of Christ" (vv. 5–6). Undoubtedly, there were again those who wished to accuse him of having ulterior motives. Some tried to say that Paul was more committed to Paul than he was to others and that he used the ministry for personal gain. He refuted that by continuing, "But we were gentle among you, just as a nursing mother cherishes her own children. So, affectionately longing for you, we were well pleased to impart to you not only the gospel of God, but also our own lives, because you had become dear to us. For you remember, brethren, our labor and toil; for laboring night and day, that we might not be a burden to any of you, we preached to you the gospel of God" (vv. 7–9). His concern for them was so evident that not only did he compare it to that of a nursing mother for her children, he even reminded them that, if necessary, he was willing to die a martyr's death for them. His concern was sacrificial, not self-serving. He spoke of how "devoutly and justly and blamelessly" he had behaved among them and then further likened his concern for them to that of a father for his children (vv. 10–12). In fact, the consistency of Paul's life and care for the Thessalonians made his concern for them even more meaningful and must have enhanced his boldness. He had lived the life in front of them both before and after their conversion.

Concern for people drives us to them, not from them—even though, like Paul, we are not certain of the outcome. It is rather trite, but true: we can give without caring, but we cannot care without giving. A caring heart is an evangelizing heart as demonstrated not only by Paul, but also Christ Himself who, when He looked at people like sheep without a shepherd, was filled with compassion (Matt. 9:36).[4] It was with that concern that He was continually seeking and saving the lost.

Obeying God Must Have Preeminence over Obeying Our Fears

Another observation made when examining passages where men were characterized by *parrēsia* appears to be the realization that, first and foremost, they must obey God before obeying their fears. That compulsion to obey Him as His disciples made them speak up in the midst of fear.

Due to the commission that had been given to him as an apostle to the Gentiles (Acts 9:6, 15–16), Paul's conviction was "Woe is me if I do not preach the gospel." Whether he did it willingly or unwillingly, he had a responsibility before the Lord (1 Cor. 9:16–17). In his mind, it was more important that he obey God rather than succumb to his fears.

That conviction is clear in his comments, noted earlier, to the Thessalonians as well. When he talked of his boldness among them and the message with which he had been entrusted, he said, "As we have been approved by God to be entrusted with the gospel, even so we speak, *not as pleasing men, but God who tests our hearts*" (1 Thess. 2:4). Paul knew that God who had examined him before entrusting him with that message was still examining him. That message was not one to keep silent; it was one to be told. It was more important that he had God's approval on everything he did than that he had man's. To Paul, there were far worse consequences in being silent than in speaking up.

Peter and John had a similar conviction. When plainly instructed by the Sanhedrin not to speak to any man in the name of Christ (Acts 4:17), they answered just as plainly, "Whether it is right in the sight of God to listen to you more than God, you judge. For we cannot but speak the things which we have seen and heard" (vv. 19–20). The ball was thrown right back in the lap of the accusers. The apostles had made their decision. Obedience to God must come first, not a surrender to the fears and threats man presented. They had made their decision; their accusers could make their own.

Believers today are not apostles in the strict New Testament sense of the term. But if, as believers, we consider ourselves Christ's disciples, we are to evangelize (Matt. 4:19; 28:19–20). We must sense a greater responsibility to the One we are following than to the fears that have a way of following us.

On the tombstone of a man noted for his witness for Christ were carved the words: "He feared men so little because he feared God so much."

CONCLUSION

Boldness in evangelism is the courage to speak with freedom, plainness, and confidence about the Lord. This side of heaven, we will likely never escape moments of fear. But God has an abundant supply of boldness for those who ask for it. As God answers those requests, we need to reflect on the truth of our message and develop a concern for those who need to hear. As we then obey Him instead of our fears, we will find ourselves speaking up in situations where previously we may have been silent. He gives the courage that enables us to speak with freedom, plainness, and confidence about the Lord.

As one experiences boldness as it is stressed in Scripture, it then becomes obvious that boldness in evangelism is related to our walk with the Lord, confidence in the Gospel, and concern for the lost. When these areas are as they should be, fear is often present, but so is the boldness needed to overcome it. As much as we might like to separate the spiritual life from evangelism, we cannot do so. The more intimate we are with the Lord, the more bold we will be in evangelism.

So What?

The tremendous ramifications of this chapter are easily seen. Who should be bolder—a Christian talking about Christ or a Buddhist talking about Buddha? Is there any doubt? Of course not. Why should a Christian be bolder? For the simple reason that, unlike the Buddhist, the Christian has a message from God. It contains no error. Only a Christian has the message that proclaims Christ's death and resurrection as the sole basis on which God will save those who come to Him in faith. Any other religion, whether it be Mormonism, Jehovah's Witness, Hinduism, Buddhism, or any of the many more recently developed cults, has man striving for acceptance by God on the basis of good deeds, sacrifices, and donations. They have no Gospel, no Good News to proclaim. Their message centers around a false gospel—what the person must do for God—and not a true gospel, what God has done for us. We of all people ought to be the boldest and most zealous in getting the Word out because we preach a message we have been entrusted with by God.

The truth of this was driven home to me in an evangelistic outreach. That night as I preached the Gospel of the grace of God, I experienced great freedom in the pulpit. It was with both power and delight I announced salvation by grace through faith. Afterward a young Christian man walked up to me and remarked, "Something just hit me as you were talking. The reason you are so bold in talking to others about Christ is that you are convinced of what you are saying." Without thinking further about what he had said or even allowing him to say more, I answered, "I really am. This [the message of the Gospel] is the truth." He then added, "I need to increase my conviction that the message we have is the only message there is. That will make me bolder." I have often thought about those comments. I have not always been as bold as I am now and there are still many times I am fearful. But when I sit down alongside a man and realize that if he doesn't hear the Gospel from me, he may not hear it at all, my boldness is increased and my fear is overcome.

We also see what makes new believers speak in the midst of fear. It is certainly not that they don't think of the consequences. Indeed they do. One of the chief reasons, though, that they speak up is that as they come to Christ, they are hit with what might be termed a nightmare. Relatives and friends are going to hell! The thought is unbearable. In a way that many times lacks tact, they speak to non-Christian friends about the Lord. They talk because they care. Regardless of whether we are one day old in Christ or fifty years old in Him, when we have the concern we need for others, we have boldness in talking about Him.

A pastor friend of mine once asked me if I would go with him to talk to a neighbor about Christ. We went, engaged him in conversation, and were soon speaking about spiritual things. The non-Christian was annoyed that the conversation had taken the direction it had. As he became increasingly agitated, my friend looked at him and said, "Let me explain something. The last thing I would ever want to do is upset you. But my wife and I have known you for years and value you as a friend. It bothers us that though we are such good friends, we have never asked you about your relationship with the Lord. I can't let it go any longer. We have even awakened at night wondering where you would go if something happened to you." The man became teary-eyed, looked at both of us, and expressed a desire for us to show him how to be certain he would live forever with God. A few moments later, he trusted Christ.

Above all, we should be reminded that in the New Testament, while believers indeed confessed their fear to one another, predominant in their minds was telling the Lord of their fear. James, in another context, reminded his readers, "You do not have because you do not ask" (James 4:2). How often is that true in the area of boldness in evangelism?

Group Discussion Questions

- When you are afraid to evangelize, what are your fears?

- Why can a lack of boldness never be an excuse for not evangelizing?

- How do your prayer life and spiritual growth affect your taking advantage of opportunities you presently have to evangelize?

- Think of those you know who consistently evangelize. If you were to ask them, "Are you ever afraid to evangelize?" what would you imagine them saying? (Why not ask them and see if you are right?)

Chapter Seventeen

What About Follow-Up?

You can lead a soul to Christ in from twenty minutes to a couple of hours. But it takes from twenty weeks to a couple of years to get him on the road to maturity.

—Dawson Trotman
The Navigator

Tragedies are before us every day. The newspapers tell of fatal automobile accidents, cold-blooded murders, brutal attacks, or construction fatalities. Within moments, a life that had so much promise can be quickly snuffed out.

Spiritually, that can never happen. Eternal life cannot be snuffed out. Jesus said, "Most assuredly, I say to you, he who hears My word and believes in Him who sent Me has everlasting life, and shall not come into judgment, but has passed from death into life" (John 5:24). Just as emphatically Christ stressed on another occasion, "And I give them eternal life, and they shall never perish; neither shall anyone snatch them out of My hand" (10:28).

There are many, however, who could be called "apparent tragedies." They are individuals who, having supposedly come to know Christ, have little to show for it. When they came to Christ, the whole town knew it. Christ was their Master, love was their motive, and the Bible was their manual. Their input in others' lives was electrifying. Now months removed from that point, quite the opposite is true. They show up in church if they are able to make it, read the Scriptures if their schedule allows, and admit they know Christ if the situation is conducive. Why?

Unfortunately, most discussions about such individuals center around the question, Are they or aren't they saved? One thing is certain. If they have not trusted Christ, they are not His. If they have trusted Christ, they are His forever! They may presently be living out of fellowship with Him and even stand in danger of being disciplined, but they are His. Perhaps we are missing the question we ought to be

asking. The question we ought to ask is, How could this tragedy have
been averted? or What was done with the new believer from the day
he trusted Christ? In light of the responsibility we have to each other
in the family of Christ, those are important questions (cf. 1 Cor. 12:25;
Eph. 4:11–16; Heb. 10:24).

Perhaps the reason we would rather not ask those questions is that
the answer may point the finger of blame at us instead of those newly
saved. Many times those who are diligent in fishing are deficient in
follow-up. I cannot recall how many Christian leaders have said to me,
in effect, "For some reason I have never thought of doing anything with
a new convert other than inviting him to church." I also cannot recall
the number of believers who have told me something such as, "I was
saved ten years ago, but for the first five years I didn't go anywhere
spiritually. Nobody followed up on me so I never knew that there was
anything more to the Christian life than coming to Christ."

What is a biblical perspective on follow-up? How did the apostle
Paul assist his new converts? He was not known as a failure in helping
people to grow. What did he do?

AN OVERRIDING PRINCIPLE: MATURITY MUST BE THE GOAL

In the present century, we have become program-oriented.
Everything from computers to churches have their program. Although
programs can be helpful, the danger they pose is that the ultimate goal
is overlooked. Sometimes it is not even discussed.

One thing that must be established at the start appears to be an
overriding principle governing Paul's follow-up of new believers. The
goal was always maturity. He spelled that out very clearly when he said,
"Him we preach, warning every man and teaching every man in all
wisdom, that we may present every man perfect in Christ Jesus. To
this end I also labor, striving according to His working which works in
me mightily" (Col. 1:28–29). *Perfect* has the idea of maturity and
completion. *Labor* refers to toil, even to the point of exhaustion. Paul's
point was that he deeply wanted each new believer to come to a point
of maturity in Christ. He labored to that end, making use of God's
power which was working in him mightily.

So much was Paul aware that maturity was the goal for each new
believer that he instructed the Ephesians that this is one reason God gives
gifted people to the body: "For the equipping of the saints for the work
of ministry, for the edifying of the body of Christ, till we all come to the
unity of the faith and the knowledge of the Son of God, to a perfect man,
to the measure of the stature of the fullness of Christ" (Eph. 4:12–13).
Only when the individual was mature in Christ could Paul feel his labors
and the labors of others had been completed. It was for this reason he

seemed keenly aware that, although evangelism might only entail a few moments, helping believers grow could entail a lifetime of work.

Many Christians and churches have found it helpful, when an individual comes to faith in Christ, to take them through a series of basic studies designed for new believers. Materials are available to assist in either booklet or tape form. These are tremendously helpful. Bear in mind, though, that these materials are only *the means*, not the end. If they are treated as the end, the new believer will often learn all that those have to teach him and then stop wherever the material stops.

One might ask, "What are the marks of maturity?" A paragraph that appears to convey what Paul had in mind by spiritual maturity is one that describes his prayer for the new converts of Colosse. He explained, "For this reason we also, since the day we heard it, do not cease to pray for you, and to ask that you may be filled with the knowledge of His will in all wisdom and spiritual understanding" (Col. 1:9). He desired that they might have wisdom and understanding, both spiritually given, that would allow them to comprehend God's will for their lives. What are the marks of such maturity? Paul went on to explain that he wanted the believers to walk worthy of the Lord; please Him in all things; be fruitful in good works; increase in their knowledge of God, through His power experience patience and longsuffering in the midst of difficulty, and be ever grateful for what God had done in transforming them from the kingdom of darkness to the kingdom of light (1:10–14). Understandably, when we have that kind of spiritual maturity because of the perspective we have on life, our walk with the Lord is a consistent one. There are times we fail, but overall, our walk with the Lord is evident, not simply when everything in life is going right but also when everything in life is going wrong.

This maturity is spiritually produced. It comes as God, through His Holy Spirit, works in the lives of His children. What, humanly speaking, can be done to encourage or enhance this growth?

A book most helpful in giving guidelines for helping new believers is Paul's first letter to the Thessalonians. By examining how Paul approached the Thessalonians, as well as looking at a few other passages, we learn what can be done so that many "tragedies" can be averted.

After three Sabbaths of explaining the Scriptures and seeing many come to Christ (Acts 17:1–14), Paul and Silas were forced to leave the city. Concerned about how the new converts were doing, Paul sent Timothy to minister to them (1 Thess. 3:1–2, 5). Timothy returned with good news. As a grateful shepherd, Paul wrote to his flock, expressing his thoughts for them, encouraging them in their growth, and discussing matters related to their work of faith, labor of love, and patience of hope (1 Thess. 1:3).

What do we continue to learn about Paul's approach to new converts?

GUIDELINE #1 – PARENTAL ATTENTION IS REQUIRED

Mature believers are not produced on an assembly line. Each one is handcrafted. The apostle Paul knew that. That is why when a person came to know Christ, not only did they become part of God's family, but in Paul's mind he also became part of Paul's family. Look at the warm words he used in describing his relationship to new believers at Thessalonica, Galatia, and Corinth:

> But we were *gentle* among you, just as a *nursing mother* cherishes her own children (1 Thess. 2:7, emphasis added).

> So, *affectionately longing for you*, we were well pleased to impart to you not only the gospel of God, but *also our own lives*, because *you had become dear to us* (1 Thess. 2:8, emphasis added).

> As you know how we exhorted, and comforted, and charged every one of you, *as a father does his own children* (1 Thess. 2:11, emphasis added).

This relationship offered him an atmosphere in which he could start where people were and take them where they needed to be. And since people are different, he could do whatever needed to be done. Since his time with the Thessalonians was rather short, one can imagine the urgency that must have been combined with his warmth and concern. Although there had been only a limited time, he had already formed a deep relationship with them.

The emphasis in the New Testament in the area of follow-up is on people, not materials. As helpful as materials are, it is the personal contact that is stressed. Dawson Trotman, founder of the Navigators, is reported to have said, "Follow-up is not done by something. It is done by someone." He was right! The one who has trusted Christ is not only a child of God, they are a brother or sister in Christ and are to be treated as such.[1] Recognizing their newly established relationship in Christ, Paul expressed parental concern toward the new converts.

GUIDELINE #2 – DO WHATEVER NEEDS TO BE DONE TO ASSIST

A combination of three words Paul used in describing his procedure in helping new believers progress toward maturity is informative. He testified, "As you know we *exhorted*, and *comforted*, and *charged* every one of you, as a father does his own children" (1 Thess. 2:11).

One has to be careful in making too sharp a distinction between these three words. They overlap each other in meaning as when we say, "I exhort you, I encourage you, I assure you . . . " Each word, though, helps us understand how Paul helped them in any way he could.

The word *exhorted* comes from the Greek root *parakaleō*. It means "to appeal to," "to urge," or "to exhort." It conveys the idea of laying before a person a particular course of conduct and urging him to pursue it.

It is not difficult to see how Paul did that with the Thessalonians. The last two chapters of his letter give us ample illustrations. We read:

> Finally then, brethren, we urge and exhort in the Lord Jesus that you should abound more and more, just as you received from us how you ought to walk and to please God; for you know what commandments we gave you through the Lord Jesus. For this is the will of God, your sanctification: that you should abstain from sexual immorality. . . . For God did not call us to uncleanness, but in holiness (1 Thess. 4:1–3, 7).

Greek cities such as Thessalonica were often known for sexual looseness, some of it even part of pagan worship services. The exhortation Paul gave was therefore most pertinent.

There are other areas in which Paul exhorted them. He wrote:

> But concerning brotherly love you have no need that I should write to you, for you yourselves are taught by God to love one another; and indeed you do so toward all the brethren who are in all Macedonia. But we urge you, brethren, that you increase more and more; that you also aspire to lead a quiet life, to mind your own business, and to work with your own hands, as we commanded you, that you may walk properly toward those who are outside, and that you may lack nothing (1 Thess. 4:9–12).

As Timothy shared his findings with Paul, Paul must have heard the evidence that they were showing love toward the believers "in all Macedonia." The geographical location of Thessalonica, as well as its political status, would have brought them many opportunities to show love toward believers coming through the city. But there is always room for an increase in love. Paul continued by mentioning such practical matters as the importance of a quiet and calm life and serving God by faithfully doing their individual tasks without meddling in the affairs of others. All of these were important in light of the way non-Christians throughout Thessalonica were watching these new converts. The impact of their example would be strong.

Paul's ministry to new converts was never weak in explaining the path they needed to walk if they wished to honor God. The closing words of his letter contain one exhortation after another concerning the kind of conduct they ought to pursue. Touching a wide range of responsibilities they had to God and to one another, he wrote:

> And we urge you, brethren, to recognize those who labor among you, and are over you in the Lord and admonish you, and to esteem them very highly in love for their work's sake. Be at peace among yourselves. Now we exhort you, brethren, warn those who are unruly, comfort the fainthearted, uphold the weak, be patient with all. See that no one renders evil for evil to anyone, but always pursue what is good both for yourselves and for all. Rejoice always, pray without ceasing, in everything give thanks; for this is the will of God in Christ Jesus for you. Do not quench the Spirit. Do not despise prophecies. Test all things; hold fast what is good. Abstain from every form of evil (1 Thess. 5:12–22).

The second word Paul used was *comforted,* which translates a form of *paramutheomai.* An examination of the word proves its meaning to be to "cheer up" or "encourage." It represents the need to encourage new believers in the midst of difficulties and problems. Paul admitted that was one reason he sent Timothy to Thessalonica. He wrote, "[We] sent Timothy, our brother and minister of God, and our fellow laborer in the gospel of Christ, to establish you and encourage you concerning your faith, that no one should be shaken by these afflictions; for you yourselves know that we are appointed to this" (1 Thess. 3:2–3). Not only did the Thessalonians suffer as non-Christians tempted them to give up their faith, but they had also witnessed firsthand how Paul and Silas were forced to leave the city. In addition, they knew of the way others apparently tried to slander Paul's ministry by rumoring that it was only done for profit (1 Thess. 2:9–10). Paul desired to comfort them so their afflictions would not result in their folding instead of standing. As he talked about the return of Christ and the certainty of that hope, twice he encouraged them to comfort one another (1 Thess. 4:18–5:11).[2]

The third word, *charged,* comes from the Greek root *martureō,* meaning "to bear witness" or "to confirm" or "to testify." As used here, it depicts a solemnity and earnestness, an urgency that is behind the encouragement. Undoubtedly, this was particularly important when new converts would begin to waver. Paul wanted them to know that it was vitally important to God, to themselves, and to him that they "walk worthy of God" (1 Thess. 2:12). Behind each exhortation he gave in 1 Thessalonians, one can detect Paul's urgency.

As these three ideas in 1 Thessalonians 2:11—"exhorted," "comforted," and "charged"—are examined within the context of Paul's letter, one finds an apostle who was willing to do whatever was necessary to assist new believers. As he did so, there was a thoroughness and urgency—what one might call an "I'll give it my all" attitude.

We too easily overlook the need for common sense in areas of evangelism and follow-up. As Paul did, we need to start where people are and do whatever needs to be done. The "exhortation," "comfort," and "charging" needed by one person may differ from what others need. One saved from a drug abuse background may demand different words and assistance from one saved who comes from a strict religious background. If we do whatever needs to be done to assist the individual in his growth to maturity, we will be following the example of Paul's approach to new believers.

GUIDELINE #3 – THE IMPORTANCE OF PRAYER

Anyone who knows the Scripture and non-Christians and reconsiders the circumstances surrounding his own conversion knows the importance of prayer in evangelism. What we dare not overlook is how essential prayer is in following up new converts. We must talk to the new convert about God and about all there is to learn about Him, but we must also speak to God about the new convert.

It is striking to notice how much emphasis Paul placed in his personal life and ministry on praying for new converts. To the people of Thessalonica he testified, "We give thanks to God always for you all, making mention of you in our prayers" (1 Thess. 1:2). To his beloved family in Christ in Philippi he stressed, "I thank my God upon every remembrance of you, always in every prayer of mine making request for you all with joy" (Phil. 1:3–4). When writing to the Ephesians, he reminded them, "Therefore I also, after I heard of your faith in the Lord Jesus and your love for all the saints, do not cease to give thanks for you, making mention of you in my prayers" (Eph. 1:15–16). As noted earlier, to the Colossians he said, "For this reason we also, since the day we heard it, do not cease to pray for you, and to ask that you may be filled with the knowledge of His will in all wisdom and spiritual understanding" (Col. 1:9).

How did Paul pray for the Thessalonians? We know his prayers for them were filled with praise. He indicated that when he said, "Remembering without ceasing your work of faith, labor of love, and patience of hope in our Lord Jesus Christ in the sight of our God and Father" (1 Thess. 1:3). He indicated that again when he said, "For what thanks can we render to God for you, for all the joy with which we rejoice for your sake before our God" (3:9). What follows gives some idea of the petitions he brought to the Lord on their behalf:

> Night and day praying exceedingly that we may see your face and perfect what is lacking in your faith. Now may our God and Father Himself, and our Lord Jesus Christ, direct our way to you. And may the Lord make you increase and abound in love to one another and to all, just as we do to you, so that He may establish your hearts blameless in holiness before our God and Father at the coming of our Lord Jesus Christ with all His saints (1 Thess. 3:10–13).

He wanted to see their faith perfected, their love increased, and their walk characterized by holiness as they awaited the return of Christ. It was therefore to this end that he prayed.

Once more, Paul's personal knowledge and involvement with them helped him pray specifically for their needs. With the ultimate goal of maturity in mind, his prayers undoubtedly progressed as the Thessalonians progressed. His parental concern manifested itself as he repeatedly brought them before the throne of grace. Those prayers were an essential part of his follow-up.

GUIDELINE #4 – TIME AND HARD WORK ARE UNAVOIDABLE

In Paul's approach to helping new believers grow, two things stand out like a neon light on a dark night. It takes a great deal of time and a great deal of hard work. The work was alluded to in Colossians 1:29 and referred to earlier, as Paul testified, "To this end I also labor, striving according to His working which works in me mightily." The "labor," which can depict work done to the point of exhaustion, reflects the fact that as enjoyable as it is to see new believers grow, it requires patient, hard work.

So much time was required that each missionary journey Paul took increased at least one year in length due to visits he made to places where he had previously ministered. In nine of the places he ministered, he returned to visit the people and confirm the churches.

In light of the time and hard work required, Paul could not do it all himself. For that reason, in the book of Acts and in Paul's writings, some one hundred names are associated with the apostle. Eliminating those with general or no designation or those who appear only in Acts, there remain thirty-six names associated with Paul under nine designations.[3] Many of these associates appear to have served with him in missions of following up new believers, just as Timothy did with the Thessalonians.

In a similar way, follow-up is a responsibility of the body of Christ today. No verse in Scripture commands that the one who leads a person to Christ has to be the one involved in his growth, but he should have a concern for the growth of the new believer. Others in the body need to assist in follow-up, even as Paul had others assisting him. Just as evangelism is not a one-man job, neither is following up new converts. When numerous ones come to Christ at one time, numerous believers are going to be needed in following up with them.

CONCLUSION

Each new believer needs to be given parental attention to grow in maturity. We need to do whatever must be done to assist. Prayer for them must be considered an essential ingredient of follow-up. When examined in this way, the work and time needed to follow up each new believer become most obvious.

One would do well to ask, "Is the time and hard work involved worth the effort?" Why not ask Paul, the one whose energy and time were so unselfishly expended? He made his answer to that question quite clear in 1 Thessalonians 2:19–20: "For what is our hope, or joy, or crown of rejoicing? Is it not even you in the presence of our Lord Jesus Christ at His coming? For you are our glory and joy." Paul's point is simple and striking. When his new converts stood before the Lord *they* would be his reason for rejoicing.

Not everyone in whose life Paul had an influence remained a radiant example of Christlikeness. For instance, Paul eventually had to say concerning his good friend Demas, "Demas has forsaken me, having loved this present world" (2 Tim. 4:10). Still, the time spent seeing new converts come to Christ and grow in His grace would be worthwhile.

So What?

W hy do we so often hesitate to get involved in the lives of new believers and give them the assistance they need? Two reasons stand out.

Patience, or rather the lack of it, is one problem. Most of us will admit that we find it easy to identify with the one who prayed, "God, give me patience and give it to me now." Our impatience is often transferred to new converts. Our attitude appears to be, "God, give me a mature convert and give him to me now." If new converts have not completed the study we asked them to do or make excuses for putting something material before something spiritual, we become frustrated. We respond with reactions such as, "If they were serious, they wouldn't let that interfere."

It would help us to remember the patience (or impatience) others exercised toward us when we first came to know the Lord. We ought to endeavor to be like those who were patient with us when we faltered and unlike those who were impatient toward us. I have had many Christians, as they reflected upon the months and years immediately after they trusted Christ and the patience a brother or sister in Christ demonstrated, say, "I'm glad [so-and-so] stuck with me. I'm sure there were days he or she felt like giving up." And, in addition to all that, if God exercises such a patient attitude toward us, surely we can be more patient toward new converts.

A second problem aside from impatience may actually be the main one. It is no secret to anyone that our age has become very materialistic and selfish. We live for things, not people, and the "what's in it for me" philosophy has crept into our churches. Following up new converts is therefore far from appealing to us. It may demand losing sleep, giving up a Sunday afternoon football game, spending time with a new believer that we would rather spend on the golf course, sacrificing money and time that could have been spent at the mall, or simply draining our physical and emotional resources. It may even mean taking the risk of lowering our image when our neighbors see the kind of "riffraff" they feel we would be better off to leave alone. Therefore, we simply would prefer to give new Christians the name and address of a church they might find helpful and hope they attend. Such an attitude and approach dishonors God and gives little or no hope to those attempting to adjust to their new life in Christ.

We need a return to the cross! If Christ died for people, why should we live for things? Besides, what would be more heartwarming to us and honoring to God than to one day point to new converts—whom

God used us to help bring to maturity—and be able to say, as Paul did of the Thessalonians, "For what is our hope, or joy, or crown of rejoicing? Is it not even you in the presence of our Lord Jesus Christ at His coming? For you are our glory and joy" (1 Thess. 2:19–20). Possessions pass but people are permanent. Which one ought to have our priority?

When we realize how personal Paul's approach to following up new believers was, the questions What do we do with new converts? and What do we study? are answered. It depends largely on their background and situation. I once led a sportscaster to Christ who immediately wanted to study Proverbs. Having glanced at that book once, he was amazed at how much it had to say about friends, finances, family life, speech, desires, wisdom, age, and so on. So we took off through Proverbs. Along with that, someone had given him a copy of C. S. Lewis's books and he became ecstatic. He is a philosophical thinker much as Lewis was. So Proverbs and some reading of C. S. Lewis's works on the side were a big help in getting him started. The point is—we must start where people are.

One thing we have learned through our evangelistic outreaches is that the best follow-up occurs when someone meets with the new convert once a week for a period of at least eight weeks. It is the contact more than the materials that makes the difference. A person who has served as a church leader and was saved years ago through our ministry once told me, "To this day I don't know what the fellow who discipled me taught me. I just know that he was at my apartment once a week for eight weeks. That really made the difference." Again, it is the contact, not the materials, that is most needed. As we meet with new believers in that context, we can determine what series of studies may be best for them.

For their personal devotional study, I usually recommend that new believers start with Philippians and read a chapter a day. Philippians is one of the easiest books for new converts to digest. It also talks about practical matters we all face in daily Christian living. Since it has only four chapters, a new believer can read it in four days. I then recommend reading it again and again—one chapter a day for a month. I alert new Christians that they will find truth going through the book the second time that they overlooked the first time. Once they have studied that book for a month, they will not only remember what they have read, but as life and events unfold, they will have occasion to reflect on what they learned and apply it to their situations.

Sometimes individuals ask, "What if new believers will not discipline themselves to study and you feel as though you are spinning your wheels?" Follow-up is obviously a two-way street. It is helpful to look at what you are doing to be certain you are not coming across in a way the new believer finds discouraging. Neither should you place too many demands too soon. At the same time, if you have done all you can and he or she continually refuses to participate, you have given it your best. You may have to discontinue meeting regularly. Be careful, however, not to write the person off! Pray fervently, asking God to show him or her the need to "grow in the grace and knowledge of our Lord and Savior Jesus Christ" (2 Pet. 3:18). God can get through where we cannot. More than one convert has testified, "I didn't see then as I do now the need to grow." Even as I write this chapter, a woman I met during one of our outreaches told me, "I wish I had the hunger for the Word ten years ago that I do now. It would have made a big difference in our family." Also, be careful not to let a bad experience with one new convert determine your opinion toward all new converts. He or she is only one person. The next new believer may be so hungry and excited to learn, that instead of leading, you may be led.

Follow-up has at least one thing in common with evangelism—it is people-oriented. A new believer is a member of the same eternal family you are. Starting where he is, you do everything you can to take him, by God's grace, where he needs to be. The expenditure of time and energy may be tremendous, but so will the eternal reward.

Group Discussion Questions

- What activities or concerns have distracted you from assisting new converts?

- Reflecting upon your life after your conversion, what has been of most help to your spiritual growth? How was it helpful? How could you have used more assistance?

- What is the difference between a person-centered approach to follow-up and a materials-centered approach? Be specific.

- Are there individuals now who will be your "hope, joy, or crown of rejoicing" (1 Thess. 2:19) when you stand before the Lord? What tangible steps can you take to begin making a meaningful impact upon a new believer's spiritual growth?

Chapter Eighteen

Do I Have To?

The greatest use of life is to spend it for something that will outlast it.
—Unknown

Some feel that the question, Does a believer in Jesus Christ have to tell others about Him? is a foolish question to ask. After all, if the heart of God yearns for the lost to be saved, then how can we *not* be concerned enough to talk to the lost?

The question of a believer's responsibility to evangelize is not a foolish one. For example, if a church decides to have a door-to-door visitation program in preparing for vacation Bible school, is a believer out of the will of God if he does not volunteer to knock on doors? When a man is going through a difficult struggle and does not seem to understand that his first and foremost need is for a relationship with Jesus Christ, should a Christian coworker who knows of his need feel guilty for not talking to him about Christ? If a believer does not always have an evangelistic tract available to give a lost person, is she neglecting to do what God wants her to do? Are pastors and church leaders the only ones who are directly commanded to evangelize, or is that something everyone in the church is supposed to do? Is there a text in Scripture that, when properly interpreted, specifically commands every believer to evangelize?

Many more such questions arise when the question is asked, Does a believer in Jesus Christ have to tell others about Him?

Perhaps we are starting at the wrong point. In considering the responsibility believers have in evangelism, we ought first to ask, "Is evangelism *commanded* of all believers? Could it be that God approaches the subject in a different way than we are accustomed to?" Once we are sure how Scripture approaches the believer's responsibility, we should have the answers to the other questions asked above.

When we study the Scriptures carefully, three observations can be made about a Christian's responsibility. These provide a clear answer to the question, Do I have to?

CHRIST DESIRES BELIEVERS TO
ENTER INTO DISCIPLESHIP AND CONTINUE IN IT

Trusting Christ is the starting point, not the stopping point. The moment we trust Christ, our eternal life is secure. Christ promised, "He who believes in Me has everlasting life" (John 6:47). Once we are God's children, it is His desire that we become His disciples. The Greek word translated "disciple," *mathētēs,* means one who learns from a master—one who is a pupil. Having come to God in faith, we are to continue learning from Him.

There were those who trusted Christ and continued learning from Him. This explains how Christians obtained their name. Acts 11:25–26 says, "Then Barnabas departed for Tarsus to seek Saul. And when he had found him he brought him to Antioch. So it was that for a whole year they assembled with the church and taught a great many people. And the disciples were first called Christians at Antioch." Since the work outgrew Barnabas's ability to handle it, he searched out Saul (later called Paul, cf. Acts 13:9), brought him to Antioch, and for an entire year they taught the people together. When one member of the populace would ask another, "Who are these people [referring to the believers]?" the answer was apparently, "These are the Christ-people, the Christians." They were referred to by the name of the One whose name was constantly on their lips.

Consider discipleship and examine what is commonly and properly referred to as the Great Commission as it is recorded in Matthew 28:19–20. As His disciples were gathered on a mountain with Him, Jesus admonished them:

> Go therefore and make disciples of all the nations, baptizing them in the name of the Father and of the Son and of the Holy Spirit, teaching them to observe all things that I have commanded you; and lo, I am with you always, even to the end of the age.

A careful study of these two verses in the original language reveals that they contain three participles and one command. The three participles are "going," "baptizing," and "teaching." The command is to "make disciples." Simply put, Jesus was commanding, "Take those who are My children and make them My disciples—those who are My pupils."

What were they to teach these pupils? He continued, "Teaching them to observe all things that I have commanded you." If we now ask what He had commanded them, the picture begins to unfold.

THE FIRST THING CHRIST TAUGHT
HIS DISCIPLES WAS EVANGELISM

When we examine the first thing Christ stressed to the first disciples He called, we discover something both thought-provoking and life-changing. We read:

> Now Jesus, walking by the Sea of Galilee, saw two brothers, Simon called Peter, and Andrew his brother, casting a net into the sea; for they were fishermen. And He said to them, "Follow Me, and I will make you fishers of men." Then they immediately left their nets and followed Him. And going on from there, He saw two other brothers, James the son of Zebedee, and John his brother, in the boat with Zebedee their father, mending their nets. And He called them, and immediately they left the boat and their father, and followed Him (Matt. 4:18–22).

Why did He desire that they follow Him? Was it so they might greatly increase in their knowledge of the Scriptures? Was it so that through Him they could one day become leaders in a local church? Was His purpose that they might learn how to be good husbands and fathers?

As desirable and commendable as all of these are, He had something else in mind. He said, "Follow Me, and I will make you *fishers of men.*"

The disciples must have recognized the eternal perspective He was giving to their lives. As fishers of fish, they were accustomed to taking something alive and making it dead. But as fishers of men, they could take something spiritually dead and, through God's Spirit, see it come alive. They could give their lives to something that would outlast them.

The disciples also knew that Christ did not expect them to be expert evangelists already. His emphasis was that He would *make* them fishers of men as they learned from Him. In fact, as we discover in Luke 5:1–11, the first thing He taught them in evangelism was obedience.

As Christ stood by the Sea of Galilee, He saw two empty boats. The fishermen were washing their nets. After a night's fishing, a fisherman always had two jobs—to clean the nets because they had become filled with pebbles during the night, and to mend the nets because they had been broken by the waves. Since these men had already accepted Christ's call to be disciples, obtaining the use of their boat was not a problem. The first one Jesus addressed was Simon because he was the owner of the craft and apparently the leader of that little fishing company. He instructed him, "Launch out into the deep and let down your nets for a catch" (v. 4). They were probably surprised that Jesus said, "Launch out into the deep," for if a night's fishing—when the fish come to the surface to feed—had not produced anything, how could they catch anything during the day? Peter's response was therefore most significant. "Master, we have toiled all night and caught nothing; nevertheless at Your word I will let down the net" (v. 5). Even though the whole night had been fruitless, he was resolved he would do what the Master said. The result was a net-breaking, boat-sinking load that left them astonished. Christ now drove home His object lesson—"From now on you will catch men" (v. 10). Using a basic principle in catching fish that become dead, He taught them a basic principle in catching men who become alive in Christ: What I need most from you in evangelism is obedience!

The message is unmistakable. If we consider ourselves His disciples—yes, we must evangelize. *Evangelism is at the heart of discipleship.* Robert Coleman writes, "Practically everything that Jesus said and did had some relevance to their work of evangelism, either by explaining a spiritual truth or revealing to them how they should deal with men."[1] Although there were many things pressing upon them as His disciples, nothing was more pressing than the need to evangelize.

Evangelism and discipleship are absolutely inseparable. One cannot be a committed disciple of Jesus Christ and not be involved in one way or another in reaching the lost. That involvement may not take the same form in each case. One person may enjoy assisting in the office of an evangelistic association because of his or her burden for the lost, while another might enjoy going door-to-door in his or her neighborhood on behalf of a visitation program of his church. One may enjoy evangelizing through the distribution of evangelistic literature while another enjoys sponsoring an evangelistic Bible study at home. An elderly widow may be involved by fervently praying for missionaries at home and abroad as they seek to evangelize. But anyone who does not look at life on earth as having the goal of influencing the lost for Christ has missed the essence of discipleship. Christ wants followers because He needs those who will fish for men. The lost were at the heart of His mission (Mark 10:45) and they are at the heart of discipleship.

When one asks, "Is every believer commanded to evangelize?" that question must be answered with another. "Do you wish to be a disciple of Jesus Christ?" If the answer is yes, understand that discipleship and evangelism go hand in hand.

Recognizing that evangelism is at the heart of discipleship, we may make a third observation that will encourage us as we follow Christ as His learners.

DISCIPLESHIP PRESENTS BOTH
OPPORTUNITY AND BALANCE IN EVANGELISM

It Presents Opportunity

A disciple is Christ's pupil. As he learns from Him, his life increasingly becomes Christlike. Something about our lives becomes most attractive to the ones outside of Christ.

In Acts 2, the conversion of approximately three thousand people occurred. We are told what then happened in the believing community.

> They continued steadfastly in the apostles' doctrine and fellowship, in the breaking of bread, and in prayers. Then fear came upon every soul, and many wonders and signs were done through the apostles. Now all who believed were together, and had all things in common, and sold their possessions and goods, and divided them among all, as anyone had need. So continuing daily with one accord in the temple, and breaking bread from house to house, they ate their food with gladness and simplicity of heart (vv. 42–46).

So close was the fellowship of these believers and so unified were they in the Messiah that they had all things in common. Each one began selling his assets, and the profits were divided among the members of the believing community, according to their individual needs.[2] What is so striking is what happened among the non-Christians as a result. The next verse explains that the believers were "praising God and having favor with all the people. And the Lord added to the church daily those who were being saved." Commending themselves to the unbelievers through their joyful and generous spirit, they enjoyed the goodwill of the non-Christians, many of whom listened to their message and became believers.

Does the Bible admonish us to this kind of living specifically with the non-Christian in mind? Very definitely. As Paul wrote to a church very close to his heart, he addressed a unity that promoted the Gospel, when he commanded, "Do all things without murmuring and disputing" (Phil. 2:14). "Murmuring and disputing" portrays someone who enjoys spending time in front of a complaint counter. Even when it comes to complaints about brothers and sisters in the body of Christ, instead of following the instruction of Matthew 18:15 to first approach the person who has sinned against him, a complainer would probably prefer to tell the whole church first. Needless to say, such behavior can be chaotic in its effect upon the unity of a church. Why was Paul concerned that such behavior be foreign to the lives of believers? He continued, "That you may become blameless and harmless, children of God without fault in the midst of a crooked and perverse generation, among whom you shine as lights in the world" (Phil. 2:15).

Paul's point was that people are watching us—people who are part of a crooked and perverse generation. Before them we shine as "lights in the world." The word *light* refers to heavenly bodies that light up the universe. Paul was explaining that what stars are to the universe, we are in the midst of the non-Christians—lights in the midst of darkness. The way we provide the light they need is explained in the next verses: by "holding fast the word of life." The participle translated "holding fast" could also be translated "holding forth" to bring out the idea Paul has in mind through his previous analogy of "lights in the world." As the sun gives forth light, we are to hold forth the Gospel for all to see and hear. With such an opportunity before us, it is important that we be blameless and harmless. "Blameless" means that we ought to be without fault before the unbelievers. There should be a holiness about our lives. "Harmless," as noted earlier, conveys the idea of innocence, harmlessness, or sincerity. Paul's admonition is that whether it be in conduct or motive, we ought to have a faultlessness and sincerity about our lives. When we loosen our tongues and fall into murmurings and disputings, we discredit our testimony and lose our influence with the non-Christian. However, if a unity free of such sin is seen, the unbeliever has no grounds for criticism and can be influenced for Christ. Christlikeness enhances effective evangelism!

Another passage deserving consideration is Peter's advice to women who have non-Christian husbands. He told them:

> Likewise you wives, be submissive to your own husbands, that even if some do not obey the word, they, without a word, may be won by the conduct of their wives, when they observe your chaste conduct accompanied by fear (1 Pet. 3:1–2).

Notice Peter's wording—"that even if some do not obey *the* word, they, without *a* word, may be won by the conduct of their wives." "*The* word" refers to Scripture. "Without *a* word" refers to the conversation of the wife. Peter pictured a man who, whether lacking understanding of the Gospel or refusing to deal with spiritual truth, was without Christ. Such a person may not listen to his wife, yet he has to see her conduct. Her conduct, therefore, ought to be as Peter described: "chaste"—meaning without fault—and accompanied by "fear," or due respect. Her submissiveness to him and honoring him as her husband may be used by the Lord to attract him to the Savior. Peter was certainly not saying that a Christian wife dare not make mistakes. Husbands and wives both do. Nor was he saying that she can never again speak to her husband about his need of the Savior. As the husband demonstrated a receptivity, she could indeed do so. He was simply challenging wives with unbelieving husbands to make Jesus Christ attractive to them by their own lives and obedience.

Instead of being "turned off" by hypocrites, the non-Christian will be "turned on" to someone whose life and conduct demonstrate that he has something to offer them. Biblically and practically, disciples whose lives exhibit a genuine holiness have some of the most prime opportunities to speak to others of the Savior.

It Presents Balance

One who as a disciple is continually learning from Christ will also increasingly develop a biblical philosophy in confronting lost people.

Often someone will contend that we have no right to talk to a person about Christ unless we have known him or her over a period of time and have won the right to be heard. Still another will insist that if we take seriously the need for others to know the Savior and the heaven-or-hell destiny that awaits each person, we should seize every opportunity we have to talk to them about the Lord. Another will contend that the issue is not how well we know the non-Christian, but how much he or she respects the Bible. Such a person would suggest that with a college crowd, for instance, one should not begin by telling of Christ's death and resurrection until determining whether they believe the Scriptures are the Word of God. Others respond, "Why defend Christ? After all, can't the Holy Spirit do His own work of convicting the lost as we are faithful in proclaiming the message?"

What does Scripture advise? The answer is simpler than we may realize. A disciple is a learner. As he learns evangelism from the One who is a fisher of men, he recognizes that some are ripe and ready for the Gospel upon their first encounter. Christ's experience in Samaria is a good example. He was there only two days (John 4:40) and did no miracles—the very thing designed to prove He was God (John 20:30–31). Yet He told His disciples, "Do you not say, 'There are still four months and then comes the harvest'? Behold, I say to you, lift up your eyes and look at the fields, for they are already white for harvest!" (John 4:35). Christ's first contact with the Samaritans led to many conversions.

A growing disciple also recognizes that some are not as prepared for what we would like to present to them. It may take a bit of time in which we "walk in wisdom toward those who are outside, redeeming the time" before we will have a chance to talk to them as we might desire (Col. 4:5). J. I. Packer, in his book *Evangelism and the Sovereignty of God*, sets forth the God-honoring balance in this area:

> You are not usually justified in choosing the subject of conversation with another till you have already begun to give yourself to him in friendship and established a relationship with him in which he feels that you respect him, and are interested in him, and are treating him as a human being, and not just as some kind of "case." With some people, you may establish such a relationship in five minutes, whereas with others it may take months.[3]

A mature Christian recognizes that at times we must be patient and pray for an open door for the Gospel (Col. 4:3). He or she also recognizes the scriptural exhortation concerning the brevity of life and how quickly it could end (James 4:14). Therefore, as they pray for that open door, there is a certain amount of urgency behind their prayers.

Another thing a spiritually growing disciple recognizes is the need to start where the non-Christian is. Of a woman who came to a well to draw water, Jesus asked for a drink, using that as a bridge to talking to her of Living Water (John 4:7–14). However, to Nicodemus, a religious man, Jesus said, "Unless one is born again, he cannot see the kingdom of God" (John 3:3). Since Nicodemus was a Pharisee, it was appropriate to bring up the subject of how one enters the kingdom of God immediately. A disciple desiring to reach others recognizes that at times he may have to reason from creation to the Creator to Christ (Acts 17:22–34). Other individuals need simply to be confronted with the declaration of Christ's death and resurrection (1 Cor. 2:1–2). Billy Graham cited this need when he once said, "The gospel is not a set of ideas to be discussed; it is a declaration. What the gospel needs, the early church concurred, was not a philosopher, but a witness—not a lawyer but a herald."[4] At all times, we must bear in mind that, ultimately, it is not the logic of an argument or the power of persuasion that brings people to the Lord. It is God who brings people to Himself (John 6:44).

CONCLUSION

The question, Is every believer commanded to evangelize? raises a far deeper issue. Evangelism is set in the context of discipleship. Once we receive Christ's invitation to life eternal through trust in Him, Christ invites us to be His disciples. The first thing He stressed to His disciples was evangelism. If we are going to follow Christ, we must evangelize.

As we learn from Him, we are presented with both opportunity and balance. Attractive lives provide appealing opportunities. Learning from One who was characterized by "grace and truth" (John 1:14) also shows us the why and how of approaching lost people.

Christ's desire is to make us "fishers of men." If we do the learning, He will do the teaching.

So What?

An understanding of the Scriptures concerning the responsibility of believers in evangelism affects the way we go about it. There are those who feel God has given a dictatorial command to every believer to evangelize and you had better do it or else! Usually those individuals approach everything in the Christian life with this oppressive perspective.

Then there are those who recognize that once we have trusted Christ, Christ challenges us to be His disciples. Accepting that invitation means that one understands that there is something eternal to live for—the salvation of the lost. I once read, "The only man worth envying is the one who has found a cause bigger than himself."[5] That is a good description of a disciple: a person who has found a cause bigger than him- or herself—assisting Christ in populating heaven. Just as others had an impact in bringing us to the Savior, what becomes exciting about His invitation to discipleship is that we can now have an impact on others. When I have spoken to believers with this outlook, their whole approach to their responsibility in evangelism is positive. They see it as a choice, not a chore. Although they often have the same fears everyone else does in evangelizing, they are confident the Lord can help them. When they "blow it" in terms of their witness, they do not feel that He regards them as disobedient or failures, but rather like those of the original twelve—ones who are still learning. With each new person to whom they give the Gospel, they realize they are one person wiser in how to evangelize.

They are overwhelmed with evangelism—for the life of them, they cannot (and have not) gotten over the fact that they can have a part in touching others for eternity. Because God could have chosen any way He wanted to get the Word out—putting it on billboards or sending angels to spread it—they are pleased that He let them do it. They would agree with Dr. R. A. Torrey, who reportedly called the winning of souls "the most worthwhile thing in life." Pastors in various parts of the world have mentioned different ones in their congregations and said to me, "I need to introduce you to him. He's really interested in evangelism." Whether a plumber or a preacher, a mechanic or a merchant, a secretary or a store clerk, these people are driven by one desire—to make an impact for Christ.

A veterinarian told me, "The veterinarian business is simply how I put food on the table. My practice exists to be a witness for Christ." Even when he took time off to enjoy his favorite sport of tennis, he first and foremost sought opportunities to play with non-Christians whom he could impact for Christ. Because of his eternal perspective on life and his desire to be a follower of Christ, evangelism was not a pain but a pleasure. He found himself welcoming Christ's invitation, "Follow Me, and I will make you fishers of men" (Matt. 4:19).

Such people are often regarded as strange by other Christians. One couple I know is approaching retirement. They are completely sold on the essence of discipleship, so they plan to sell their house, live off the proceeds, and make themselves available as camp personnel. They want to have an impact on the world for Christ and are convinced that camp ministry is one way to do that. When they shared their vision with another couple in their church, they met the response, "Good to hear of your plans, but aren't you wasting your retirement years?" The truth is, those with whom they shared their plans were actually the ones wasting their years—investing everything in sixty to eighty years on earth instead of in eternity. As my friends remarked to me, "They don't know what they're missing. They've missed out on the purpose of living."

We now understand why, biblically, if one is a church leader one must be involved in some way in evangelism. The Great Commission is, "Make disciples . . . teaching them to observe all things that I have commanded you" (Matt. 28:19–20). Church leaders are those who, as Christ's disciples, have given themselves to discipling others. Since the first thing Jesus taught His disciples was evangelism, they too must evangelize and see that others are taught to do the same. Furthermore, who are the leaders of the church? They are the ones who are noted for their Christian growth (1 Tim. 3:6), solid testimony (1 Tim. 3:7), blameless character (Titus 1:6–8), and knowledge of the Scriptures (Titus 1:9). Simply put, they of all people should understand both Christ's mission and theirs. If the church leaders are not in some way involved in evangelism, they have reason to question if they ought to be in a leadership position in the church. How committed are they to discipleship and the first thing Christ taught His disciples?

Paul told Timothy as a gifted pastor-teacher, "Do the work of an evangelist" (2 Tim. 4:5). That command would directly apply to church leaders today. Why was Timothy to evangelize? That paragraph does not tell us. It does not need to. Matthew 4:19 and 28:19–20 already have. A pastor or teacher is one who has accepted Christ's call to be a disciple who, in turn, disciples others. Again, the first thing He taught His disciples was evangelism. The winning of the lost must be foremost in leaders' minds. Everything done in and through their church is to be done with the ultimate goal that the community will be touched for Christ.

What we have learned about a disciple's walk as he or she learns how to live—and how it affects the impact he or she has on others—could constitute a book in itself. I led a man to Christ who told me a sad story with a happy ending. "For years," he said, "I'd been thinking about Christ. But every fellow businessman I met who was a Christian didn't live like it. In fact, I can honestly say that I was more ethical in my business dealings than they were. I said to myself, 'Why become a Christian if you already live better than they do?' Then I met some men who attend the church where you are speaking. I couldn't get over them. They not only freely talked about Christ but also actually lived the life. I was determined they were fakes and tried my best to find something to prove they were as deceitful and underhanded as the rest. I couldn't find a thing. Did that ever have an impact on me! So when they invited me to come hear you speak, I accepted. I felt that if they appreciated you, you must be all right. Am I ever glad I did." To that example could be added many more. It is difficult to argue against the testimony of an attractive life.

Disciples learning from Christ and growing to maturity increase both in their sensitivity to the Holy Spirit and also to the lost. In each situation, they attempt to sense where the individual is spiritually and what the proper approach to take would be. How many times have you heard someone say of another believer, "He is much more tempered in his approach than he used to be. He used to come on too strong and turn a lot of people off"? New converts may often evangelize without a great deal of sensitivity—though with commendable enthusiasm—simply because they are not yet mature; but as they grow spiritually, they learn to be more sensitive.

On the one hand, we can take on our shoulders the responsibility that belongs to the Holy Spirit and attempt to "rush" someone into a decision to trust Christ. That person may not be spiritually prepared to trust Christ. On the other hand, we can fail to realize how ripe someone is for the Gospel. Two situations I have reflected on while writing this chapter are prime examples of how we can meet people in both realms.

My wife and I once decided to invite our new neighbors over for dinner with the goal of talking to them about the Lord. As the evening and conversation progressed, it was easy to sense the husband's tremendous apprehension that I might ask him questions concerning his spiritual condition. Sensing that that night was not the time, I simply used the evening to cement our friendship. My wife and I later found out that as they walked home that night, the man said to his wife, "I can't believe Larry did not hit me with the Gospel. I was so scared he would." Since then, having won that respect and friendship, I have had the opportunity on three occasions to clearly present the Gospel and invite him to trust Christ. Although he has yet to do so, he has talked, listened, and interacted about his need.

In contrast, while returning from a speaking engagement, I took a seat on the plane alongside a high school student. He told me, "Today I had a rude awakening. My parents are divorced and I'm staying with my aunt. This morning she walked into my bedroom and said, 'It's time somebody else keeps you for a while. We're flying you to Texas for the summer.'" Frustrated, he added, "So here I am headed for Texas." As we talked, he asked, "By the way, what do you do?" "I'm a minister," I answered. "I'm just returning from a speaking engagement." When I noted his interest, I asked, "Are you interested in spiritual things?" He immediately explained that he had just begun to think about the Lord because of some Christian classmates who were zealous in talking to him about Christ. So I asked, "Well, has anybody ever taken a Bible and shown you how you can know that you're going to heaven?" When he answered, "No," I asked, "May I?" "Would you?" was his eager response. When the Good News was explained, there seated in a plane thousands of feet above sea level, the teenager trusted Christ as his Savior. I had the privilege of reaping where others had sown. Just thirty minutes earlier he had been a total stranger to me.

The answer to knowing how to handle these varied situations is to be a growing disciple. Through a study of the Word we gain a maturity that helps us handle what is a spiritual work—evangelizing the lost. I wish I could tell you that I have always had that sensitivity. I cannot because I have not. But thanks to the grace of God and his patience with me, my sensitivity is increasing.

After I became a Christian, I wanted to tell others what I now knew—salvation is a free gift. Because of being spiritually only a few months old, the way I handled some of those situations left a lot to be desired. Although I would not apologize for doing what I could to reach the lost, I thank God for showing me through concerned friends my need to grow. I would testify firsthand that as I have grown, not only has my burden for the lost increased, but the balance between tact, boldness, confrontation, sensitivity, and all the matters related to our conversation and conduct with the lost has become more obvious. I must give Him the credit, not myself.

As I have spoken in evangelistic outreaches to the lost and in seminars to train believers how to evangelize, many times I've been asked, "How can I know what to say if . . ." People then explain particular situations they have either faced or contemplate facing. I am more convinced than ever of the answer I have given hundreds—there are some things that can be learned, and there are other things that only God through His

Holy Spirit can teach us as we begin interacting with the unbelievers. Nothing can substitute for a close walk and growing relationship with Him. If we will only live for Him as His disciples, seeking to reach the lost and learning from Him how to do it, we will make an impact on non-Christians. He is ready to use us if we are willing to be used.

When we consider the question, Do I have to? and understand how Scripture approaches evangelism and sets it in the context of discipleship, we ought to respond: "In comparison, what could be more satisfying, rewarding, or permanent?" If a contractor lays a sidewalk, someone can tear it up. If a carpenter builds a house, someone can tear it down. But if as Christ's disciple in the midst of those activities, a carpenter or contractor leads a person to Christ, nobody can undo that. Therefore, to give ourselves to evangelism is the most worthwhile and eternal cause in life. As every believer comes to understand evangelism and discipleship from a biblical perspective, he or she can approach acquaintances with a gratitude that says, "Guess who I am privileged to represent—just wait 'til I tell you what He's asked me to explain!" Others will get the distinct impression that we are on a mission—a mission that preoccupies our mind, affects our priorities, and alters our schedules. It is a mission to tell everyone the Good News that is so exciting *and* so FREE and CLEAR.

Group Discussion Questions

- Thoughts about evangelizing are often more negative than positive. How will a proper understanding of discipleship affect *your* positive attitude toward evangelism?

- How does understanding that Christ wants to *make* us fishers of men and does not expect us to know everything there is to know about evangelism affect our attitude toward presenting the Gospel? Are there times you needlessly criticized yourself for what you felt was a poor job in evangelism instead of simply learning from the experience? Where, when, and how?

- Why does Christ need disciples in every profession who are committed to evangelism?

- Think of your contacts you have through your work. In what specific ways will a commitment to evangelism cause that job to take on an eternal perspective?

Chapter Notes

Chapter 1

1. C. H. Spurgeon, *Lectures to My Students*, 3 vols. in 1 (reprint, Grand Rapids: Associated Publishers & Authors, 1971), 2:28.
2. Gerhard Friedrich, *"euangelion,"* in *Theological Dictionary of the New Testament*, ed. Gerhard Kittel, 10 vols. (Grand Rapids: Eerdmans, 1964), 2:722.
3. Ibid., 724.
4. Greek translators of the Old Testament even used forms of *euangelion* to speak of announcing the Lord's universal victory over the world and His rule as a king (Ps. 40:9; 68:11; 96:2; Isa. 52:7). For further study see Ulrich Becker, "Gospel," in *The New International Dictionary of New Testament Theology*, ed. Colin Brown, 3 vols. (Grand Rapids: Zondervan Publishing House, 1976), 2:109.
5. See also Romans 1:16; 10:15; 1 Corinthians 9:12, 18; 2 Corinthians 2:12; 4:4; 10:14; 11:7; Galatians 1:6-7; Ephesians 6:15; Philippians 1:27; 1 Thessalonians 2:2, 8-9; 3:2; 2 Thessalonians 1:8; 1 Timothy 1:11; 1 Peter 4:17; Revelation 14:6.
6. In Galatians 2:7 Paul said, "The gospel for the uncircumcised had been committed to me, as the gospel for the circumcised was to Peter." He was not referring to two different gospels. He was saying, "I had a ministry to the Gentiles as Peter did to the Jews." As Peter made clear, "We believe that through the grace of the Lord Jesus Christ we [Jews] shall be saved in the same manner as they [Gentiles]" (Acts 15:11). The New Testament has several different ways of describing this aspect of the Gospel. Romans 1:1 calls it "gospel of God" because He initiated it. Romans 10:15 calls it the "gospel of peace" because it concerns how people, although they are sinners who have rebelled against God, can be at peace with Him. Still another verse, 2 Corinthians 10:14, refers to it as the "gospel of Christ" because His atoning work makes the proclamation of this good news possible. All of these are ways of referring to the Gospel that manifests the grace of God (Acts 20:24).
7. Philip Yancey, "Whiteout on Mt. Ranier," *Reader's Digest*, January 1976, 106-10.

Chapter 2

1. *Dallas Morning News*, August 20, 1987, p. 4A.
2. Quell notes this when he says, "This limited aspect of the usage of [*hatta't*] is fundamental to our understanding of the religious meaning of the term, and in essence of the whole thought of sin in the OT." Gottfried Quell, "Sin in the OT," *Theological Dictionary of the New Testament*, ed. Gerhard Kittel, 10 vols. (Grand Rapids: Eerdmans, 1964), 1:273.
3. B. F. Westcott in his commentary on the gospel of John makes this helpful observation: "The idea of 'conviction' is complex. It involves the conceptions of authoritative examination, unquestionable proof, of decisive judgment, of

punitive power. Whatever the final issue may be, he who 'convicts' another places the truth of the case in dispute in a clear light before him, so that it must be seen and acknowledged as truth. He who then rejects the conclusion which this exposition involves, rejects it with his eyes open and at his peril." B. F. Westcott, *The Gospel According to St. John* (Grand Rapids: Eerdmans, 1973), 228.

4. *Time*, February 22, 1971, 23.
5. *Time*, July 25, 1977, 18.

Chapter 3

1. Alva J. McClain, "Christian Faith—Its Nature, Object, and Intellectual Medium," *Bibliotheca Sacra* 90 (April-June 1933): 152.
2. The one verse in the Bible that uses the term "receive" immediately explains that the issue is trusting Christ. John 1:12 begins, "But as many as received Him," and continues, "to them He gave the right to become children of God, even to those who *believe* in His name."
3. Revelation 3:20 is sometimes used to support this wording. Jesus said, "Behold, I stand at the door and knock. If anyone hears My voice and opens the door, I will come in to him and dine with him, and he with Me." The preceding verse says, "As many as I love, I rebuke and chasten." The word "chasten" means "to child-train" and is used throughout the New Testament of believers, not unbelievers. Therefore, it becomes clear that Revelation 3:20 is addressed to Christians concerning their fellowship with the Lord, not to the non-Christians concerning their salvation. The passage as a whole addresses a church: "And to the angel of the church of the Laodiceans write" (v. 14). Although the church may have had non-Christians in it, there is no reason to project unbelievers into the passage. Frankly, in light of the persecution a person encountered once he assembled with believers, it is more probable to have non-Christians in today's church than in the church of the New Testament day. We ought not read this passage, though, through modern-day spectacles.

Chapter 4

1. Velma Barfield, *Woman on Death Row* (Minneapolis: World Wide Publications, n.d.), 93-97.
2. Larry Moyer, *How to Tell the Bad News/Good News*, reprinted with permission of EvanTell, Inc., and the author. Copyright 1987 by EvanTell, Inc. This Bad-News/Good-News approach is also available through EvanTell in a tract designed for non-Christians entitled "May I Ask You a Question?"

Chapter 5

1. "These things I have written to you" in 1 John 5:13 is not a reference to the entire epistle. John has made it clear in the opening remarks of his epistle that he is writing to speak about fellowship with the Lord. In 1 John 1:3-4 he says, "That which we have seen and heard we declare to you, that you also may have fellowship with us; and truly our fellowship is with the Father and with His Son Jesus Christ. And these things we write to you that your joy may be full." In 2:1 and 2:26, "these things" clearly refers to the immediately preceding context. Likewise, "these things" of 5:13 refers to the immediate context, where we are simply told, "And this is the testimony: that God has given us eternal life, and this life is in His Son. He who has the Son has life; he who does not have the Son of God does not have life" (vv. 11-12).
2. Charles C. Ryrie, *So Great Salvation* (Wheaton, Ill.: Victor Books, 1989), 52.
3. R. V. G. Tasker, *The Gospel According to St. Matthew*, Tyndale New Testament Commentaries (Grand Rapids: Eerdmans, 1961), 62.

4. This in no way allows a Christian an excuse for not living for the Savior, as is dealt with elsewhere in this book. Sin in the life of Christians invites God's discipline, while faithfulness will receive eternal reward.

5. Romans 8:16 states, "The Spirit Himself bears witness with our spirit that we are children of God." Some have taken that to mean that unless one senses the Holy Spirit at work within him, he is not a child of God. Once again, the meaning is explained by the context which is that of prayer. We are told one verse prior, "For you did not receive the spirit of bondage again to fear, but you received the Spirit of adoption by whom we cry out, 'Abba, Father.'" *Abba* is a term that denotes intimacy, tenderness, security, similar to when a child today addresses his father as "Daddy." When we come to God in prayer we do so saying, "You are our father, please help us." As we do so the Holy Spirit who also enjoys a special relationship with the Father bears witness to God *along with* our spirit of the special relationship we have with Him as His children and intercedes on our behalf.

Note that the word translated "with" has just that idea—along with our spirit, not *to* our spirit. It has the same meaning in Romans 2:15 in the phrase "their conscience also bearing witness." So much does the Holy Spirit intercede along with our spirit and cries out to God on our behalf, that even if we don't know how to express what we desire, the Holy Spirit expresses that for us on our behalf. In Romans 8:26-27 we read, "Likewise the Spirit also helps in our weaknesses. For we do not know what we should pray for as we ought, but the Spirit Himself makes intercession for us with groanings which cannot be uttered. Now He who searches the hearts knows what the mind of the Spirit is, because He makes intercession for the saints according to the will of God."

Instead of ever addressing the issue of whether or not a person is a Christian, Romans 8:16 gives powerful instruction concerning the ministry of the Holy Spirit in the life of a believer, particularly as we cry out to God for His help in the midst of our problems (cf. Rom. 8:18).

Chapter 6

1. A fourth word, *ametameletos*, is used only twice (Rom. 11:29; 2 Cor. 7:10). It is used in an adjectival sense in both places.

2. A. T. Robertson, *Word Pictures in the New Testament* (Nashville: Broadman Press, 1930), 1:24.

3. William Howard, "Is Faith Enough to Save?" *Bibliotheca Sacra* 99 (January 1942): 96.

4. It is worth noting that study of the extra-biblical usage of repentance is not as instructive as one might hope, mostly because unlike the New Testament, usage of repentance is not tied to anything specific. One scholar summarizes the frustration here: "In pre-biblical and extra-biblical usage [*metanoeo*] and [*metanoia*] are not firmly related to any specific concepts. At the first stage they bear the intellectual sense of 'subsequent knowledge.' With further development both verb and noun then come to mean 'change of mind,' 'repentance,' in an emotional and volitional sense as well. The change of opinion or decision, the alteration in mood or feeling, which finds expression in the terms, is not in any sense ethical. It may be for the bad as well as the good. . . . Whether linguistically or materially, one searches the Greek world in vain for the origin of the New Testament understanding of [*metanoeo*] and [*metanoia*]." J. Behm, "*metanoeo* and *metanoia* in the New Testament," *Theological Dictionary of the New Testament*, ed. Gerhard Kittel, 10 vols. (Grand Rapids: Eerdmans, 1964), 4:979-80.

5. The breakdown of these uses looks like this:
    8 times in Matthew

      4 times in Mark
      14 times in Luke
      11 times in Acts
      1 time in Romans
      3 times in 2 Corinthians
      1 time in 2 Timothy
      3 times in Hebrews
      1 time in 2 Peter
      12 times in Revelation

6. Other references the reader may want to examine are Mark 1:15; Luke 13:3-5; Acts 3:19; Acts 17:30; and Acts 26:20. Note that in Acts 2:38 Peter is not giving an additional requirement for salvation. The significance of the verse as it relates to the need for baptism will be explained in the chapter "Is Baptism Essential to Salvation?"

7. William Evans, *Great Doctrines of the Bible* (Chicago: Colportage Association, 1912), 40.

8. Acts 8:22 gives further insight. Although the author understands Simon to be a believer (Acts 8:13), the use of *metanoeo* in verse 22 clearly demonstrates the need for a change of mind. As Simon witnessed the facts that those on whom Peter and John laid their hands received the Holy Spirit, he reduced the gift to a department store item. Offering to purchase it, he asked, "Give me this power also, that anyone on whom I lay hands may receive the Holy Spirit" (v. 19). Peter rebuked him for entertaining the thought that a gift from God could be purchased with money. He made clear that Simon's real problem was not his money, but his heart. Confronting him directly, he told Simon, "You have neither part nor portion in this matter, for your heart is not right in the sight of God. Repent therefore of this your wickedness, and pray God if perhaps the thought of your heart may be forgiven you. For I see that you are poisoned by bitterness and bound by iniquity" (vv. 21-23). It could hardly be clearer that Peter was asking Simon to change his mind concerning not only his sinful thought, but the degree of sinner he is—as evidenced by the fact that he would even entertain such an idea. Simon needed to change his mind and recognize that as a person "poisoned by bitterness and bound by iniquity," he had a heart that was not right with God.

9. R. A. Torrey, *What the Bible Teaches* (New York: Fleming H. Revell, 1898), 355.

10. Various writers note how repentance in salvation contexts either implies faith or is associated with faith when they say:

> "It is a great mystery; faith is before repentance in some of its acts, and repentance before faith in another view of it; the fact being that they come into the soul together."

C. H. Spurgeon, "Faith and Repentance Inseparable," *Reformation Herald* 3 (February 1978), 34.

> "Moreover, true repentance never exists except in conjunction with faith, while, on the other hand, wherever there is true faith, there is also real repentance . . . It should be borne in mind, however, that the two cannot be separated; they are simply complementary parts of the same process."

L. Berkhof, *Systematic Theology* (Grand Rapids: Eerdmans, 1941), 487.

> "If in Jesus conversion includes faith, in Paul [*metanoia*] is comprised in [*pistis*, faith], the central concept in his doctrine of salvation."

J. Behm, "*metanoeo* and *metanoia* in the New Testament," *Theological Dictionary of the New Testament*, 4:1005.

All this is not saying that when *metanoia* and *metanoeo* are used, they always refer to eternal salvation. In Luke 17:3-4, Christ used repentance in terms of our relationship with one another as He stressed the need for forgiveness. In Revelation 2:5, where John addressed the church at Ephesus, he emphasized the need for repentance on the part of believers who had lost their first love. As in Acts 8:22, cited earlier, in none of these examples is eternal salvation the issue.

11. Lewis Sperry Chafer, *Systematic Theology*, 8 vols. (Dallas: Dallas Seminary Press, 1948), 3:376.

12. Matthew 21:29, 32; 27:3; 2 Corinthians 7:8 (twice); Hebrews 7:21.

13. In short, as Mantey states, "*metamelomai* has the basic connotation of feeling different, or remorse." Julius R. Mantey, "Repentance and Conversion," ed. Carl F. H. Henry, *Basic Christian Doctrines* (Grand Rapids: Baker Book House, 1971), 193. Michel agrees with these observations when he says: "[*Metanoein*] and [*metamelesthai*] are distinct in class. [*Metanoein*] means a change of heart either generally or in respect of a specific sin, whereas [*metamelesthai*] means 'to experience remorse.' [*Metanoein*] implies that one has later arrived at a different view of something, . . . [*metamelesthai*] that one has a different feeling about it. . . . But it is easy for the two ideas to come together and even merge since a change of view often carries with it an uncomfortable feeling."
Michel, "*(metamelomai, ametameletos)*," *Theological Dictionary of the New Testament* (Grand Rapids: Eerdmans, 1967), 4:626.

14. In the Septuagint, *metanoeo*, the prominent word for repentance in the New Testament, is rarely used, but one can notice the concept of conversion. Behm states: "The linguistic material leads to the conclusion that for the Jewish Hellenistic world of the 2d cent. A.D. (*metanoeo*) was a common and even preferred equivalent of (*epistrephomai*=shub), 'to turn, to convert'" [("*metanoeo/metanoia*) in Hellenistic Jewish Literature," Behm, 990].

15. A second passage also often cited in studying the Old Testament concept of salvation is Habakkuk 2:4. The prophet Habakkuk said, "The just shall live by his faith." Referring to the judgment forthcoming on Judah through the Babylonian invasions, Habakkuk reminded the people of how one escaped the judgment. Are the just those who are received by God on the basis of their humble acts of obedience? No. Instead, Habakkuk said, "The just shall live by his faith." Their righteous standing with God came from placing simple faith in Him, the same as the New Testament exhorts one to do (Rom. 4:5). They were then to live in a way that represented the righteous standing they had with God. Paul quoted Habakkuk in Romans 1:16-17, "For I am not ashamed of the gospel of Christ, for it is the power of God to salvation for everyone who believes, for the Jew first and also for the Greek. For in it the righteousness of God is revealed from faith to faith; as it is written, 'The just shall live by faith.'" Paul's point as he echoed what the Old Testament also said is that we are justified by faith. As we live a life in accordance with the new standing with God we have by faith, we save ourselves from the consequences of daily sin, a subject we will discuss in chapter 8 when we examine Romans 10:9-10.

16. Second Corinthians 7:8-10 and Hebrews 12:16-17 represent probably the two most well known New Testament passages on repentance. What now, in light of our present study, do these two passages mean?

In 2 Corinthians 7:8-10, Paul discussed both his and his readers' reaction to a previous letter he had sent them. In so doing, he used a form for both words for repentance—*metamelomai* and *metanoia*. The verses read: "For even if I made you sorry with my letter, I do not regret it [*metamelomai*]; though I did regret it [*metamelomai*]. For I perceive that the same epistle made you sorry, though only for a while. Now I rejoice, not that you were made sorry, but that your sorrow led to repentance [*metanoia*]. For you were made sorry in a godly manner, that you might suffer loss from us in nothing. For godly sorrow produces repentance [*metanoia*] to salvation, not to be regretted [*ametameletos*]; but the sorrow of the world produces death."

When reading verse 10, "For godly sorrow produces repentance to salvation, not to be regretted," commentators are divided over whether "not to be regretted" refers to the repentance or to the salvation. The sentence structure favors salvation. The context favors repentance, however, and most commentators prefer this view. Regardless, this verse does not enter into discussion of repentance as it relates to eternal salvation. Since Paul referred to his readers as believers (2 Cor. 6:14-16), the salvation spoken of here is not a salvation from damnation, but a salvation from the consequences of sin in a believer's life. After writing 1 Corinthians and noticing that the problems in Corinth had not been resolved, Paul paid the Corinthians a very painful visit. Afterward, he wrote them the severe letter to which he referred in 2 Corinthians 2:4 which has been lost to us. It is this letter Paul discussed in this passage. What he was saying in context was, "Although I had regretted writing you, I don't regret it now. I am now grateful that the letter produced the kind of godly sorrow that led to repentance—a repentance not to be regretted, because it led to salvation." He even spoke of how his rebuke and their repentance brought about a change of behavior (7:11) and encouraged them to forgive the offending brother (2:10).

The repentance spoken of in Hebrews 12:17 was that of Esau in the Old Testament. Concerning him we are told, "For you know that afterward, when he wanted to inherit the blessing, he was rejected, for he found no place for repentance, though he sought it diligently with tears." The birthright in Jewish families always went to the eldest son and gave him privileges over his brothers as well as guaranteeing him a double part of the inheritance. The birthright could be forfeited by serious sin or it could also become a bartering item. The above verse refers to Genesis 25:29-34 in which hungry Esau sold his birthright to his brother Jacob for some food. The privileges of the birthright were then given by Isaac to Jacob instead of Esau. When Esau realized the gravity of his action, with tears he sought a repentance or a change of mind on his father's part but found none. Having solemnized his decision with an oath, Isaac could not and would not reverse what he had done (Gen. 27:39-40). It is worth noting that (1) the repentance sought was a change of mind on Isaac's part, not Esau's, and (2) although Esau sought that repentance with tears, he never received it. The birthright went to Jacob and remained there.

Chapter 7

1. When considering the nature of salvation, many are troubled by Mark 10:17-22. This passage relates the story of a wealthy and prominent ruler who questioned Christ: "Good Teacher, what shall I do that I may inherit eternal life?" Christ answered, "One thing you lack: Go your way, sell whatever you have and give it to the poor, and you will have treasure in heaven: and come, take up the cross, and follow Me." At first glance, this passage would appear to teach that in order for a man such as this to enter heaven, his money as well as his life must belong to Christ.

Once again, the context must be carefully studied. The rich young ruler's question about what he must do to inherit eternal life reflected the very common Jewish thought that eternal life belonged to the future age and was not a present reality. Furthermore, the ruler's use of the word *inherit* reflects the Jewish understanding that in order to obtain this future eternal life, one must meet certain conditions.

For further study on the Jewish study of inheritance, I would suggest the following resources: Arthur Marmorstein, *Studies in Jewish Law* (London: Oxford University Press, 1952) and Roy A. Stewart, *Rabbinic Theology* (Edinburgh: Oliver and Boyd, 1961).

Notice again what he asked: "What shall I *do* that I may inherit eternal life?" As He frequently did, Jesus answered a question with a question: "Why do you call Me good?" Jesus realized that the man was using the word *good* too lightly. On the one hand, he too quickly attached the word to Christ without realizing to whom he was talking. On the other hand, he did not realize deeply enough his own lack of goodness. So Jesus dealt with both areas. He first told the young ruler, "No one is good but One, that is, God." Foremost in Jesus' mind was that the man recognize that if Jesus were good, then He must also be God. Because Christ claimed to be equal with the Father (John 14:11), if He were not God, He was the farthest thing from good—a liar.

With that classification, Jesus now set out to show the man his own lack of goodness by how far short he fell of God's holy standard. Romans 3:20 explains that "by the law is the knowledge of sin." In order to show the young man his sin, Christ gave him six commandments that dealt with his relationships with his fellow man. Jesus said, "You know the commandments: 'Do not commit adultery,' 'Do not murder,' 'Do not steal,' 'Do not bear false witness,' 'Do not defraud,' 'Honor your father and your mother'" (v. 19). As the man reviewed his life, he proudly announced, "Teacher, all these I have observed from my youth." That may well be one of the most self-righteous statements found in the Bible. For someone to claim that he has never failed in honoring his parents and has never had a lie come from his lips shows an appalling absence of honest self-examination. The young man obviously had a problem with pride.

It is crucial to understand what happened at this point. Jesus made clear in His ministry that one receives eternal life simply by faith (John 3:36; 5:24; 6:47). For this reason, He could say to the multitudes just prior to talking with the wealthy ruler, "Assuredly, I say to you, whoever does not receive the kingdom of God as a little child will by no means enter it" (Mark 10:15). Jesus knew the young ruler lacked faith. At the same time, He knew the man was not prepared to receive what he needed to know. The love for riches that would keep him from following Christ if he were a Christian was the same love for riches that prevented him from coming to Christ. Therefore, in order to attract his attention and show him his real problem, Jesus gave the young ruler a demanding call to discipleship: "Then Jesus, looking at him, loved him, and said to him, 'One thing you lack: Go your way, sell whatever you have and give it to the poor, and you will have treasure in heaven; and come, take up the cross, and follow Me'" (v. 21). By use of the word *treasure,* Christ showed He had gone beyond the man's original question to explain how reward or treasure is received in heaven. The young man probably knew he might have to give up some things, but to be told to give up everything accomplished exactly what Jesus wanted: it arrested his attention. The young man was so grieved to hear this that he walked away (v. 22).

Reflecting on what happened, Christ put His finger on the man's real problem as He told His disciples, "Children, how hard it is for those who trust in riches to enter the kingdom of God!" (v. 24). The most widely used critical editions of the Greek New Testament (and the English translations based on them) omit the phrase "for those who trust in riches" mainly on the authority of two old Greek manuscripts (Aleph and B). But the phrase is found in the large majority of the surviving Greek manuscripts of the New Testament. The inclusion of the phrase has good support, and evidence indicates that the words were part of the original text of Mark. The man, distracted by his wealth, was trusting in his riches as a basis for meritorious entrance into the kingdom of God. He desired riches to be an indication of divine favor—a very prominent Jewish standard. Christ added, "It is easier for a camel to go through the eye of a needle than for a rich man to enter the kingdom of God" (v. 25). The camel was the largest animal they knew. The eye of the needle was the smallest opening. So the point was clear: it is as difficult for a man who trusts in riches to enter into heaven as it is to put the biggest animal you know through the smallest opening you know!

One can understand the dismay of the disciples at this point. If rich men cannot make it to heaven, how are we poor men going to get in? For that reason, "They were astonished beyond measure, saying among themselves, 'Who then can be saved?'" (v. 26). Instead of leaving them in despair, however, Jesus offered them the hope they needed: "With men it is impossible, but not with God; for with God all things are possible" (v. 27). Although we cannot save ourselves, He, indeed, can save us.

When understood in context, the paragraph becomes a beautiful illustration of how heaven is freely given and is a miracle of God's grace. One who is distracted by and trusts in wealth as a means of salvation is as hopeless of obtaining eternal life as a camel is of going through the eye of a needle. Only God cause someone to see their need of Christ and extend to them the gift of eternal life.

2. This is what gives the warning in Galatians 1:6-9 such importance.

> I marvel that you are turning away so soon from Him who called you in the grace of Christ, to a different gospel, which is not another; but there are some who trouble you and want to pervert the gospel of Christ. But even if we, or an angel from heaven, preach the gospel to you than what we have preached to you, let him be accursed. As we have said before, so now I say again, if anyone preaches any other gospel to you than what you have received, let him be accursed.

In this paragraph three groups of individuals are represented. One group adhered to the gospel of the "grace of Christ," which Paul preached—the only true Gospel. Then there was the group listening to the gospel spread by Judaizers, which Paul called "a different gospel" (v. 6). The reason Paul said it was "not another" gospel is that "another" in verse 7 means another of the same kind and so not actually good news. Paul was saying that the gospel spread by Judaizers was not another gospel of the same kind, but one of a different kind. This different gospel began by exhorting the lost to believe in Christ. Then as a requirement for salvation, it added circumcision and observance of feasts and ceremonies referred to in the remaining chapters of Galatians. For the Judaizers, the gospel was therefore not Christ *period* but Christ *plus*.

But there was still a third group, the ones Paul referred to in verse 6 as "turning." These people has listened too long to the Judaizers and now were giving people a garbled gospel. Concerning anyone who would pervert the Gospel of grace, Paul said, "But even if we, or an angel from heaven, preach any other gospel to you than what we have preached to you, let him be accursed"

(v. 8). The word *accursed* in this passage does not mean forever damned. Bear in mind, Paul entertained the idea he could so stray from the Lord that he could begin preaching another gospel: He said, "Even if *we,* or an angel from heaven, preach any other gospel, . . . let him be accursed." Paul understood that he could not lose his salvation. In Romans 11:29 he testified that "the gifts and the calling of God are irrevocable." The clause "let him be accursed" conveys the idea "let him be the victim of God's displeasure." The situation and people involved would determine how that divine displeasure would be manifested.

For the one preaching a different gospel who has not met the Savior, that divine displeasure is in the form of the eternal hell awaiting him. For the true believer who has strayed from preaching the Gospel of grace, salvation is secure, but the displeasure of God upon him would be manifested in other ways. Discipline might resemble what the children of Israel experienced during their repeated times of disobedience (Num. 14, 16) or what the Corinthians experienced as a result of their disorder at the Lord's table (1 Cor. 11:30). Paul was simply saying that when a man preaches another gospel, he deserves God's discipline, however it is exercised.

3. Bear in mind that the entire paragraph as it relates to false prophets is set in the context of there being two ways, two gates, and two destinies. Jesus had just told the people, "Enter by the narrow gate; for wide is the gate and broad is the way that leads to destruction, and there are many who go in by it. Because narrow is the gate and difficult is the way which leads to life, and there are few who find it" (vv. 13-14).

Chapter 8

1. "The favorite Johannine construction, however, is *[pisteuein eis]* followed by the accusative. This expression can be said to be original with the New Testament writers, and an important construction for their message. It is used by them 45 times. There is no similar example in the LXX, unless one would consider the sentence in Ecclesiasticus 38:31 as parallel: *[panted autoi eis cheiras auton enepisteusan]* and C. H. Dodd adds that so far as he has been able to discover, there is no parallel to *[pisteuein eis]* in profane Greek either.

The astonishing thing, however, is that this new and original construction is monopolized by the Fourth Evangelist. Out of the 45 New Testament examples, John accounts for 36 of them." Gerald F. Hawthorne, "The Concept of Faith in the Fourth Gospel," *Bibliotheca Sacra* 116 (April 1959): 119.

2. The other two places are John 2:23-25 and John 8:30-31. John 8:30-31 was examined in chapter 5. John 2:23-25 states: "Now when He was in Jerusalem at the Passover, during the feast, many believed in His name when they saw the signs which He did. But Jesus did not commit Himself to them, because He knew all men, and had no need that anyone should testify of man, for He knew what was in man." Since the construction *episteusan eis* (believed in) is normally used by John to refer to genuine conversion, we have no reason to suspect genuine faith is not in view here. Nothing in the text indicates that Christ did not regard them as true believers. Instead, the passage is simply indicating that these who had come to faith were not prepared for a full disclosure of who He was—the kind of disclosure that would lead to a greater intimacy with Him. This kind of intimacy is referred to in John 15:14: "You are My friends if you do whatever I command you." Therefore, "Jesus did not commit Himself to them," as one would do for his friends. Since the text says "He knew all men" and "knew what was in man," perhaps He realized that, like the ones referred to in John 12:42, they did not have the courage to stand behind their convictions.

Whatever His reason, knowing they were unprepared for this kind of intimacy, He chose not to commit Himself to them. It is worth noting that this paragraph precedes the account of Nicodemus, a Pharisee coming to Jesus by night. Undoubtedly, already there were those who felt the pressure not to speak openly on behalf of Christ—the kind of pressure referred to in John 7:13: "No one spoke openly of Him for fear of the Jews."

3. Leon Morris, *The Gospel According to John*, The New International Commentary on the New Testament (Grand Rapids: Eerdmans, 1971), 605-6. It should be noted, however, that this excellent comment on John 12:42 is not entirely consistent with his view of John 2:23.

4. One might legitimately ask, "Could Paul have been referring to an eschatological deliverance—that deliverance believers will experience when they stand before the Lord unable to be condemned for their sin?" The answer is that, unlike passages such as 1 Thessalonians 5:9, these words in Romans are not set in a context of future eschatological events.

5. Theologians have often found it helpful to explain that there are three tenses to salvation. Our past salvation, referring to the moment of conversion, delivered us from the penalty of sin; our present salvation delivers us from the power of sin, and our future salvation will deliver us from the presence of sin. Addressed in these terms, it is our present salvation that is in view here.

6. Other such usages one might want to examine include Acts 25:11-12, 21, 25; and 28:19.

7. Our understanding of the phrase "whoever calls upon the name of the Lord" is enhanced when we study the corresponding Hebrew phrase as it is found in Joel and other places. Schmidt speaks of this phrase: "While the number of such passages is relatively small in the NT, and in the LXX so far as it corresponds to the Hebrew [*epikaleisthai to onoma kuriou*, "to call on the name of the Lord"] occurs much more frequently. The NT usage suggests that this is a technical term, and this impression is heightened and confirmed when we turn to the LXX." K. L. Schmidt, "(*epikaleo*)," *Theological Dictionary of the New Testament* ed. Gerhard Kittel, 10 vols. (Grand Rapids: Eerdmans, 1965), 3:499.

The corresponding Hebrew phrase is used in contexts of prayer, adoration, and worship in which need for God's assistance is openly acknowledged and His character is proclaimed. When Abraham was seventy-five, God called him to travel to Canaan. Upon reaching the land of Canaan and seeing its wicked and numerous inhabitants, Abraham must have welcomed the Lord's promise, "To your descendants I will give this land." So "there he built an altar to the LORD, who had appeared to him. And he moved from there to the mountain east of Bethel, and he pitched his tent with Bethel on the west and Ai on the east; there he built an altar to the LORD and called on the name of the LORD" (Gen. 12:7-8).

Nine chapters later Abraham met Abimelech who, although militarily superior to Abraham, recognized that God's hand was upon Abraham and sought a good relationship with him. After settling the matter of a well Abimelech's servants had stolen from Abraham, the two "made a covenant at Beersheba. So Abimelech rose with Phichol, the commander of his army, and they returned to the land of the Philistines. Then Abraham planted a tamarisk tree in Beersheba, and there called on the name of the LORD, the Everlasting God" (Gen. 21:32-33).

And the LORD appeared to him the same night and said, "I am the God of your father Abraham; do not fear, for I am with you. I will bless you and multiply your descendants for My servant Abraham's sake." So he built an altar there and called on the name of the LORD, and he pitched his tent there; and there Isaac's servants dug a well (Gen. 26:24-25).

8. From time to time similar questions (about confession as a condition for salvation) are raised in connection to Matthew 10:23-33 and 2 Timothy 2:11-13.
In Matthew 10:32-33 Christ said, "Therefore whoever confesses Me before men, him I will also confess before My Father who is in heaven. But whoever denies Me before men, him I will also deny before My Father who is in heaven." Any question about whether Christ was demanding confession as a requirement for eternal salvation in these verses is easily answered by examining the context. Christ was speaking on the subject of discipleship (cf. vv. 22-25, 35-42). He warned His hearers pointedly of the ridicule and persecution they would encounter as His disciples. In light of that persecution, He told them that if they were willing to confess Him before men, He would confess them before the Father (vv. 32-33). However, if they denied Him before men out of fear of persecution, He would deny them before the Father. His concluding remarks clearly show that what He would "deny them" was the *believer's rewards*:

> He who finds his life will lose it, and he who loses his life for My sake will find it. He who receives you receives Me, and he who receives Me receives Him who sent Me. He who receives a prophet in the name of a prophet shall receive a prophet's reward. And he who receives a righteous man in the name of a righteous man shall receive a righteous man's reward. And whoever gives one of these little ones only a cup of cold water in the name of a disciple, assuredly, I say to you, he shall by no means *lose his reward* (vv. 39-42).

What the reward is we are not told. It could have to do with honor or responsibility in His kingdom in light of John 12:26 where we are told, "If anyone serves Me, him My Father will honor." But that this "confession" or "denial" is totally unrelated to salvation from damnation is obvious from the context of Matthew 10.

The relationship of confession or denial to discipleship and reward is also found in other passages. In the parable in Luke 19:11-27, which we will examine later in greater detail, a nobleman went abroad to receive a kingdom. Before leaving he gave each of his ten servants a mina (approximately what a working man would earn for three months of labor) with which to conduct his business until he returned. Upon receiving his kingdom, the nobleman returned and examined each servant concerning his stewardship.

The servant who had used his one mina to earn ten minas was commended ("confessed" to be good and faithful) and rewarded: "Well done, good servant; because you were faithful in a very little, have authority over ten cities" (v. 17). On the other hand, the servant who had done nothing with his one mina was denied reward by the nobleman: "Out of your own mouth I will judge you, you wicked servant. You knew that I was an austere man, collecting what I did not deposit and reaping what I did not sow. Why then did you not put my money in the bank, that at my coming I might have collected it with interest?" (vv. 22-23).

The faithful servant was given greater reward while the unfaithful one suffered great loss (vv. 24-26). The "confession" the nobleman made of his servants was in regard to their service. The thought of gaining or losing reward is not only consistent with Luke 19:11-27, but is promised in 1 Corinthians 3: "If anyone's work which he has built on it [the foundation, which is Jesus Christ] endures, he will receive a reward. If anyone's work is burned, he will suffer loss; but he himself will be saved, yet so as through fire" (vv. 14-15).

In 2 Timothy 2:11-13, Paul exhorted Timothy, "This is a faithful saying: 'For if we died with Him, We shall also live with Him. If we endure, We shall also reign with Him. If we deny Him, He also will deny us. If we are faithless, He remains faithful; He cannot deny Himself.'" The sentence that obviously would alarm some is the latter part of verse 12, "If we deny Him, He also will deny us." Considered by itself, it appears to say that if one does not profess Christ publicly, he is not one of His and Christ will deny the fact that he belongs to Him.

Again, however, examining the context removes our confusion. The beginning of verse 12 reads, "If we endure, we shall also reign with Him." By "endure" Paul referred to endurance of hardships and trials. He used the same word two verses earlier as he spoke of his imprisonment for preaching the Gospel: "Therefore I endure all things for the sake of the elect, that they also may obtain the salvation which is in Christ Jesus with eternal glory" (v. 10). The meaning of verse 12, therefore, is that if we endure (trials and hardships), we will reign with Christ.

In that same context of reward, 2 Timothy 2:12 continues, "If we deny Him, He also will deny us." The denial here is similar to that spoken of in Matthew 10:33. That individuals who are "denied" are nevertheless recipients of heaven is seen in the next verse: "If we are faithless, He remains faithful; He cannot deny Himself." We can go back on our word. God cannot go back on His. He does not go back on His promise that we have eternal life. Once He has accepted us upon our simple trust in Him, He will not toss us back. As Romans 11:29 has encouraged us, "The gifts and the calling of God are irrevocable."

By Paul's use of the word "faithless," it cannot be certain whether he meant denial or "unbelief," as the word can be translated. Paul may have been thinking of a believer who gets so far out of fellowship with the Savior that he denies who Christ is or that he ever trusted Him as Savior. Whatever Paul meant, one thing is clear. Our salvation does not rest on our faithfulness to God but upon His faithfulness to us. Once we become a child of God by faith, we are never cast out of His family. Even if we turn our backs on Him, He promises never to turn His back on us—He cannot deny Himself. We know He does not turn His back on us because, since we are His children, He may have to discipline us severely (Heb. 12:5-11).

Far from teaching that if one does not publicly profess Christ, one does not know Him, passages such as Matthew 10:32-33 and 2 Timothy 2:11-13 teach a truth close to that found in Romans 10:9-10. Consistently and publicly acknowledging our faith in Christ is essential to both our present victorious Christian walk and our future reward. But any such acknowledgment, or lack of it, in no way affects our eternal salvation.

This is not the first mention in the New Testament of such an idea. Romans 8:17 tells us that since we are God's children we are also "heirs—heirs of God and joint heirs with Christ, if indeed we suffer with Him, that we may also be glorified together." The idea of deserved reward for those who suffer for Him is inherent in both Romans 8:17 and 2 Timothy 2:12.

Chapter 9

1. T. M. Lindsey, "Baptism," in *The International Standard Bible Encyclopedia* (Grand Rapids: Eerdmans, 1939), 1:389.
2. Geoffrey W. Grogan, "Baptism for the Dead," *The Zondervan Pictorial Encyclopedia of the Bible*, ed. Merrill C. Tenney, (Grand Rapids: Zondervan Publishing House, 1975), 1:470. Note that the apostle Paul was not condoning baptism on behalf of the dead. He was simply citing the contradiction between practicing such a baptism—expressing the hope of a resurrection from the dead—while denying the resurrection of Christ.

3. A. T. Robertson, "Baptism," in *The International Standard Bible Encyclopedia*, 1:385.
4. F. F. Bruce, *New Testament History* (Garden City, N.Y.: Doubleday and Company, 1972), 100.
5. Ibid., 108.
6. Lindsey, "Baptism," 389.
7. Cited by Robertson, "Baptism," 386.
8. Some might ask, "Is it possible that Paul simply downplayed baptism or led others to do it, in light of their partisan spirit, but at the same time remained convinced himself that it was necessary for salvation? That is hardly a possibility. To downplay or remove from his personal involvement anything required for salvation is unlike the apostle Paul. He was far too zealous for whatever concerned Christ. For example, one can hardly imagine the fervent and faithful apostle Paul not preaching Christ because through his preaching a person might develop a partisan spirit toward Paul himself.
9. Interestingly enough, in Acts 10 among a Gentile audience, forgiveness and the gift of the Holy Spirit took place at the moment of faith (vv. 43-44). Cornelius, the first Gentile convert, was a centurion in the Italian regiment (v. 1). No doubt disgusted with the Gentile paganism of his day, he embraced the monotheism of the Jews. Scripture describes him as "a devout man and one who feared God with all his household, who gave alms generously to the people, and prayed to God always" (v. 2). His house apparently became a meeting place, his family and friends being in sympathy with him. There may even have been some devout soldiers who gathered with them (v. 27). Though devout, Cornelius lacked a full understanding of the Gospel of grace. Upon trusting Christ and receiving forgiveness and the gift of the Holy Spirit, he was then baptized (vv. 47-48). In no way, though, was baptism made a requirement for either forgiveness or the bestowal of the Spirit. When Paul wrote to the Romans, he reminded them that all Christians possess the Spirit of God (Rom. 8:9). There was yet a different situation in Samaria. In Acts 8:14-17, the Samaritans who had been baptized with water (v. 12) were indeed not baptized with the Holy Spirit until Peter and John came and laid hands on them. The reason appears to be so that the Samaritan believers could be seen to be of the same faith as those of the Jerusalem church, so that there would be no rival church in Samaria. Through the delay in the giving of the Holy Spirit, the unity of the church was preserved. Apart from Acts 2:38, the experience of the Samaritans is the only exception to the pattern of the indwelling of the Spirit beginning at the moment of conversion.

Consider also Acts 19:1-6. Paul met those in Ephesus who were ignorant of the Holy Spirit and were not even believers in Christ. They had simply heard John's message, which Paul explained to them was preparatory to their believing in Jesus. When Paul explained to them what they had not understood about John's ministry and preached Christ to them, they believed and were baptized in Christ's name. Instantly, as Paul laid hands on them, they received the Holy Spirit. Thus, as is the norm throughout the New Testament, they received the Holy Spirit at the moment of faith.
10. Although this question of Paul's does not appear in many of the early manuscripts of verse 6, it is found in the manuscripts of Acts 22:10, where Paul recounts his conversion.
11. In our day, confession alone is the only requirement for forgiveness (1 John 1:9). It must be stressed that the confession and forgiveness spoken of are not referring to deliverance from hell. The moment an individual trusts Christ, his eternal life is secure (John 5:24). If a believer does not confess his sins, his fellowship with God is jeopardized, but not his eternal home in heaven.

12. Some late manuscripts omit verse 37, but the textual evidence argues for its inclusion.

13. The fact that baptism tells others we desire to be Christ's disciples gives significance to Paul's words denouncing the divisive spirit in Corinth. He asked the Corinthians, "Is Christ divided? Was Paul crucified for you? Or were you baptized in the name of Paul?" (1 Cor. 1:13). If the Corinthians had focused on the One who had died for them, they would have realized that they belonged to Christ. Their baptism announced that they were His disciples, not Paul's or Peter's or Apollos'.

Chapter 10

1. Cited in *Bible Expositor and Illuminator,* January–March 1965, 189.

Chapter 11

1. Joel E. Romero, "Evangelism with a Purpose," *The King's Business,* September 1970, 9.

2. In Philippians 1:15, Paul said, "Some indeed preach Christ even from envy and strife, and some also from good will." This should not be confused with what an atheist or a cultist does. The preachers to whom Paul referred were indeed evangelizing, although the *motives* with which they did it were not God-honoring.

3. First Peter 3:1 says, "Likewise you wives, be submissive to your own husbands, that even if some do not obey the word, they, without a word, may be won by the conduct of their wives." Peter was not saying a person can be saved simply by looking at another person's life. Whether it be through his or her own study of the Word, evangelistic literature, or a verbal witness, the Gospel must be explained to him or her. Peter was simply reminding wives with non-Christian husbands that men who will not listen to the Word must look at the Word as it is lived out in their wives' lives. In so doing, they may be attracted to the Gospel through the testimony of their mates' actions and activities.

Chapter 12

1. Rev. Richard C. Halverson, sermon preached at the World Congress on Evangelism, Berlin, October 1966.

2. Robert Leslie Sumner, *Evangelism: The Church on Fire* (Chicago: Regular Baptist Press), 85.

3. Arthur P. Johnston, *The Battle for World Evangelism* (Wheaton: Tyndale House Publishers, 1978), 207.

4. Mark McCloskey, *Tell It Often—Tell It Well* (San Bernardino: Here's Life Publishers, 1985), 182.

Chapter 13

1. Some Bible teachers feel the list given here is not one of gifts but rather of offices within a church—one person holding the office of pastor-teacher, another holding the office of evangelist. Regardless of how one describes the list, however, it remains clear that God has given individuals to the church to evangelize the lost and equipped them accordingly.

2. G. Campbell Morgan, *Evangelism* (New York: Fleming H. Revell, 1904), 55.

Chapter 14

1. Other passages we could consider are Matthew 24:22; Mark 13:27; Luke 18:7; Romans 8:33; 9:11; 11:5, and Colossians 3:12.

2. It would be helpful if we could simply say that God's determination of who constitutes the elect is based on His knowledge beforehand of who would trust Christ and who would not. That is, He knows beforehand who is going to trust

Christ and thereby elects them. Although God does indeed know who will and will not trust His Son, to say that particular item of knowledge is the idea behind "whom He foreknew" is reading more into the phrase than can be proven from the verses. Romans 8:29 is worth looking at a bit more closely: "For whom He foreknew, He also predestined to be conformed to the image of His son, that He might be the firstborn among many brethren." In context, Paul's purpose in that verse was not explaining a definition of how people become Christians. To make the passage define that was not his purpose in that verse. Paul's point was that those whom God foreknew, He has predestined to come into conformity to the image of Christ. Paul had a similar emphasis in Ephesians 1:3-4: "God . . . has blessed us with every spiritual blessing in the heavenly places in Christ, just as He chose us in Him before the foundation of the world, that we should be holy and without blame before Him in love." Paul's point was not how God chose us, but that everything He has for us is in Christ. Individuals are indeed chosen, but Paul had in view what we were *chosen to*, not how we were chosen. Elsewhere he wrote, "The Spirit Himself bears witness with our spirit that we are children of God, and if children, then heirs—heir of God and joint heirs with Christ, if indeed we suffer with Him, that we may also be glorified together" (Rom. 8:16-17). Is Paul talking there about how to become a child of God? Not at all. He is simply saying that as children of God, we have a special opportunity before us—that of being heirs of God and joint heirs with Christ.

3. Christ's condemnation of the cities that refused to believe the evidence concerning Him also makes it clear that He holds individuals totally responsible. His miracles were designed to elicit faith in Him (John 20:30-31). When the cities of Chorazin, Bethsaida, and Capernaum rejected Him, He warned:

Woe to you, Chorazin! Woe to you, Bethsaida! For if the mighty works which were done in you had been done in Tyre and Sidon, they would have repented long ago in sackcloth and ashes. But I say to you, it will be more tolerable for Tyre and Sidon in the day of judgment than for you. And you, Capernaum, who are exalted to heaven, will be brought down to Hades; for if the mighty works which were done in you had been done in Sodom, it would have remained until this day. But I say to you that it shall be more tolerable for the land of Sodom in the day of judgment than for you (Matt. 11:21-24).

Tyre and Sidon, heathen cities of Phoenicia, were noted for their idolatry, pride, and luxury as well as their cruel mockery of Israel at a time when God had to deal severely with His people (cf. Ezek. 26:1-28:10). He told those of Chorazin and Bethsaida that Ezekiel done in Tyre and Sidon—as wicked as they were— the miracles Christ had performed, those in Tyre and Sidon would have repented. Hence, though all face judgment, Christ is clear that Chorazin and Bethsaida will receive the greater condemnation because they had greater opportunity. Likewise, Sodom and wickedness were synonymous. Yet in the same passage Christ told those of Capernaum, His home place, that due to the greater opportunity they rejected, they would receive greater condemnation than those in Sodom. In each of the cities Christ addressed, He held the people totally accountable for rejecting the Son of God. As those in each city suffer in hell, it is due not to His rejection of them but, first and foremost, to their rejection of Him.

4. Willard M. Aldrich, "Grace" booklet, 14-15.

5. Lewis Sperry Chafer summarized well the "partnership arrangement" we have with God in prayer as it relates to evangelism: "The reason for human intercession in this divine plan has not been wholly revealed. The repeated

statements of Scripture that it is a necessary link in the chain that carries the divine energy into the impotent souls of man, in addition to its actual achievement as seen in the world, must be the sufficient evidence of the imperative need for the prayer in connection with the purpose of God. Thus in the Scriptures and in experience it is revealed that God has honored man with an exalted place of cooperation and partnership with Himself in His great projects of human transformation." Lewis Sperry Chafer, *True Evangelism* (Grand Rapids: Dunham Publishing Company, 1919), 89.

Chapter 15

1. The word *sophia* is used six times in Colossians: 1:9, 28; 2:3, 23; 3:16, and 4:5.
2. Trench makes a noteworthy observation that *sophia* "is never in Scripture ascribed to other than God or good men, except in an ironical sense. . . . cf. 1 Corinthians 2:1, 4, 5, 6." Richard Chenevi Trench, *Synonyms of the New Testament* (Grand Rapids: Eerdmans, 1953), 283.
3. Trench calls it "The mean between craftiness and folly . . . it skillfully adapts its means to the attainment of the ends which it desires." Ibid., 282, 284.
4. Josh McDowell, *Evidence That Demands a Verdict* (San Bernardino: Campus Crusade for Christ, 1972), 373.
5. Josh McDowell, *More Than a Carpenter* (Wheaton, Ill.: Tyndale House Publishers, Inc., 1977), 108.

Chapter 16

1. C. H. Spurgeon, *The Early Years—C. H. Spurgeon Autobiography: 1* (Edinburgh: Banner of Truth Trust, 1962), 373.
2. H. C. Hahn, "Openness, Frankness, Boldness," in *The New International Dictionary of New Testament Theology* (Grand Rapids: Zondervan Publishing House, 1967), 2:736.
3. D. Edmond Hiebert, *The Thessalonian Epistles* (Chicago: Moody Press, 1971), 85.
4. See also Matthew 14:14; 15:32; 20:34; Mark 1:41; 6:34; 8:2; and Luke 7:13.

Chapter 17

1. Compare 1 John 3:17-18; James 2:15-16; Rom. 14:10, 13, 15, 21; 1 Cor. 6:6-8; 12:25-27.
2. Both of these references use the earlier Greek word translated "exhort" but here translated "comfort." This is another reason one must be careful not to make too sharp a distinction between these three words found in 1 Thessalonians 2:11.
3. E. Earle Ellis, "Paul and His Co-workers," *New Testament Studies* (July 1971): 437-52.

Chapter 18

1. Robert E. Coleman, *The Master Plan of Evangelism* (Old Tappan, N.J.: Fleming H. Revell Co., 1964), 77.
2. There is no record of this pooling of property outside of the early years of the Jerusalem church. Some feel it was necessitated by the circumstances of the time. For example, as word of the Christian faith spread, pilgrims may have come to Jerusalem to learn more, lingered there, and found themselves in need of provisions.
3. J. I. Packer, *Evangelism and the Sovereignty of God* (Chicago: InterVarsity Press, 1961), 81.
4. Arthur P. Johnston, *The Battle for World Evangelism* (Wheaton, Ill.: Tyndale House Publishers, 1978), 267.
5. Guy Wright, cited in *Reader's Digest* (October 1965), 232.